CONTRADICTION IN MOTION

CONTRADICTION IN MOTION

Hegel's Organic Concept of Life and Value

SONGSUK SUSAN HAHN

CORNELL UNIVERSITY PRESS
ITHACA AND LONDON

Material from the following previously published essays has been adapted for use in this book with permission of the publishers: A version of "Organic Holism and Living Concepts" and "Living Concepts and Living Selves" in *Internationales Jahrbuch des Deutschen Idealismus*, editors Karl Ameriks and Jürgen Stolzenberg, metaphysics issue, Band 5, 2007.

"Hegel on Saying and Showing" was originally published in *Journal of Value Inquiry* 28 (1994) and reprinted in *International Library of Critical Essays in the History of Philosophy: Hegel*, vol. II, editor David Lamb (Aldershot, Eng.: Ashgate, 1998), with kind permission of Springer Science and Business Media.

"Value Conflicts and Belief Revision" in *CLIO* 24, no. 4 (1995).

First published 2007 by Cornell University Press
Printed in the United States of America

Library of Congress Cataloging-in-Publication Data

Hahn, Songsuk Susan.
    Contradiction in motion : Hegel's organic concept of life and value / Songsuk Susan Hahn.
        p. cm.
    Includes bibliographical references and index.
    ISBN–13: 978–0–8014–4444–9 (cloth : alk. paper)
    1. Hegel, Georg Wilhelm Friedrich, 1770–1831.   2.   Contradiction.
I. Title.
    B2949.C64H34 2007
    193—dc22

                                                    2006039787

Cornell University Press strives to use environmentally responsible suppliers and materials to the fullest extent possible in the publishing of its books. Such materials include vegetable-based, low-VOC inks and acid-free papers that are recycled, totally chlorine-free, or partly composed of nonwood fibers. For further information, visit our website at www.cornellpress.cornell.edu.

Cloth printing   10 9 8 7 6 5 4 3 2 1

For my mother and father
Whang Byung-Ryang (in memoriam) and Hahn Sangduk

Contents

Acknowledgments

I always knew that when the ideal editor came along I would know it; I just didn't know by what signs. All the signs were valid when I met Roger Haydon. I knew by the intelligence and care with which he handled this manuscript that it had found an editor and a house (home). He lifted that massive unknown off my back fairly early on and carried it himself throughout years of ambiguity. That gave me the mental freedom I needed to step back from the race long enough to bring this work to a more natural finish. Thanks first of all to Roger for breaking this beast gently and bringing it in from the cold.

Many thanks to Teresa Jesionowski for editing this manuscript with art and understanding. Her discriminating eye and unobtrusive judgment made the crawl down the homestretch as graceful as possible.

I essentially wrote this manuscript backward, with the chapters on ethics drafted first. Thanks to those who took it on faith that the earliest, roughest sketch was worth reading: Harry Frankfurt, Allen Wood, Frederick Neuhouser, Jerry Schneewind, Susan Wolf, Dennis Des Chene, and P. J. Ivanhoe. Richard Bett and Theodore Buttrey commented expertly on the ancient bits with a scrupulous eye for detail and historical truth.

I remember Raymond Geuss: his charismatic teaching at Columbia is what brought me to Hegel in the first place. Without Charles Parsons' subtle and profound influence, the book would have been stalled interminably. From him, I learned of the importance of coming to grips with Hegel's logical apparatus and looking there for the deeper motivation driving his views on contradiction. He was my touchstone throughout.

Sally Sedgwick and Béatrice Longuenesse kindly encouraged the chapters on logic by providing vital insights about Hegel's logic viva voce. I have learned much from Bob Brandom's *Leben und Tod Kampf* with this difficult author. I show my gratitude in the opening chapter by criticizing him (dialectically and admiringly). Aaron Preston gave rather good comments on that chapter that led to a nice revision.

Harry Frankfurt and Susan Wolf set living examples for me of what philosophy can be at its best when kept grounded by the highest human values. Harry has been one of my greatest heroes since graduate school. Susan set the tone for me of a way of talking and writing philosophy: without vanity, without ego.

The Goethe-Hegel connection in the opening chapter is due to Eckart Förster's inspiration. Förster's involvement with the project came in the endgame when I most needed a Lieblingskollege, a Second, and a wartime consigliere all rolled into one. He kept me trained impersonally on the configuration of the pieces, not personalities, and gave me the heart to play hard through a losing position.

Karl Ameriks' and Jane Kneller's NEH Summer Institute marked the turning point at which I began thinking about contradiction organically, not formally. Many thanks to Karl, Jane, and the celebrants, especially Ted Kinnaman and Deirdre Maloney, for much enlightenment and laughter in the Rocky Mountains.

Good friends I've had along the way. Maria Phillips and Franc Nunoo stayed up with me all through the longest day's journey into night. My brother, Charles McCreight, watched the drama unfold without judging, and with a uniquely absurd sense of humor that kept me laughing through it all.

Thanks to one of the masked reviewers for his heroic good deeds behind the scenes. His timely intervention gave me the perspective I needed on how all the parts of the book came together as a comprehensive whole. Knowing there was at least one rare individual out there with enough feeling and discernment to catch this book when it fell, gave me the assurances I needed to make one last hard push to see the final revisions through.

Allen Wood's involvement with the project has been sustained and unwavering from beginning to end. At the beginning, he sent me two sets of knowledgeable criticisms of the ethics chapters. In the end, he prepared an expert reviewer's report. Throughout a vast middle stretch of dead writing time, he took the bad with the worse, especially during my Wanderjahre out in the Ohio wilderness. Heartfelt thanks to Allen for his expert advice over the years, for the lavish effort it has cost him, for making the world a safer place to do Hegel scholarship, and for being exactly what I think a human being in the profession should be like.

If one is lucky in life, one meets that special person early enough for them to have a formative influence on one's work from that point on. For me, that special person was Michael Forster. At an earlier, critical period he was my dissertation adviser. His books and seminars gave me something I could respect. Later, he contributed most to causing my own book to come into being. He made me feel its life. Life is short, but he devoted as many hours to discussing this book as there are grains of sand rushing through the hourglass now seen darkly through a mist of gratitude. I will long remember our marathon consultations. And if he should remember, let him recall how his Spartan discipline, uncompromising rigor, and terrible clarity sometimes made things difficult—but beautiful! I count among the biggest things he gave me: an impersonal sense of being part of something far more important than myself and a desire to take on the risks and responsibilities that go with that feeling of belonging. Most of all, thanks to Michael Forster, from now until forever, for believing in me.

S.S.H.

Abbreviations

Primary Writings by G. W. F. Hegel (1770–1831)

All texts and translations are from standard English translations listed below, unless indicated otherwise. Works will be cited by paragraph or section number (§); remarks (*Anmerkungen*) are indicated by "R," and additions (*Zusätze*) by "Z." In writings cited by paragraph (§), a comma is used before a remark or addition to indicate "and." Thus, for example, "PR §269, Z" means "both the paragraph PR §269 *and* the addition to §269." Whereas, when the paragraph number and the Z are closed up, as in "§324Z," that means "only the addition to §324, not the paragraph proper." Where I find it necessary to cite the original German, the English pagination will be followed by a slash (/) and the volume and page from Hegel's *Werke* (Frankfurt am Main: Suhrkamp Verlag, 1969–1971).

B   *Hegel: The Letters* [*Briefe*]. Edited by Clark Butler and Christiane Seiler. Bloomington: Indiana University Press, 1984.

D   *The Difference between Fichte's and Schelling's System of Philosophy.* 1801. Translated by H. S. Harris and Walter Cerf. Albany: State University of New York Press, 1977.

EL   *Encyclopedia, Part I: Hegel's Logic* [*Wissenschaft der Logik*]. 1817. Translated by T. F. Geraets, W. A. Suchting, and H. S. Harris. Indianapolis: Hackett, 1991.

EN   *Encyclopedia, Part II: Philosophy of Nature* [*Naturphilosophie*]. Translated by Michael J. Petry. New York: Humanities Press, 1970.

EG   *Encyclopaedia: Part III: Philosophy of Mind* [*Philosophie des Geistes*]. Translated by William Wallace and A. V. Miller. Oxford: Oxford University Press, 1971.

ETW   *Early Theological Writings.* Translated by T. M. Knox. Chicago: University of Chicago Press, 1975.

GW   *Faith and Knowledge* [*Glauben und Wissen*]. Edited by Walter Cerf and H. S. Harris. Albany: State University of New York Press, 1977.

JS   *The Jena System, 1804–5: Logic and Metaphysics.* Edited and translated by John Burbridge and George di Giovanni. Kingston: McGill-Queen's University Press, 1986.

NL   *Natural Law.* Translated by T. M. Knox. Philadelphia: University of Pennsylvania Press, 1975.

PhG   *Phenomenology of Spirit* [*Phänomenologie des Geistes*]. 1807. Translated by A. V. Miller. Oxford: Oxford University Press, 1977.

PR   *Philosophy of Right.* Translated by T. M. Knox. Oxford: Oxford University Press, 1952.

SL   *Science of Logic.* 1812. Translated by A. V. Miller. London: George Allen and Unwin, 1969.

SS   *System of Ethical Life* (1802/3) [*System der Sittlichkeit*], and *First Philosophy of Spirit (1803/4).* Edited and translated by H. S. Harris and T. M. Knox. Albany: State University of New York Press, 1979.

VA   *Lectures on Fine Art* [*Vorlesungen über Ästhetik*]. Translated by T. M. Knox, 2 vols. Oxford: Oxford University Press, 1975.

Werke   *Werke.* 20 vols. Edited by Eva Moldenhauer and Karl Marcus Michel. Frankfurt am Main: Suhrkamp, 1969–1971.

Writings by Immanuel Kant (1724–1804)

CJ   *Critique of the Power of Judgment.* Edited and translated by Paul Guyer. Cambridge: Cambridge University Press, 2000. English translation will be followed by volume and page number in the Akademie edition of Kant's collected works (abbreviated Ak).

CPR   *Critique of Pure Reason.* Edited by Paul Guyer and Allen Wood. Cambridge: Cambridge University Press, 1997.

G   *Groundwork of the Metaphysics of Morals.* Edited by Mary Gregor with an Introduction by Christine Korsgaard. Cambridge: Cambridge University Press, 1998.

LM   *Lectures on Metaphysics.* Translated and edited by Karl Ameriks and Steve Naragon. Cambridge: Cambridge University Press, 1997.

CONTRADICTION IN MOTION

Introduction

One of the most intractable problems in understanding this already obscure author is his repeated insistence that "Everything is contradictory." Hegel thinks that, if we pay attention to our experience, we'll see that we're confronted by contradictions all the time. He insists that contradiction pervades all natural life-forms, including human life-forms and their aesthetico-cultural and moral forms of expression. We already intuitively experience unity in organic life-forms; now properly philosophical thinking must be brought to see an element of contradiction in every growing, living thing. He acknowledges this in his repeated tributes to Heraclitus: "*Everything* in my logic is indebted to Heraclitus" (SL 83; EL §88Z). In oversimplified terms, this book is about why we can't "think" a contradiction, why we should try, and the conceptual resources that Hegel offers to take the sting out of doing so.

In this book, I try to make Hegel's doctrine of contradiction, once widely dismissed as heretical, into a plausible doctrine deserving serious consideration, particularly in its application to value. I reject the standard interpretations and develop a new line that avoids thinking about contradiction as beholden to a formal, classically bivalent logic. Unlike the authors of standard criticisms and defenses, I don't wish to portray Hegel as offering a philosophical position that either denies or affirms the law of contradiction. Instead, my strategy is to give plausible motivations for his claims by linking his theme of contradiction to interrelated elements in his *Logic* and *Naturphilosophie* in the service of constructing an organic-holistic view of nature and cognition. On my naturalized

1

reading, once contradiction is properly understood as a living unity of opposites in organisms undergoing change and development, contradiction is not a sign of error to be avoided but of life itself to be embraced.

This book falls into three main parts. In Part I, I argue that the motivation for Hegel's doctrine of contradiction is lodged deeply in his logical apparatus: namely, at that intersection where he tests his abstract logical and methodological apparatus against the more concrete, unmanageable aspects of empirical nature. Hence, the main title of this book, *Contradiction in Motion*—a line taken from his larger *Logic* (*SL* 441). His views on contradiction have systematic connections to many parts of his System, especially to his dialectical method in the *Logic*. To make Hegel's views on contradiction more plausible, I naturalize them in a way that makes it possible to incorporate them into his logic of organic wholes with systematic ties to his *Philosophy of Nature*.

It will become evident in the course of this book that my interest is in Hegel's logic of contradiction not just for its own sake, but in relating contradiction to his *Philosophy of Nature* and then applying this organic picture of cognition to the realm of value. My view is that we have to take the theoretical and practical dimensions of Hegel's thought as a package; and what we may gain from a joint study of his *Logic, Naturphilosophie,* aesthetics, and ethics are insights that would not be attainable if each were studied in isolation. Once I have his logic of organic wholes in place, I apply his revisionary logic to practical issues that arise in the realm of value to make sense of conflict and contradictions arising there.

In the two remaining practical parts, I examine the extent to which Hegel's organic model informs his aesthetics and ethics. Although his reflections on art and artistic expression make up only a fragment of his whole philosophical system, aesthetics provided him with a rich field for discovering a kind of intuitive knowledge that mediates between discursive and nondiscursive knowledge in its judgments about beauty. Art forms represent to him our first attempt to represent to ourselves, prelinguistically and pictorially, a special unified consciousness of life and life-forms in the nonconceptual products of the human imagination. Thus, art forms and artistic expression enjoy a privileged status in his System because of their pivotal role in developing the revisionary language we need to articulate our unified consciousness of life and life-forms.

In applying Hegel's doctrine of contradiction to value, I extend to art forms the holistic methodology that he derived from a special teleology of organic forms, in order to bring out problems concerning the discursive articulation of unified aesthetic wholes. In this, and many other important respects, I argue that Hegel's aesthetics was influenced by Kant's understanding of beauty on the analogy of the purposiveness of living organisms. On the model of living organic wholes, whose unities can't be understood by purely mechanistic laws, but whose parts and organs function in an organic unity, art forms have a wider nonpropositional, pictorial content which embodies our intuitive knowledge of unity. Not everything we know is, in principle, accessible to rational cognition and concepts. Hegel has a wider sense of propositional content, not restricted to a narrow content that is fully articulable and conceptualizable in ordinary concepts; rather Hegel's sense falls into an intermediate area between propositional and nonpropositional thought.

Finally, to the extent that dialectical method systematically informs all the interconnected parts of Hegel's System, in Part III of the book, I explore the extent to which his ethics has to be reconfigured, if not altogether abandoned, in the light of his methodological and logical commitments. Given the dependency of action and agency on the ordinary laws of logic, I explore the extent to which Hegel's revisionary understanding of classical logical principles—such as the law of contradiction, the law of excluded middle, and the principle of identity—is threatening to spread and infect ordinary logic, the kind of logic that makes action possible. A logical principle in our conceptual scheme may be revised for theoretical reasons unless it happens that we have to invoke it as a practical principle. But certain classical laws of logic are so central to our conception of action and agency that without them our very conception of action seems jeopardized. If Hegel's logic rejects bivalence, yet we accede to the dependency of action and agency on the ordinary laws of logic, then what becomes on his ethics of our commitments to morally determinate verdicts and a principle of moral bivalence? To my knowledge, no other English-language study on Hegel squarely faces the strain his revisionary logic puts on his ethical commitments.

In the practical application, I argue that the relevance of relating Hegel's organic holism, with its distinctively contradictory operation, to his ethics is felt especially in conflict situations, where irresolvable conflicting moral principles are driven into contradiction. The strain of trying to relate his holistic method to his ethics is felt when we try to make sense of our unified consciousness of agency and action on an organic-holistic ethics which has the peculiarity of construing moral opposites, vice and virtue, evil and good, as essentially inseparable terms.

The deeper intuitive consciousness we have of organic unities extends to a self-conscious awareness of our own self-unity and unified actions, but our understanding of this unity outstrips our ability to articulate it in discursive concepts and logical laws. I argue that Hegel's revisionary logic influenced his views on action and agency in a striking and radical way—not so radically as to undermine our very concept of unified action and agency, but rather so as to enlist certain negative reactive attitudes toward contradiction, like guilt and regret, to play a key psychological role in revising moral concepts.

The atemporal, theoretical considerations about logic and concepts will interact with the more practical parts in a complex way. A certain amount of ambiguity is inevitable in relating Hegel's logical categories to historical-empirical phenomena. This may reflect an ambiguity in the way he himself relates his *Logic* to historically contingent empirical phenomena in the second and third parts of his System. It would be distorting to try to extract the logical parts of his System in abstraction from their empirical-historical instantiations. Thus, I've tried to steer a cautious course midway between the diverse range of literary, historical, philosophical, social, and political phenomena that he had in mind in his discussions of value, and the abstract realm of "timeless" logical forms. I am not a classicist by training, but I felt it was imperative to take some of the abstractness out of Hegel's logico-aesthetico-moral reflections by testing them, as he does, against real-world cases drawn from a diverse range of sources in the early Greek classical literature. I am also not just a historian by temperament. What I have offered in this book is not meant to be a strict historical exegesis of Hegel's thought and texts, but rather a rational reconstruction of Hegel's organics in a form in which I, as a philosopher, would want to defend it.

Although it was logical for me to proceed through the three parts of the book in the way I have just described, moving from the theoretical, methodological considerations to the more concrete practical applications, the reader unfamiliar with some of the more technical aspects of Hegel's System may find it more useful to read the chapters in the opposite order: starting with the practical chapters to get an intuitive grip on the kinds of historically contextualized cases that Hegel had in mind. Hegel's preoccupation with the ancient tragic conflicts, in particular, and the repetition of these structures in modern analogues are a good starting point for someone with no background in Hegel to acquire a felt-sense of what was important to him about the irresolvable structure of such cases that could have led him to certain logical considerations about contradiction. After exploring the practical consequences of Hegel's analysis, I suggest that the lay reader then go back and read Part I about the deeper methodological motivations that gave rise to his preoccupation with irresolvable conflicts in the first place. Reading the book this way—if the chronology of Hegel's own works serves as any indication—follows the way that he himself thought through these matters: His early moral-theological works were followed by his later theoretical considerations. But the more logical, systematic way to see how the parts of his System hang together, without implying that one part presupposes another, was to reverse the order as I have done here: Starting from theoretical considerations arising at the intersections of Hegel's *Logic* and *Naturphilosophie* and then deriving from them the more general methodological commitments underpinning the practical parts of his System.

This book has been long in gestation. Anyone who has been eviscerated by this author will know exactly why. If at times this material seems hard to read, let the reader take some comfort in knowing that it was even harder to write. The length of time it took me to write this book marks the distance I have traveled since embarking on my epic wanderings. I traveled along an uncharted and torturous path that took me through a quite different set of logical and methodological issues at some distance from my point of departure. Conflict situations for Hegel, I realized along the way, were symptomatic of ontological contradictions embedded at a deeper level of reality. This required me to resituate some earlier reflections about the surface symptoms of contradiction in an entirely different theoretical framework in order to try to give them the rigorous logical and epistemological grounding that Hegel had in mind. My mature reflections aren't meant to dislodge, only to deepen, my earlier work. Whatever the risks, this is the book I wanted to write.

PART I

HEGEL'S LOGIC OF ORGANIC WHOLES

1

Organic Holism and Living Concepts

What does Hegel mean when he says we must regard concepts as "living"? Hegel's way of reconciling the material and spiritual qualities of nature is to find in nature a spiritual reflection of human life-forms. Concepts are not abstract, static, lifeless things for him, but living, pulsating, self-generating things perpetually in motion. He attributes to concepts "life," "inner life," and "immanent life," a "living essence," a "self," even a "self-moving soul."[1] He thinks that concepts (like natural organisms, which undergo growth, reproduction, self-disruption, and self-repair) possess an internal principle driving them to undergo development, self-generation, self-disruption, and revision. The direction of this development follows a similar teleological pattern, which exhibits lawlike regularities that aren't explicable according to traditional laws and principles observable at the level of inanimate things. That means that concepts are less like stones and more like us.

But why does Hegel say this and what does he mean by it? Is this just an animistic figure of speech? Strictly speaking, concepts don't grow or reproduce. *Omne vivum ex vivo.* Two possible strategies come to mind to

[1] In German, the phrases are "das lebendige Wesen der Sache" (PhG §51/ *Werke* 3:51); "das eigne Leben des Begriffs" (PhG §53/ *Werke* 3:52; SL 764–774/ *Werke* 6:474–487); and "selbstisch" (PhG §37/ *Werke* 3:39). G. W. F. Hegel, *Phenomenology of Spirit*, trans. A. V. Miller (Oxford: Oxford University Press, 1977); *Phänomenologie des Geistes*, in *Werke* 3 (Frankfurt am Main: Suhrkamp Verlag, 1970); *Science of Logic*, trans. A. V. Miller (London: George Allen and Unwin, 1969); *Wissenschaft der Logik* I, II, in *Werke* 5, 6 (Frankfurt am Main: Suhrkamp Verlag, 1969).

explain what Hegel means. On a Kantian strategy, what is living must be something that only consciously designing agents can supply in their living awareness of concepts. The sense in which concepts are living must refer to something amenable only to human cognition. We can't give a sense to concepts being alive apart from the suitability of our cognitive faculties for cognizing their living nature. Thus, this strategy doesn't subscribe to an anthropomorphic, animistic view of concepts as possessing an objective living essence; rather, their living nature depends on our subjective cognition of them "as if" they were living.

However, regarding concepts as living by heuristic analogy to living organisms isn't without its own problems. Even if the sense in which concepts are alive *were* amenable to animate organisms, a problem would still arise concerning the status of organic nature itself. Even supposing we could give sense to living nature by referencing the suitability of our cognitive faculties for cognizing nature, the Kantian strategy only fits on the assumption that there is already a relation of appropriateness or "fitness" between our cognitive faculties and living nature.

Alternatively, a second possible strategy is to question this very assumption. Instead of bringing the regularities we observe in nature closer to something amenable to our human faculties, Goethe for one insists that we must make our human faculties more adequate to the task of cognizing living unities already existing in nature. On Goethe's strategy, concepts must be regarded as living in an objective sense, not "as if" they were living. There is no preestablished "fit" or harmony between organic nature and our cognitive faculties. Rather, our human faculties are inadequate as is; thus Goethe exhorts us to *extend* our cognitive faculties and concepts, in order to make them more suitable for the empirical cognizability of nature. According to Goethe, our recognition of the organic unities can't consist of a perceptual experience of them under traditional concepts and laws that apply at the level of static, inert matter, such as "Being"; instead, to capture their living unities we must subsume them under the idea of the "Becoming" of nature.

Of the two possible strategies for getting clearer on what Hegel means, Goethe's organic-holistic model is the more promising. In the Jena correspondence, Hegel's own botanical studies were encouraged directly by Goethe's essays on the metamorphosis and morphology of plants.[2] Early

---

[2] Johann Wolfgang von Goethe, *Scientific Studies*, ed. and trans. Douglas E. Miller (New York: Suhrkamp, 1988).

in Hegel's career when he needed to supplement his income, he solicited Goethe to arrange for him to assume Schelver's responsibilities of overseeing the ducal botanical gardens. The advantage, Hegel explains in the correspondence, would be to facilitate his own lectures on botany.[3]

My aim in this opening chapter is to use this organic paradigm to make sense of Hegel's claim that concepts are living. "Organics," as he calls it, was absolutely fundamental to his thought from Jena right up through his later works, as the following texts indicate: he gives a brief account of life in the *Phenomenology of Spirit* first as an object of Consciousness (PhG §§168–173/*Werke* 3:139–143); then at a later stage in the Reason chapter, in a long subsection titled "Observation of Nature," he discusses cognition of life as it displays itself in organic nature (PhG §§244–297/*Werke* 3:187–226). Although Goethe's influence in Jena belongs to a youthful stage of Hegel's development, well before his mature logic, the categories of Life and Teleology appear in the first part of his mature System, the *Encyclopedia Logic* (EL §§204–208; §§216–222/*Werke* 8:359–365, 373–377). Goethe's organic model of nature is explicitly discussed in the second part of Hegel's System, the *Naturphilosophie*. In "Organics," he discusses Goethe's theory of metamorphosis (EN §§343–349) and shows an intimate familiarity with the problem of recognizing living unities in organic wholes as it initially got worked out in Goethe's botanical writings. Hegel's preoccupation with organics persists and reappears at the end of his *Science of Logic*, where he develops an account of how life and living organisms relate to the logical concepts of Life and Teleology (SL 761–774/*Werke* 6:436–461, 469–486). He carries over this organic paradigm to a practical context, where it serves as a model for the State in *Philosophy of Right* (PR §256, §267, Z; §324 R, Z; §269, Z/*Werke* 7:412–413, 493, 414). Finally, he applies his organic conception to aesthetics in his late Berlin *Lectures on Fine Art* in the section "Naturschöne" (VA 116–152).

My task is to expound the sense in which Hegel thinks concepts are living, as can be gathered from the array of texts just cited. My strategy will be to show how Hegel recasts Goethe's intuitive insight about the being and becoming of nature into the more precise, logical idiom of the first two concepts of his larger logic, Being and Becoming. While

---

[3] Letter from Hegel to Goethe, Jena, end of January 1807, in *Hegel: The Letters*, ed. Clark Butler and Christiane Seiler (Bloomington: Indiana University Press, 1984), 686–687.

certain conceptual intersections between Hegel's *Logic* and *Naturphiloso-phie*, the first and second parts of his System, have already been charted,[4] and while the role of the logical concept of Life in the philosophical cognition of nature has been noticed,[5] little attention has been paid to relating single logical concepts to specific empirical phenomena from the neglected *Naturphilosophie*. We get a prime example, I'll argue here, of the sense in which Hegel thinks concepts are living in the opening dialectical triad of his larger Logic, in the motion of Being toward Becoming.

To avoid a monolithic picture of influence, the scope of influences on Hegel's holistic method should include a much broader range of his contemporaries than just Goethe. One line of influence consists of the romantic *Naturphilosophen*, Fichte, Schelling, Schlegel, Hölderlin, and Novalis.[6] Another line extends from Kant to include more of Hegel's contemporaries such as Hamann, Herder, and Schiller, whose holism originated largely out of their preoccupation with aesthetics.[7] Kant, in particular, is an unrecognized precursor of the Goethe-Dilthey tradition, especially in Kant's use of the idea of life as a central aesthetic category.[8] In Chapter 4, I'll weave in some additional strands

---

[4] George di Giovanni, "More Comments on the Place of the Organic in Hegel's *Philosophy of Nature*," in *Hegel and the Sciences* (Dordrecht: D. Reidel, 1984), 101–107; M. Drees, "The Logic of Hegel's Philosophy of Nature," in *Hegel and Newtonianism*, ed. Michael J. Petry (Dordrecht: Kluwer, 1993), 91–101; and George Lucas Jr., "A Reinterpretation of Hegel's Philosophy of Nature," *Journal of the History of Philosophy* 22, no. 1 (1984): 110–111.

[5] John Findlay, "Hegelian Treatment of Biology and Life," and Milič Čapek, "Hegel and the Organic View of Nature," in *Hegel and the Sciences*, ed. R. S. Cohen and M. W. Wartofsky (Dordrecht: D. Reidel, 1984). Murray Greene, "Hegel's Concept of Logical Life," in *Art and Logic in Hegel's Philosophy* (Atlantic Highlands, NJ: Humanities Press, 1980), 121–149.

[6] Frederick Beiser identifies the young Hegel, at least in connection with his organic view of nature and before 1804, as a romantic to be classified with these other romantics. In *The Romantic Imperative*, Beiser cites as the crucial texts for Hegel's defense of the organic view of nature the sections on Fichte and Schelling's systems in the *Differenzschrift* and the section on Kant in *Glauben und Wissen*. Frederick C. Beiser, *The Romantic Imperative* (Cambridge: Harvard University Press, 1993), esp. chaps. 8 and 9.

[7] Daniel Dahlstrom, "The Aesthetic Holism of Hamann, Herder, and Schiller," in *The Cambridge Companion to German Idealism*, ed. Karl Ameriks (Cambridge: Cambridge University Press, 2000).

[8] Rudolf Makkreel, "The Feeling of Life: Some Kantian Sources of Life-Philosophy," *Dilthey-Jahrbuch für Philosophie und Geschichte der Geisteswissenschaften*, Band 3/1985, 84–86.

of influence by stressing the extent to which Kant's organic holism in the third *Critique* had a decisive impact on Hegel's aesthetics. But first I wish to untangle from this complicated skein the single Goethean thread of influence in order to show how Hegel appropriated Goethe's organic holism in the natural sciences for his philosophical purposes of understanding organic unities. Although my reading of Hegel will portray him as significantly departing from Kant's theory of concepts, this is not meant to put it at odds with certain Kantian readings of Hegel, which can accommodate this specific revision.[9]

1.1 Two Methodologies: Organic Holism and Strict Empiricism

In Jena, both Goethe and Hegel were preoccupied with the problem of how we recognize the essential unity of a living thing throughout the metamorphosis of its parts. The perception of a plant confronts us with a bewildering manifold of parts—seed, root, leaves, stalk, stem, stamen, pistils, bud, blossom, fruits. The plant germinates, grows, bears fruit, and then dies and decomposes. The diversity of its parts during its life cycle would seem to contradict its unity. To reduce the essence of the plant to any single part in isolation or to a sequence of parts strung together in an unconnected unity would be arbitrary. What constitutes our psychological experience of the plant at a given moment isn't just confined to the substantive parts—what is most evident to consciousness. When a plant's substantive parts undergo growth and change, we can't literally see or perceive with bare perception the blind spots at the transitions. Just as we can't "see" a blind spot while driving, to put the point anachronistically, our experiential, phenomenological experience doesn't consist of experiencing anything salient in the transitions. But like a driver who has just been blindsided by what he can't see, the blind spots are felt omissions, not dead omissions. We still feel their absence as an active presence. Distinctive features of Goethe's brand of holism, worth singling out from among many strands of influence on the young Hegel, are the psychological considerations Goethe invokes to account for the invisible aspects of the process of developing organisms. Elements of Goethe's holism appear in the method of rational reflection that Hegel uses to explain how we grasp a plant's parts in relation to a sequence of

[9] Cf. Robert Pippin, *Hegel's Idealism* (Cambridge: Cambridge University Press, 1989), 7.

interrelated parts taken as a completed whole. This involves a process of reflecting on what the mind is really doing when it holistically understands these organic unities: namely, engaging in a mental activity of reconstructing the whole as a sum of its disparate parts, which involves a higher experience of its unity that is not reducible to the parts.

As is already well known, Hegel applied his logic of organic wholes to his theory of the State in *Philosophy of Right*, where he uses the model of a healthy organic unity to explicate the part/whole relation between individual members and the collective whole.[10] To raise the conception of the State from an inert and mechanical "organization" to a purposively organized living organism, he models the inward organization and structure of social items on the analogy of organs in a healthy body, whose individual members can't function independently as distinct and detachable apart from that from which they derive their social sustenance (PR §269, Z; §324Z). Unfortunately, Hegel's organics got tainted with conservative associations of the very model it opposed: a clock-work mechanism, whose innumerable lifeless parts get oppressively subordinated to a mechanical kind of collective. This misreading, run together with his misunderstood identification of the rational with the actual (PR, pp. 10, 11), led the old orthodoxy to a bad organicist reading of Hegel's political theory. On it, organic holism was regarded as a recipe for social conformity.[11] Whether right or wrong, I make no apologies for Hegel's political organicism and wish to assess the merits of his organic theory of concepts independently of it.

[10] Hegel, *Philosophy of Right*, ed. Allen W. Wood (Cambridge: Cambridge University Press, 1991); *Grundlinien der Philosophie des Rechts*, in Werke 7 (Frankfurt am Main: Suhrkamp Verlag, 1970); PR §324R, Z; §269, Z.

[11] The old orthodoxy finds a textual basis for a totalitarian reading especially in Hegel's remark that "This is the same as the ideality of every single class, power, and Corporation as soon as they have the impulse to subsist, and be independent. It is with them as it is with the belly in the organism. It, too, asserts its independence, but at the same time its independence is set aside and *it is sacrificed and absorbed into the whole*" (PR §267). Also see Hegel, "On the Actuality of the Rational and the Rationality of the Actual," *Review of Metaphysics* 23 (June 1970): 698. For examples of the orthodox reading, see Ernst Tugendhat, *Self-Consciousness and Self-Determination*, trans. Paul Stern (Cambridge: MIT Press, 1986), 311, 315–316, and Karl Popper, *The Open Society and Its Enemies*, vol. 2, chap. 12 on Hegel (New York: Harper and Row, 1962). For a good antidote to this misreading of Hegel's organicism as a conservative attempt to justify the status quo, see Michael Wolff, "Hegel's Organicist Theory of the State: On the Concept and Method of Hegel's 'Science of the State'" in *Hegel on Ethics and Politics*, ed. Robert Pippin and Otfried Höffe (Cambridge: Cambridge University Press, 2005), 294,

What has been overlooked, as far as I know, is that he extends a model of healthy organic unity along the dimension of logical concepts to explain how we know that a concept's parts are unified in relation to what he calls "the real organic Concept or the *whole*" (PhG §266/*Werke* 3:204). Sometimes he calls life itself "the whole organic concept." As life develops historically in a temporal dimension, so he thinks will the concepts and categories we use to articulate its dialectical structures. The real organic Concept, understood also as his philosophical System, understands concepts not in isolation but holistically encompasses them in a system of related, interlocking, interconnected elements. Each concept has implied in it distinct parts or determinations of other concepts, by virtue of being embedded in a more complex nexus of interconnecting inferences and beliefs. What is really involved in our knowing the unity of a concept's parts is that we're implicitly drawing on this web of inferences and beliefs. Reflection on this process produces a dynamic movement in thought, which Hegel describes in the preface to the *Phenomenology of Spirit* as a process of becoming:

> This movement of pure essences [concepts] constitutes the nature of scientific method in general. Regarded as the connectedness of their content it is the necessary expansion of that content into an *organic whole*. Through this movement the path by which the concept of knowledge is reached becomes likewise a necessary and complete process of *becoming*. (PhG §34/*Werke* 3:37–38, italics added; cf. §20, §56)

By reflecting on the movement of the mind in relation to a completed sequence of interrelated concepts taken as a whole, methodological holism accounts for the unity of a concept's parts and the direction of their development and modification. This involves examining what the essence of a thing is, not at the superficial level of the ordinary understanding, but at the profounder level of reflection. There, "intelligent

and Frederick Neuhouser, *Foundations of Hegel's Social Theory: Actualizing Freedom* (Cambridge: Harvard University Press, 2000), esp. chap. 7, "The Place of Moral Subjectivity in Ethical Life." Against the conservative interpretation of Hegel's identification of the rational with the actual, and practical efforts to bring the actualization of a social item in line with its concept or rational essence, see Allen W. Wood, *Hegel's Ethical Thought* (Cambridge: Cambridge University Press, 1990), 10, and Sean Sayers, "The Actual and the Rational," in *Hegel and Modern Philosophy*, ed. David Lamb (London: Croom Helm, 1987), 143–160.

reflection," as Hegel calls it, reflects on itself or thinks about what the mind is really doing when it undergoes certain "steps" or "moments" of this process—steps that involve taking up concepts in conceptual order, breaking them down into further components and, finally, connecting them up in a successive synthesis. It is specifically the business of Hegel's *Logic* to track the rational patterns underlying what the mind is really doing when it grasps a concept's multiple determinations in relation to a series of inferentially related concepts taken as a completed whole. Occasionally Hegel describes the holistic method implied in his logic using the technical term "dialectic." But more often, he calls it more naturally "experience" (*Erfahrung*, PhG §86/*Werke* 3:79)—albeit, experience reflected upon at a deeper level.

By bringing in the tendency of reflection to move the mind rationally toward logical structures, Hegel's holism gives concepts a psychological dimension that effectively shifts us away from seeing concepts in Kantian terms. For Kant insisted that logic deals with nothing but the form of thought alone. Thus, psychological considerations, at least of the kind that Frege had in mind, could play no role in explaining the objective nature of logical concepts. Hegel criticizes the Kantian approach to predication in the first *Critique* for involving what he calls a "pigeon-holing understanding" (*der tabellarische Verstand*, PhG §53/*Werke* 3:52), which he thinks intrudes on the natural flow of thought by imposing onto objects a static table of a priori categories, a "lifeless schema" frozen and fixed outside of time. Imposing a Kantian notion of formal negation, predication, and rationality on living organisms disturbs the spontaneous movement of thought by giving concepts a rigid fixity and false determinateness that is incompatible with growing organisms constantly in flux.

Thought has its own natural, instinctive rhythm—"the rhythm of the organic whole" (PhG §56)—which, if allowed to develop undisturbed, will seek its natural course. To shift to organics, Hegel thinks we must loosen our grip on false metaphysical commitments and presuppositions associated with traditional forms of judgment, which lead to thinking of a priori concepts as in a dead, external relation to their objects. To undertake the shift to organics, we must naturalize the fundamental principles underlying dialectic. In Chapter 4, I'll stress that Kant's shift to an organic approach in his third *Critique* provided Hegel with an organic terminology that is more adapted to the conditions of life developing on its own terms. But here, in the context of revising Kant's theory of concepts, Hegel's revision is aimed at Kant's conditions on knowledge in the first *Critique,* and designed to shift us away from a formal, Kantian model of concepts toward Goethe's organicism.

A second methodological influence on Hegel in Jena was Goethe's demand for strict empirical observation. In the *Metamorphosis of Plants,* Goethe insists that direct perceptual experience and careful observation, not a priori theorizing, are essential to revealing the deeper forms of nature. Over this issue, Goethe and the *Naturphilosophen* clashed with Kant, who thought that logic involves a priori concepts and logical relations to be grasped abstractly by the intellect in the medium of pure thought alone.[12] As a corrective, Goethe urges us not to overintellectualize in abstraction from living phenomena or to move too hastily away from living forms to abstract judgment and interpretation. Rather, he insists on deriving the essences of objects by continuous contact with the real thing. He wrote, "[M]y thinking is not separate from objects; . . . the elements of the object, the perceptions of the object, flow into my thinking and are fully permeated by it; . . . my perception itself is a thinking, and my thinking a perception."[13] To keep what is dead from displacing what is living, to keep our abstract logical categories from doing violence to natural living forms, Goethe insists that we must "stay with" the object and "work from life." We may fashion his demand for careful empirical observation into a kind of prime directive, a policy of noninterference in the life of nature: Look, but don't disturb!

Goethe's prime directive has important bearings on how Hegel relates his logical concepts to their empirical instances. Hegel credits Goethe with an insight into the identity between concepts and objects.[14] In keeping with Goethe's directive to stay with the object, to work from life, Hegel renounces the distinction between pure categories and concepts

[12] On this issue, see Frederick C. Beiser, "Kant and the *Naturphilosophen,*" in *The Romantic Imperative* (Cambridge: Harvard University Press, 2003), chap. 9.

[13] See Johann Wolfgang von Goethe, "Significant Help Given by an Ingenious Turn of Phrase," 39; "The Experiment as Mediator between Object and Subject," 12, 13–14; and "Empirical Observation and Science," 25, in *Scientific Studies,* ed. Douglas E. Miller (New York: Suhrkamp, 1988).

[14] In the *Lectures on Fine Art,* Hegel credits Goethe's methodology in his scientific writings with the insight that idea and (intuitive) perception coincide: "Of this sort was Goethe's observation and demonstration of the inner rationality of nature and its phenomena. With great insight he set to work in a simple way to examine objects as they were presented to the senses, but at the same time he had a complete divination of their connection in accordance with the Concept" (VA 129/*Werke* 13:174).

and the objects they depict (PhG §166/ *Werke* 3:137).[15] Hegel emphasizes time and time again that he thinks through the logical concepts and categories not analytically, but *synthetically* through continuous contact with cases *in concreto* (SL 414–415/ *Werke* 6:42–43). The concepts are synthetic in the sense that they are answerable to and disconfirmable by their empirical instantiations (EN §246R). If the truth of the logical categories lies in their application to empirical instances, then the function of the empirical examples—many of them conceived of in infinitely rich empirical detail in the *Naturphilosophie*—is to justify the logical counterparts, even at the sparest level of logical treatment. His empirical examples are more than minor illustrations of the logical concepts and categories for purposes of making them more comprehensible, as some commentators claim.[16] Far from being "astonishingly weak" and unconvincing in his examples, as one critic claims,[17] the concepts gain their very meaning and justification by corresponding to objects of possible experience (EN §246R/ *Werke* 9:15).

As we proceed, however, we'll see that it would be as gross a simplification to label Hegel an uncritical empiricist as it is for Karl Popper to label him a rabid rationalist.[18] For Hegel isn't bent on debunking a priori intellectualist claims in favor of adopting an uncritical empiricism wholesale (cf. EL §§37–39/ *Werke* 8:106–111; EN §248R). In fact, later we'll see him dialectically criticize Goethe's strict empiricism in a position in the *Phenomenology* that he calls "Perception." As it will become increasingly clear, the way that Hegel's organic concept analysis relates the logical determinations to their empirical instances is far from ambiguous. Many of Hegel's observations, for better or worse, blur the line between where elements of pure conceptualization end and empirical issues begin—as well they should, since a false contrast between the conceptual and the

[15] In the prefatory sections to the Self-consciousness chapter in the *Phenomenology*, Hegel writes, "If we give the name of concept to the movement of knowing, and the name of object to knowing . . . not only for us, but for knowing itself, *the object corresponds to the concept*" (PhG §166, italics added). See also SL 765–766.

[16] On this issue, see John Findlay, *Hegel: A Re-Examination* (London: George Allen and Unwin, 1958), 70. See also Richard Norman, who dismisses Hegel's use of natural examples as "minor illustrations" (Richard Norman and Sean Sayers, *Hegel, Marx, and Dialectic* [Atlantic Highlands, NJ: Humanities Press, 1980], 162).

[17] Thomas Bole, "Contradiction in Hegel's Science of Logic," *Review of Metaphysics* 40 (March 1987): 515, 526, 527.

[18] Karl Popper, "What Is Dialectic?" in *Conjectures and Refutations* (London: Routledge and Kegan Paul, 1963), 324.

empirical would commit him to a metaphysical dualism of the kind that he strenuously avoids. If concepts are to "stay with" and "move with" their empirical instances, as they must in a naturalistically construed dialectic, then the line between what is logical and what is empirical will inevitably become blurred. Indeed, Hegel's renunciation of the very distinction between concept and object will cost him the sharp distinction between what is logical and what is empirical. The price he'll have to pay just to play will be to ante up new conditions for the very possibility of cognizing concepts in terms intermediate between logic and empiricism.

1.2 Hegel's Organic Concept Analysis

Now both Goethean methodologies, holism and empiricism, are implied in Hegel's exposition of the first two concepts of his larger *Logic*: Being and Becoming (SL 82–108/ *Werke* 5:82–114). In keeping with methodological empiricism, Hegel thinks through the concept Being synthetically through continuous contact with empirical instantiations of Being. These empirical examples aren't mere illustrations of Being, but rather vital realizations of the concept itself (EN §246R). Since his argument is meant to generalize, and any living entity that satisfies the general features of Being counts as an instantiation of it, his argument could, and probably should, be repeated, taking all of his examples as subject matter.[19] But since my specific purpose here is to demonstrate (by analogy with Goethe's botanical model) the organic sense in which Hegel thinks concepts are living, I'll focus throughout on Hegel's favorite example, the plant. A plant, he thinks, possesses an essential organization and connection among its aggregate parts, which, when taken as an organic totality, reveal essential aspects of the dialectical process within itself.[20]

---

[19] The argument in "Being" is meant to be quite general and apply to any living entity that undergoes growth and change. Besides sentient animals and geological examples, Hegel also draws his examples of Being from the spiritual, social, philosophical, and scientific realms, including the Being of God or the Absolute Being (SL 100, 481; EL §86), thinking man (SL 441), life and death, life and self-consciousness (SL 83), Fichte's first originary principle, I = I (EL §86).

[20] Hegel favors certain concepts that come in mutually entailing pairs of opposites, where the truth of these pairs of opposites consists only in their interdependent relation to each other. Each is implied in the concept of the other (SL 437–438). While these relational properties are artificially kept apart as

In this connection, we may ask of the first concept of the larger *Logic*: "What is the *Being* of a plant?" (SL 415). Alternatively, drawing on the first sense that Hegel gives to the concept Being, we may ask: "What is the *essence* of the plant?"[21] Methodological empiricism constrains us to make sense of this question from within ordinary perception. But a plant's parts are infinite, and divisions within the subparts are infinite, and divisions within the divisions give the organism an infinite complexity. Since the mind can't take in infinite complexity, naturalists of Hegel's day sought to simplify the sensory barrage by reducing it to a single characteristic or capacity, rather than a whole complex of characteristics. *Which* part of the plant, they inquired further, can serve to define the simple essence of the plant?

Hegel's preliminary answer occurs in a passage from his *Naturphilosophie*, where logic and natural history come together in his discussion of Goethe's theory of metamorphosis and morphology in relation to the logical concepts Being and Becoming. In the passage called "The Plant Nature," Hegel takes as his dialectical jumping-off point an answer given

---

discrete and disunified by the ordinary understanding, when taken holistically, Hegel writes, "The whole is not equal to them as this self-subsistent diversity, but to them together" (SL 516). Hegel favors concepts that come in the following pairs of opposites: true/false, light/dark, morning/night, white/black, virtue/vice, good/evil, life/death, male/female, right/left, above/below, assets/debts, positive/negative, east/west, immediacy/reflection, necessity/contingency, organic/inorganic, acid/base, north pole/south pole, and so on (PhG §39; EL §119Z1, EL §376, Z; SL 83–84, 437). He adopts Goethe's polarizations of light and dark from the *Farbenlehre*, where dark is just the determinate absence of light: "Pure light and pure darkness are two voids which are the same thing" (SL 93, 102). Problems of indeterminacy also arise with respect to other garden-variety concepts, like plant and mud, which can't be conceived in terms of pairs of clear opposites. Although there is no clear opposite of plant, Hegel conceives of the parts of the plant in terms of difference, opposition, and self-contradiction. He cites the plant as a clear example of how the stages of growth and change result in an internal disruption that captures aspects of the dialectical process.

[21] The first sense that Hegel gives to the concept Being is dictated by the need to start from a presuppositionless starting point, one that will justify the beginning from within the theory. But as the concept undergoes dialectical treatment, we'll see that its meaning will shift along a continuum of meanings depending on our place in the dialectical process, ranging from "simple essence," to "to be," "is," "what is," "what primarily is," to, more strongly, "exists" and "existing." With Aristotle's influence in evidence, Hegel rejects the idea that Being has a single, unitary meaning (cf. *Physics*, Bk. Alpha) but goes further than Aristotle and implicates the concept in its opposite meaning, "Non-being."

by preformation theory, one of the dominant theories in the first half of the eighteenth century about the genesis of life:

> The germ [seed] is the unexplicated *being* [*das Unenthüllte*] which is the entire concept [Begriff]; the nature of the plant which, however, is not yet Idea because it is still without reality. In the grain of seed [*Samenkorn*] the plant appears as a simple, immediate unity of the self and the genus . . . . The development of the germ is at first mere growth, mere increase; it is already in itself the whole plant, the whole tree, etc., in miniature. The parts are already fully formed, receive only an enlargement, a formal repetition, a hardening, and so on. For what is to *become*, already is; or the *becoming* is this merely superficial movement. (EN §346a, 323–324/ *Werke* 9:§346Z2, italics added)

The essence of the plant is its seed or germ. Key to preformation theory was the belief that the germ is already a preformed embryo of the plant in miniature, a view which is consistent with a view of nature as static and pregiven. Selecting out this single characteristic from the manifold of diverse parts is nonarbitrary because the seed is in some sense already itself the whole plant ("the entire Concept"). That is, we see in an acorn a foreshadowing of the species of oak tree it will become. We can know this about the seed already before witnessing its subsequent history unfold. The plant's complex of characteristics may be defined in terms of this single characteristic—its seed—because the plant is already "fully formed" at the embryonic stage, according to a pregiven mold and development, and further development consists in little more than enlargement and repetition.

The problem facing preformation theory—largely discredited toward the close of the eighteenth century—was that it couldn't account for a problem of growth and generation. The theory of epigenesis, largely Aristotelian in its form, was meant to account for precisely this problem. Namely, how does the seed move from a merely potential, inchoate, indeterminate seed to a fully actualized, determinate plant with an articulated, differentiated structure? As Hegel puts it here: "The nature of the plant . . . , however, is not yet Idea because it is still *without reality*." Even in its purest, simplest form, the seed already has to carry within it the power (*Kraft*) not to remain in its earliest, inchoate, potential stage, but to effect an expansion of its content to include all of its differentiated, determinate articulations: as germinating seed, seed-root, seed-leaf, stalk, foliage, cluster of green, leaf-like petals, flower-bud, blossom, petals, fruit, and so on. The mere potential of the seed to metamorphose into its future forms, existing as a dormant causal efficacy, doesn't yet commit it actually to any one of its future physical forms to the exclusion of all others. For one can't visibly observe in the potential seed a preformed mold in such a way as to give the mind a higher experience that references the completed whole. How, then, on a psychologically motivated brand of holism, do we get the mind to reflect on the preformed germ in a way that moves it from an empty, potential, inchoate mass to a fully actualized, differentiated structure in a way that references the completed whole? What could move us to this reflective experience of a higher sort? What introduces movement into the dialectic at this point?

What produces reflection in the dialectic at this point is Hegel's claim that the preformationist's belief in the preformed seed is "empty" and "abstract." Notice that calling the preformationist's belief "empty" and "abstract"—terms taken from Hegel's *Logic*—doesn't by itself carry a threat of vacuity. The holistic requirement, recall, demanded precisely that the concept be free of all determinate content if the seed is to carry within it the potential to metamorphose equally into every one of its future variations in order to incorporate all of its parts equally. This feature of emptiness and abstractness is only a defect, understand, if the goal of concepts is to strive to acquire greater determinacy of meaning. As Robert Brandom rightly argues, this is in fact Hegel's goal.[22]

We see anticipations of the goal in the Spinozistic idea that every living organism has a *conatus*, which is driving it toward unfolding and intensifying its further articulations, where there is no rational goal or necessity to this striving other than a blind endeavor to preserve its existence. Hegel assimilates categories applying to life—the goal of self-preservation and self-reproduction—to concepts. But to do this, he must translate the idea of a blind drive or instinct for self-preservation into the more conceptual idiom of empirical concepts striving *rationally* toward the goal of bringing about determinacy of content. The goal of self-preservation

[22] Robert Brandom, "Holism and Idealism in Hegel's *Phenomenology*," *Hegel-Studien* (Summer 2002). References are to the reprinted version in *Tales of the Mighty Dead: Historical Essays in the Metaphysics of Intentionality* (Cambridge: Harvard University Press, 2002), chap. 6, pp. 178–179. Also see Robert Brandom, "Some Pragmatist Themes in Hegel's Idealism," *European Journal of Philosophy* 7, no. 2 (1999): 164–189.

gets translated into the idea of concepts striving *rationally* toward main-taining their self-unity or selfsameness throughout a dialectical revision that threatens them with contradiction and self-disruption. Thus, given our rational commitments to determinacy of content, the static concept Being must strenuously undergo revision in order to move us from an awareness of the seed's being merely potential, inchoate, and indetermi-nate to its becoming a dynamically actualized, determinate form.

In response to this demand for revision, thought doesn't scatter in any direction. What directs its movement, Hegel thinks, is something internal to the concept that is driving it to become more adequate to the goal of conceptual determinacy. Fortunately, every concept, he thinks, comes equipped with an inherent rationality—in keeping with his organic model, he calls it a "rational *kernel*" or "rational *germ*"—which is inwardly driving it to develop more determinate articulations from within. To capture the rhythm of the organic whole, Hegel derives from this internal rhythm one of the most fundamental principles governing dialectical process—what he calls the "the principle of determinate [*bestimmte*] negation."

One compelling interpretation of this principle is represented well by Brandom's holistic account. Take a color concept, say red, whose deter-minate conceptual content can't be grasped in an immediate abstract re-lation of self-identity: "red is red." On Brandom's inferentialist interpre-tation, we steadily advance from this empty, tautologous understanding of red, in which almost nothing seems to be said, to the richer determi-nations from within a complex, holistic system of inferences, articula-tions, and determinations in which the color concept is contextually em-bedded. Grasping the self-identity and self-unity of red nonvacuously really involves these much richer, more complex inferences, articula-tions, and determinations. Hegel makes this explicit to consciousness by running through the instinctive logic implicit in our understanding in the following further steps of reflection: *Determinate* content is intel-ligible only against the background of mediating relations of exclusion that tell you all that the thing is not, in the sense of Spinoza's dictum, "Omnis determinatio est negatio" (SL 113/*Werke* 5:121). Red is what it is, *and not another thing*. But an infinite number of things stands to red in a relation of "indifferent" (*gleichgültig*) exclusion—red is not black, white, green, purple, and a potentially infinite array of diverse colors and things. This would require the mind to take in infinite diversity. This it cannot do. What drives red toward the goal of conceptual determinacy, on Brandom's account, are strongly incompatible commitments and judgments arising from bringing it into mutually exclusive opposition with its determinate opposite. Enter the principle of determinate negation to direct our thought about what a thing nonarbitrarily excludes ("repels"), by invoking further concrete entailments and inferential relations in certain contexts that are methodically ordered to bring "red" into a relation of "strong incompatibility" and "mutual exclusion" with its determinate opposite, "green." So far, so good.

But Brandom's key terms "strong incompatibility" and "mutual exclusion" lead him to claim further that Hegel's notion of determinate negation must be implied in, or closely related to, the notion of negation implied in the law of contradiction, which he understands as "P rules out not-P; they are incompatible." That is, one and the same thing cannot exhibit mutually exclusive properties, P and not-P, because they stand to each other in a relation of strong incompatibility, where one and the same thing can't be both P and not-P at the same time and in the same respect. This is a very natural thought. Since Hegel equates the principle of negation with an "inherent rationality" or "rational germ," which is driving concepts toward the goal of conceptual determinacy, it's very natural to want to relate the principle of determinate negation to the law of contradiction, the most fundamental principle guiding and constraining all *rational* thought. "So far from rejecting the law of contradiction," Brandom insists, "I want to claim that Hegel radicalizes it, and places it at the very center of his thought."[23] So far, so good, if all you want to do is capture the static essences of inanimate objects that don't undergo change.

But what we can't do is extend Brandom's notion of determinate negation, with its ties to the formal law of contradiction, along the temporal dimension of living organisms undergoing change and motion. Since methodological holism seeks to understand how living organisms change over a complete lifetime, from germination to decay, through a fluid sequence of developing opposed parts, a formal notion of negation that excludes or repels opposites won't do. It's true that Hegel sensibly acknowledges that the law of contradiction is indispensable for analyzing a restricted domain of objects and situations, namely, inert, inanimate bodies at rest and "finite situations"—by which I take him to mean inanimate objects that don't undergo change or development. But life-forms, not inert bodies, represent the primary class of objects for Hegel. As early as his doctoral thesis, *De orbitis planetarum*, Hegel is preoccupied

---

[23] Brandom, "Holism and Idealism in Hegel's *Phenomenology*," 179, 182.

with the relation between rest and motion of the celestial bodies. To overcome a false opposition between the concepts of permanence and change, one of his central metaphysical aims is to criticize the concept of permanence of substance as involving inert, static objects; rather, the concepts are inseparably related because substance may be seen to be in continuous, unbroken movement. By being a momentary phase within movement, rest is implicated in the concept of motion.[24] Rather than think of permanent substances as primary, and bodies undergoing change as a special case of bodies at rest, the special case of permanent substances is reducible to the primary case of change. Thus, if motion is the primitive case for Hegel, not reducible to rest, this would make life-forms the *primary* case, not the special limiting case.

The primacy of life-forms for Hegel bears directly on Brandom's account because life-forms require a revisionary, nonbivalent logic that allows one to see P as identical to not-P in some way that is internally related to not-P, yet not reducible to not-P. Conceptual determinacy in life-forms is achieved by relating the thing negatively to its determinate opposite in such a way as to be connected internally to that very thing which it excludes. Thus, if the principle of determinate negation were construed formally so as to *exclude* from the seed what is not related to it (not being a seed, but being a germinating root), as it is on Brandom's account, then it would exclude from our totalizing understanding the plant's next vital growth stage at which the plant is not a static pre-formed seed, but a germinating root developing in time. Determinate negation, viewed naturalistically, not formally, involves the mediation of relations of negation that bring a concept into continuity with its opposite—not to repel, restrict, or exclude it—but to bring it into a negatively charged relation of elective affinity with its opposite so as to include the difference in a holistic, unifying understanding that allows an organism to have its opposite implied in it in some speculative sense of identity-in-difference.[25]

---

[24] On comparisons between Zeno's arrow paradox concerning motion and Hegel's position, see Adam Schaff, "Marxist Dialectics and the Principle of Contradiction," *Journal of Philosophy* 57, no. 7 (March 1960): 248–249.

[25] Many thanks to Bob Brandom for responding to this material and stimulating some revisions. I've accentuated the differences between Brandom's analyses and my own for purposes of being dialectical. We don't disagree over fundamentals, especially, over the holistic and pragmatic elements central to Hegel's thought. I see hints and telltale signs of a softening in Brandom's stance toward

1.3 Negation Naturalized

But giving up formal negation is hard to do. It means seeing that Hegel's naturalized notion, arising out of his commitments to an organic concept of rationality, must involve a fluid way of seeing an organism internally becoming that very thing which it excludes. Hegel seeks a dialectical principle that will capture a relation of mutual interdependence of opposites, not mutual incompatibility. Rather than arbitrarily choose the principles governing dialectic, Hegel seeks to derive the principle of determinate negation directly from nature. In the passage of "The Plant Nature" already discussed, starting from the position of nature and taking nature on its own terms, he cites the relevance of the opposed biological forces of attraction and repulsion to the dialectical process:

> [T]he individual [plant] destroys itself, converts itself into its non-organic nature, and through this self-destruction [*Aufzehrens*] comes forth into existence—the process of formation. (EN §346Z/ *Werke* 9:394–395; cf. EN §§375–376Z/ *Werke* 9:535–538)

In this formative process, the plant undergoes a spontaneous process of "self-repulsion," which has the function of negatively relating it to its opposed force (*Kraft*) or antithetical tendency occurring within the same organism, not in a way that formally excludes or repels its contrary tendency, but in an organic way that relates it inseparably to that very thing which it excludes. A natural force or tendency seeks to express itself but does so only when its expression is elicited by a contradictory force. In order for a force to be what it is, that which elicits its expression must be a force itself equal in power to the force it opposes. The reciprocally opposed forces, attraction and repulsion, have negatively charged effects only in opposition to one another. Change in nature is generated by the interaction of these conflicting forces.

Out of this organic process of self-repulsion, Hegel naturalistically, not formally, derives a principle of teleological development that orders

---

contradiction in his most recent work on Hegel: "A Sketch of a Program for a Critical Reading of Hegel" (*Internationales Jahrbuch des Deutsches Idealismus*, Band 3, 2005, ed. Karl Ameriks and Jürgen Stolzenberg), and in his earlier work with Nicholas Rescher, *Logic of Inconsistency* (Oxford: Basil Blackwell, 1980).

the concept's inner progress. The principle of determinate negation reflects a naturalized process of thought that *strenuously* seeks to adapt itself to this natural tendency toward self-negation that Hegel thinks is present in every living thing. Following nature's example, the concept Being exhibits an internally self-contradictory motion that develops precisely in the way that life appears in organisms. The concept's "rational kernel"—to take up his organic terminology again—meaning the inner logic or rationality ordering the concept's progress—moves it away from its initial abstractness and emptiness and drives it toward acquiring greater determinacy of content by disruptively relating it to its opposed concept: "Non-Being" or "Nothing" (*Nichts*).[26] "Non-Being" seamlessly incorporates the next vital growth stage of the seed at which it becomes something indeterminate in content with respect to its previous form. In passing from not being a seed to becoming a seed-leaf, the plant has directed its energy against itself by becoming something other than what it was.

"Contradiction" (*Widerspruch*) is Hegel's key technical term for this relation of strong ontological opposition arising out of this natural process, where two realities combined in one subject cancel one another's effects such that the two parts can't coexist within a unity at the existing level (EN §248 R). The seed-leaf is seen to be the negation or "contradiction" of the seed, standing in a relation of conceptual, not formal, incompatibility to its previous form. In passing from being a seed to a seed-leaf, the plant has in effect canceled out (negated) its former part and contains the negation or destruction of its previous form. Notice saying that the plant is a "seed-leaf" indicates more than just a negation,

---

[26] To conform to Hegel's German usage, I've capitalized his key concepts, Being, Non-Being, and Becoming. I'll use the term "Non-Being" in order to generate in the starkest terms a flat contradiction between Being and Non-Being. By doing so, I mean to stress that Hegel sees himself drawing on the ancient history of this problem beginning with Heraclitus and its subsequent history in Plato's *Parmenides* and Aristotle's *Physics* (Bk. Alpha) (SL 83; cf. PhG §71; EL §88Z, §81Z). Of his incorporation of Heraclitean and Parmenidean ideas, Hegel writes: "There is no proposition of Heraclitus that I have not adopted in my Philosophy," *Lectures on the History of Philosophy*, trans. E. S. Haldane (London, 1892), 279, 285. Cf. Heraclitus: "I am as I am not," fragment 81 (Heraclitus, 2001, p. 51). On this issue, see Milič Čapek, "Hegel and the Organic View of Nature," in *Hegel and the Sciences*, ed. R. S. Cohen and M. W. Wartofsky (Dordrecht: D. Reidel, 1984), 114–116; and Anthony Manser, "On Becoming," in *Hegel and Modern Philosophy*, ed. David Lamb (London: Croom Helm, 1987), 65–67.

privation, or lack of being a seed. The positive constituent parts of the plant stand to each other in a relation of *real* opposition, not merely of privation or lack, by not being determinately a seed, but now a seed-leaf. Goethe himself never speaks of contradictory parts, but rather of opposing tendencies and polarizations among heterogeneous parts being weakly in opposition.[27] Whereas, Hegel shows in further steps of reflection in his *Logic* that the mere diversity and heterogeneity that Goethe speaks of actually involve richer episodes of consciousness that lead to opposition, and then develop into determinate opposition, and then finally pass over into bona fide contradictions (SL 442). Thus, Hegel insists that a relation of strong, "real contradiction" exists between the plant's constituent parts, not as *logical* contradictories, as black is to white, but rather, as *conceptual* incommensurables, as red is to green in Wittgenstein's color puzzles, which defy consistent visualization and conceptualization.

From this, it doesn't necessarily follow that Hegel's naturalized concepts and norms, with their distinctively contradictory operation, are incompatible with the law of contradiction and other related laws of classical logic. I'll argue further in Chapter 3 that he must still be pragmatically employing the law of contradiction, not in its analytic form, but in the form of what he *does* in dialectical practice. If this fundamental law weren't pragmatically in force in dialectical method as a commonsense principle to impose minimally normative constraints on our consciousness of unity by holding apart opposite meanings, then the simultaneous assertion of two contradictories would collapse into the same meaning. If dialectic were resigned to putting up with contradictions, there would be no need to resolve our incompatible commitments in the third, synthesizing concept, Becoming. Just to distinguish between Being and Non-Being involves implicitly accepting a whole network of inferences and beliefs with systematic connections to other beliefs. By acknowledging

[27] In Goethe's botanical writings, these polarizations and contrasts consist of the root embryo developing downward and the leaf embryo upward. The root embryo always stays simple, whereas the leaf embryo develops diversely. Roots require darkness and moisture to develop, and, by contrast, the leaf requires light and aridity. The upward development of the plant from seed to blossom is a further intensification and "perfection," whereas, by contrast, the downward movement of the root system is an uninteresting conglomeration of fibers and tubes. Goethe, "On Morphology," in *Goethe's Botanical Writings*, trans. Bertha Mueller (Woodbridge, CT: Ox Bow Press, 1989), 95.

the incompatibility of our commitments at the transitions, we acknowledge an obligation to do something to remove the offending incompatibility. What our rational commitments compel us to do when faced with
a contradiction is to remove the defect that led to contradiction. With
just this much in place, ignoring the details for now, I'll proceed on
the supposition that Hegel can't be affirming contradictions in a way
that is incompatible with the law of contradiction since the presence of
contradictions, as well as the *elimination* of them, is at the center of his
dialectical practice.

Since natural contradictions are seen as natural and not formal, they
are not seen as defects in an organism but as positive natural catalysts
that direct an organism's change and development. Hegel praises the
mutually enlivening benefits arising from this interplay of natural forces:
"[C]ontradiction is the root of all movement and vitality; it is only in so
far as something has a contradiction within it that it moves, has an urge
and activity" (SL 439/*Werke* 6:75). The internal motor of concepts, with
its distinctively contradictory operation, is grounded naturalistically in
life or "experience." For Hegel writes, "Yet whoever claims that nothing
exists which carries in itself a contradiction, in the form of an identity
of opposites, is at the same time requiring that nothing *living* shall exist"
(VA 120/*Werke* 13:167). What Hegel thinks he has gained by modeling
his dialectical principles naturalistically on the way nature responds to
contradiction is insight into this positive role that contradiction plays in
moving concepts toward the goal of conceptual determinacy.

Now, tracking what nature does, working from life, Hegel derives the
principle of determinate negation directly from nature. Among the features of living organisms that he thinks carry over to concepts—causality,
self-generating power, self-disruption, self-repair, self-regeneration, and
contradiction—contradiction is the most pertinent feature to something's
being alive: "Something is therefore alive only in so far as it contains
contradiction within it, and moreover is this power to hold and endure
the contradiction within it" (SL 440/*Werke* 6:76). Hegel captures this antithetical tendency of the concept Being to "turn against itself" ("self-
destruct," or "repel itself from itself" from within), in a way that tracks
the manner in which the corresponding empirical object relates itself to
its inner opposed forces. He describes the aporetic role that contradiction plays in moving concepts toward the goal of conceptual determinacy in the following naturalistic terms: "Only when the manifold terms
have been driven to the point of contradiction do they become active

and lively towards one another, receiving in contradiction the negativity which is the indwelling pulsation of self-movement and spontaneous activity [*Lebendigkeit*]" (SL 442/*Werke* 6:78). In the logical-conceptual parallel, living concepts track nature's spontaneous, self-healing response to contradiction thusly: When pent-up forces within the concept Being are brought into a negatively charged relation of elective affinity, our natural abhorrence of violations of our rational commitments to consistency and determinacy produces a spontaneous corrective movement in rational thought. The concept spontaneously disrupts itself from within in the sense of our no longer being able to describe the concept as self-identical. Following what nature does in response to the way contradictions exhibit themselves in organisms, the concept repairs itself by seeking resolution of the offending contradiction in a third, middle concept: Becoming (*Werden*).

The concept Becoming involves introducing the least amount of conceptual revision from the outside needed to repair the incommensurability between Being and Non-Being.[28] Becoming appears as the third term of the dialectical triad that preserves both concepts, not in an unstable relation of mutual exclusion or mutual incompatibility, but as unified coherently under a synthesizing temporal concept that allows for change and transmutation. The seed is neither a seed nor not a seed in Becoming. The seed's potential to become a leaf, as well as any one of its present or future manifestations, is immanent in its stages of coming to be and passing away. The concept Being initially appeared as a simple, indivisible, all-encompassing unity, but in a static and indeterminate way.

---

[28] Becoming, not, say, Beginning, has the greatest proximity to the preceding concepts. Beginning doesn't introduce enough new conceptual distinctions to synthesize Being and Non-Being because it only encompasses the initial phase of the plant as coming to be a seed-leaf but fails to include its terminal stage when it passes away. This explains why we can't skip Becoming and go right to the next concept after Becoming, Determinate Being (*Dasein*), because Determinate Being has loaded into it many more conceptual distinctions than are needed to resolve the ambiguity with the least amount of conceptual revision. Whereas Becoming is inclusive enough to capture both initial and terminating phases in a more all-encompassing unity while introducing the least amount of conceptual revision with respect to the two previous concepts. The significance of minimizing conceptual revision at each transition is to avoid introducing anything conceptual *from outside* the dialectic in progress. On this issue, see Forster, "Hegel's Dialectical Method," in *The Cambridge Companion to Hegel*, ed. Frederick C. Beiser (Cambridge: Cambridge University Press, 1993), 147–148.

The transition to the complex dynamism in Becoming cancels out its indeterminateness and emptiness. What makes the mutability of Becoming an advance over the motionlessness (*Bewegungslösigkeit*) of Being is the introduction of a temporal dimension that gives Becoming a more complex, internally articulated structure that permits negation, mediation, and relations of difference, which allow it simultaneously to incorporate the contradictory stages of coming to be and passing away.

In the triadic movement we've just witnessed, the concept Being moved in our reflection beyond its initial, static emptiness. A further relation with its opposite concept is an implied determination of the organic unity of the concept Being. The concept thus acquired a more articulated structure involving richer determinations permitting negation, mediation, and a relation of difference, which canceled out the initial claim about the seed's emptiness and indeterminateness under the concept Being.[29] By tracking the movement of Being in our reflection, we have arrived at a nonmetaphorical sense in which Hegel thinks concepts are living. Organics is not just an animistic figure of speech, with a meaning merely derived from living organisms.[30] Hegel doesn't distort the concept of an organism in nature to make it less of a stretch to apply to inanimate objects, such as concepts. I've tried to show that, owing to Goethe's influence, Hegel's method of natural science was to derive the concept of the organism from strictly observing nature's objective living structures and then to radically reconstitute our ordinary understanding of concepts so that we can envisage the possibility of their developing *precisely as* living organisms.

If the triadic movement we just witnessed is to count as a true dialectical movement, then Hegel should not be seen as coming out on the side of preformation theory or epigenesis. In classic dialectical fashion,

---

[29] In the parallel phenomenological argument in the *Phenomenology*, introducing relations of negation and mediation into Sense Certainty gives the object of Perception a much more articulated structure than the bare, unmediated object of Sense Certainty.

[30] Hegel applies the concept of organism quite broadly, not just to concepts and living organisms, but also to inanimate crystals and minerals, artifacts, and the state or political community. Michael Wolff argues convincingly that Hegel's use of the term "organic" is not merely metaphorical at least in connection with the state. See Wolff, "Hegel's Organicist Theory of the State: On the Concept and Method of Hegel's 'Science of the State,'" in *Hegel on Ethics and Politics*, ed. Robert Pippin and Otfried Höffe (Cambridge: Cambridge University Press, 2004), 300, 312.

he brings two theories that were originally thought of as opposed closer together by showing that preformation theory—which staged a comeback in the late eighteenth century—already had contained within its concepts some of the key concepts implied in epigenesis. As it turns out, the concept of being a preformed embryo had a more complex internal structure that had implied in it all along the more complex temporal concept, Becoming, which epigenesis invoked to account for growth and generation.

This being the case, if the living motion of concepts is to conform to the indivisible motion of living organisms, not merely by analogy or metaphor, then the concept Non-Being had to be already contained in the concept Being, not in an analytic sense, but in some teleological sense of necessity that already guarantees that the oak tree was foreshadowed in the acorn. We see in an acorn a foreshadowing of the species of oak tree it will become. We can know this about the seed already before witnessing its history unfold. Even in its earliest, embryonic form, the seed of the plant contained a relation to its own negation or nothingness, in the sense that it was already penetrated through and through with the potential to become what it was not: not an acorn, but a germinating root. Since nature follows regular, predictable patterns, regular causal correlations between the seed and its future appearances allow us to predict what the seed will necessarily become. But these lawlike causal regularities in nature won't play an explanatory role of the necessity for revision at the level of concepts. Necessity at the conceptual level will have to be explained by conceptually necessary inferential connections among concepts, not causal connections. Like the seed that necessarily carries within its internal structure its entire evolving history, the rational kernel of the concept Being necessarily—not in the sense of logical necessity but in the sense of teleological necessity already guaranteed by nature—carries within its structure an already completed series of concepts. This returns us to the grain of truth in preformation theory that we began with: "What is to become already is." In the fluidity of Becoming, the transition has "always already" taken place. ◆

What I've tried to show so far, through a sustained empirical example, is how Hegel recasts Goethe's preoccupation with the move from Being to Becoming in nature into the conceptual idiom of his dialectical logic. Hegel's key concepts are consistent with the Goethean view of nature, not as static and pregiven, but ever-changing in a process of becoming. The peculiar sense in which Hegel thinks concepts are alive is exemplified in the living motion from the static Being of nature—what has already taken a preformed shape—to the fluid Becoming of nature—what is perpetually undergoing growth and change.

Although I focused on the dialectical structure of the opening triad in the *Logic*, one encounters in every concept in the series the same generic structure. On my naturalistic reading, Hegel gives his dialectical principles and concepts a developmental structure continuous with the self-developing, self-correcting power of nature. He fashions them out of the tendencies he observes still from a position inside nature, in a way that tries to impose onto nature the least amount of conceptual revision from the outside. By first establishing contradictions empirically and accepting the basic, prerational structure of nature, organics doesn't "leave nature behind," as a dualistic reading of reason and nature would have it. Rather, from a position *immanent* in nature, Hegel sees himself relating to its modes logically, that is, *rationally*, by conceptualizing into rational dialectical principles the dynamic movement from Being to Becoming.

1.4 Nature as a Source of Rational Norms

Still, my naturalistic reading might look as if Hegel runs the risk of leaving nature "as is"—as inchoate, bare, and uninterpreted. But naturalizing underlying dialectical principles doesn't mean leaving nature "as is"—for how could we fail to do that? Hegel doesn't need to fashion a principle out of what we already do out of inertia. Laying stress on the bare natural facts alone would reduce organics to a mechanistic view of nature, precisely the view that organics was supposed to reject. We can't ignore Hegel's insistence that philosophy must give an a priori character to the natural empirical sciences and human sciences (EL §12/*Werke* 8:55–56).[31]

Thus, further clarification is needed: Organics first operates at the immediate level of unconscious nature, accepts its basic structure, and then exposes its contradictions on its own terms—not by animistically imposing onto nature concepts and categories that don't apply to unconscious

---

[31] On Hegel's rejection of an uncritical empiricism involving the bare, unformed contents of raw nature, Sally Sedgwick cites as textual support in the lesser *Logic*: EL §§37–39, §38Z, §24Z1 §24Z1). Cf. Sally Sedgwick, "Hegel's Treatment of Transcendental Apperception in Kant," *Owl of Minerva* 23, no. 2 (1992).

natural life, but by making explicit in human awareness nature's affinity for human reason from a standpoint already immanent in nature. To avoid leaving nature as is or worse, behind, Hegel starts from a descriptive notion of the presence of contradiction as a powerful life force (*vis viva*) in nature, which aims spontaneously to generate and eliminate contradictions as part of its own self-correcting development. At this purely descriptive level, Hegel appears to be empirically affirming the existence of contradictions as a neutral, ontological feature in a physical world devoid of self-conscious subjects. We can't say, strictly from a position inside nature, that nature reacts emotively with abhorrence to contradiction, without lapsing into a kind of anthropomorphism. At this level, nature is a blind, nonrational mechanism, and negation and contradiction appear to nature differently than they do to rational discursive beings such as ourselves. Since nonrational nature is morally neutral with respect to the presence or elimination of contradictions, Hegel seeks to derive from nature a normative notion which is appropriate to a rational self-consciousness who can react moralistically with abhorrence to contradictions and pursue the rational goal of eliminating them.

To reconcile the normative, evaluative response to contradictions with the natural, descriptive notion, without mechanically reducing the former to the later, Hegel deduces the evaluative sense of contradiction from the lower, prerational, unconscious tendencies in nature. To keep our normative responses grounded stably in the lower, prerational tendencies of nature, dialectical principles get their naturalized rational content from being a powerful emanation of the rationality hidden in and implicit in nature's self-correcting principles. But since nature has no conscious awareness of its latent rationality, it takes a higher-order commentary, given from a self-conscious standpoint of human reason, to read thought processes out of (not into) nature in order to give logical form to what nature has really achieved. Without lapsing into animism, anthropomorphism, or metaphor, Hegel claims that nature is already in some sense invested with an immanent rationality (a latent "rational kernel"), which has an affinity for human reason. This inherent rationality as it "shows," "displays," or "presents" itself in nondiscursive form in nature prefigures the rational progress and development of the concepts in his *Logic*. It takes the "cunning of reason," that is, the mediation of rational reflection and a psychological motivation, to derive this rational content from the uninterpreted results of unthinking, unconscious, prerational nature. This involves further reflection on the significance of the descriptive facts in a way which isn't available just by examining the neutral presence and elimination of contradictions in nature. Hegel supplies this higher-order commentary at the level of his *Logic* by reproducing nature's enlivening response to contradiction in the form of certain laws and judgments that seek the elimination of contradictions: namely, the principle of determinate negation, the identity-in-difference principle, and the principle of the interpenetration of opposites—the very rational norms that make explicit nature's blind goal to eliminate contradictions.

Therefore, far from giving us a crude naturalism that leaves nature as is, Hegel's higher-order commentary takes us beyond unthinking nature, by *completing and fully realizing* at a conscious interpretive level what nature has really achieved—even though it doesn't know it. All the while, he's building on what happens at the lower, prerational level by giving our higher, normative response to contradiction a grounding in the lower, prerational self-correcting power of nature.

Feel privileged to be allowed to look upon nature from a respectful distance. Look, but don't disturb! But never feel ashamed before the power of Nature. Nature is becoming self-conscious.

2

Living Concepts and Living Selves

2.1 Transition Problems

Everything, I would venture, turns on how Hegel has characterized the pure structure of the transitions (*Übergänge*) as that paradoxical juncture of the dialectic at which a unified concept necessarily passes over into contradictory parts. Something paradoxical is happening at the thought transitions at which we are required to hold a concept's opposed determinations firmly in thought in an internally related synthesis that doesn't repel, but holistically includes, the contradiction in an unstable equilibrium (SL 440/*Werke* 6:76). While the parts are conceptually pulled apart and kept separate in ordinary thinking, thinking a contradiction, Hegel insists, is the essential moment of the concept (SL 835) at which the parts are held "firmly" together in intelligent reflection (SL 441–442/*Werke* 6:77–78).

One of the greatest transition problems is thought to occur in the movement from Being to Becoming that we have just analyzed. Hegel himself admits that "the proposition: 'Being and nothing are the same' appears to be such a paradoxical proposition" that we can't speak or represent the thought in a coherent proposition (EL §87R, §88R/*Werke* 8:188). We can grasp the thought, comprehend it, think it, and even *mean* it through our use of the word "Becoming." But there is nothing prima facie in this paradoxical proposition, as is, to justify the thought that a third, intermediate term with a temporal dimension, like Becoming, can supersede the contradictoriness of the two previous static concepts, rather than simply repeating, combining, or running them together in disregard of their opposed meanings. No surprise, then, that many astute commentators have taken issue particularly with the transition to Becoming.[1]

Yet Hegel asks us to consider this in-between situation, falling in the cracks of the transition as it were, as giving rise to a new object in its own right (PhG §279/*Werke* 3:212). Each term is what it is only in virtue of being defined reciprocally in contrast with its determinate opposite. But while the constituent parts are strongly incompatible, the relation itself that connects Being with Non-Being can't be one of mutual exclusion. For no such distinctions or oppositions are present in true organic unity, which is just the relation in transition. This inseparable codependency between the terms is not a relation of mutual incompatibility, where the terms would come into conflict and cancel each other out, but rather a relation of mutual entailment, where the terms are brought together necessarily into an unstable equilibrium (EL §119). Hegel thus considers the *relation* of strong contradiction connecting Being and Non-Being as pure transition, as an object in its own right (PhG §279). He calls this transition a "nonactual" object ("*Unwirkliche*," PhG §32/*Werke* 3:35–36), drawing as he is on the tradition of Plato's *Parmenides* (PhG §71; SL 83, 94–95, 100; EL §81Z1, §104Z3), which generates a paradox about whether an object with such contradictory determinations could really exist, or whether we can coherently refer to a thing that does not exist. The concept Being would seem to refer to an object that both "is" and "is not"—i.e., a self-contradictory, hence unrealizable, object not existing in physical or logical space. This "non-actual" object in transition, consisting in just the relation of real opposition, "falls apart" or "falls to the ground," Hegel puns (SL 437), in the sense that we lose our ground or justification for subsuming the object under a self-unified concept (SL 440; PhG §54).

How, then, do we integrate the effects of contradiction at the transitions without doing violence to our rational commitments to conceptual determinacy? Hegel's doctrine of contradiction is not meant to leave us stuck in aporiai at the transitions, for he writes in the lesser Logic, "contradiction is

---

[1] On the transition problems afflicting Becoming, see John Findlay, *Hegel: A Re-examination* (London: George Allen and Unwin, 1958), 158–159; John McTaggart, *A Commentary on Hegel's Logic* (Cambridge, 1910), 20; Charles Taylor, *Hegel* (Cambridge: Cambridge University Press, 1975), 232; Michael J. Inwood, *Hegel* (London: Routledge and Kegan Paul, 1983), 310; and Anthony Manser, "On Becoming," in *Hegel and Modern Philosophy*, ed. David Lamb (London: Croom Helm, 1987).

not the end of the matter, but cancels itself" (EL §119Z).[2] Contradiction is not the end of the matter, but a transitional point of instability, an aporetic moment in the movement of reflection that must cancel itself out at a higher ground than can be afforded by any of the concepts at the present level (EL §119Z2; VA 97).

But how do we extend Hegel's rejection of a bivalent contrast between the pairs of opposites—e.g., truth/falsity, good/evil, virtue/vice—to the false contrast between conceptual determinacy and the effects of contradiction? The goal of striving toward determinacy of meaning and contradictory effects at the transitions seem opposed because thinking a contradiction sends the mind scattering in all directions instead of settling on a univocal, determinate result. Trying to conceive of an object under an unrealizable concept, which refers to an as-of-yet indeterminate object, would seem to violate our most basic conditions on determinacy of meaning. Namely, the antecedent condition under which a potential object can be thought of as unified is that it can't exceed logical possibility. If the appropriate test of the truth of a concept lies in its empirical actualization, as it does for Hegel,[3] then concepts must refer to a determinate, contentful something, not to a nihil negativum.

In the light of this paradoxical situation, let's check what's happening at the transitions against common sense. Even before philosophical reflection finds a ground for recognizing organic unity in the plant's heterogeneous parts, Hegel means to keep theory in check by insisting, with common sense, that we already grasp the plant as unified. Notice he doesn't call the object in transition a "hypothetical object," an "indeterminable x," or an "object in general" (*Gegenstand überhaupt*). What is required psychologically, if not logically, to keep this "non-*actual* object" from unraveling in consciousness is a commonsense form of perceptual realism represented as "Perception" in the *Phenomenology* (PhG §131). One sign that he means to stick close to common sense is that the law of contradiction, what Aristotle called a "principle of common sense," is still in force at the transitions, at least in one form or another. Though

---

[2] Hegel confirms this in the *Lectures on Aesthetics*: "Life . . . only becomes affirmative in its own eyes by obliterating the opposition and the contradiction. It is true that if it remains in mere contradiction without resolving it, then on contradiction it is wrecked" (VA, Intro., 97).

[3] Hegel writes, "Truth entails that the concept shall be, and that this existence shall correspond with the concept" (EL §104Z).

this is not to say, as we'll see later, that Hegel himself identifies formal logic with sound common sense (EL §115R).

But Hegel's views on the relationship of speculative philosophy to common sense are complicated.[4] It's not enough for philosophical reflection simply to accord with a commonsense perceptual realism, as we'll see later. Philosophically speaking, Hegel thinks there can be no such immediate or original unity in an object prior to a conscious subject's recognizing that unity through a process of deeper reflection (PhG §18). Later I'll clarify this relationship between philosophical reflection and common sense in the context of relating formal logic, which Hegel associates with a species of the ordinary understanding, to dialectical logic, which he associates with speculative Reason. For now, suffice it to say we know immediately and unreflectively with common sense that there just are these organic unities. But we are not yet able to express or represent our thoughts about them coherently in propositions. Thus, to avoid a Sense-Certainty style refutation—that is, giving the object undergoing change and becoming a false determinacy that is ultimately self-undermining and self-refuting—something more philosophical than common sense is needed to express the ground of our consciousness of this unity in a more "reflected" way.

My task in this chapter is to inquire more *reflectively* into the ground of our consciousness of unity in Becoming. We are faced with only two choices, at least on a traditional metaphysics: Either we know a thing's unity by the way the object is in logical terms a priori and independently of consciousness or by the way the object presents itself to consciousness a posteriori. That is, every statement is either an analytic principle known a priori or a synthetic principle known by empirical experience a posteriori. (We note in passing a class of statements not easily classifiable as either analytic or synthetic.)[5] I'll argue that Hegel thinks both

---

[4] Cf. PR §2R, §317, §318, Z, §319R, §360. Common sense, Hegel thinks, contains a germ of truth, but it takes a "great man of the age" to find and recognize the grain of truth in it (PR §318Z). For common sense has no criteria for discriminating between true and false opinion (and half-truths). Philosophy must first gain critical distance and independence from common sense, he thinks, and then accept it afterward, but only after certain key philosophical concepts have undergone a transformation enabling them to express new Hegelian meanings (PR §317–318; cf. "On the Essence of Philosophical Criticism," 280, 283).

[5] Hilary Putnam marks out a "large" class of statements not classifiable as either analytic or synthetic in "On the Analytic and Synthetic," in *Minnesota Studies in the Philosophy of Science*, 3: 358–397. Minneapolis: University of Minnesota Press, 1962.

alternatives have to fail; thus, to avoid the "fork" of traditional meta-physics, he was motivated to give an Idealist analysis of our conscious-ness of unity, one which relates concepts to selves. I end this chapter with a brief sketch of what this unifying ground must look like to have the structure and unity peculiarly characteristic of living selves.

2.2 Logic of Contradiction

If empirical concepts refer to organisms that exhibit rational, lawlike movements in Becoming, then it would seem that our rational com-mitments require us to take these regularities as unfolding according to some kind of logic. Thus, consider first whether we can articulate the *log-ical* basis for our consciousness of the unity of a plant undergoing meta-morphosis with the law of the excluded middle (and indirectly, the law of contradiction, to which it is related).[6] Hegel understands the law of the excluded middle as Aristotle does, as asserting that something must be either P or not-P, and that there is no third possibility (SL 438–439; cf. Aristotle, *Metaphysics*, Gamma, 1011b25–27).

But this first move is blocked by Hegel's insistence that the concept of Becoming involves incompatible commitments at the transition that can't be mediated by logical laws. Hegel cites metamorphosing plants, along with other garden-variety concepts, as clear exceptions to the law of excluded middle (EL §119R/ *Werke* 8:246): "Instead of speaking in ac-cordance with the law of excluded middle (which is a law of the abstract understanding), it would be better to say 'Everything stands in opposi-tion.' There is in fact nothing, either in heaven or on earth, either in the spiritual or the natural world, that exhibits the abstract 'either-or' as it is maintained by the understanding" (EL §119, Z2).[7] The law rules out precisely the indivisible middle phase we seek to capture at which the

---

[6] SL 438. See Adam Schaff on converting the law of the excluded middle into the law of contradiction using the law of de Morgan. "Marxist Dialectics and the Principle of Contradiction," *Journal of Philosophy* 57, no. 7 (March 1960): 241.

[7] Hegel cites other notable exceptions to the law of the excluded middle, such as "ignorance" as indifferent to truth and error; "grey" as neither dark nor light; "innocence" as neither good nor evil; and "motion" itself (SL 437–438/HW 6:72–73). Kit Fine also cites as exceptions "red" and "tall," among others. Cf. Fine, "Vagueness, Truth, and Logic," in *Vagueness: A Reader*, ed. Rosanna Keefe and Peter Smith (Cambridge: MIT Press, 1997), 130–131.

plant is neither a seed nor not a seed (in symbols: neither P nor not-P), but is ceasing to be a seed (P) as equally coming to be a seed-leaf (not-P). The seed does not now gradually pass over into not being a seed. For that would imply falsely a sharp separation under the concept Becoming between being a seed and ceasing to be a seed (EL §87Z). Organic holism rules out this artificial separation by guaranteeing that the seed "always already" has its opposite determinations indivisibly and causally implied in it. The transition in nature is indivisible, and the difference is dissolved in the fluid movement of one becoming the other. Quite the opposite of excluding this in-between middle phase, thinking this contradiction as a relation is an essential moment of consciousness of the organic unity in Becoming (SL 835).

Consider alternatively whether a disjunctive judgment of the form "The plant is A or B or C or D or . . ." can logically mediate our incompatible commitments in Becoming. No matter which way we interpret the connective "or" we run into problems. The "or" can't be exclusive because organic holism requires us to understand the plant's parts (disjuncts), not as subordinate to any other, but as symmetrically coordinated in the in-between phase during which the plant is neither a seed nor not a seed, but is *equally* one of these disjuncts as well as any other. Nor can the "or" be interpreted inclusively because, we've said, the plant undergoing change has contradictory parts, and an inclusive "or" would unify mutually exclusive disjuncts in violation of the law of contradiction. This would put a disjunctive judgment in conflict with itself, since by its own lights, to assert a relation of mutual exclusivity between disjuncts carries with it implied judgments and norms that pragmatically uphold certain principles of common sense, such as the law of contradiction. By trying to avoid a contradiction, by doing so, the principle would thereby commit one (EL §119R).

Thus, Becoming belongs to a class of concepts, far larger than is usually supposed, which confronts us with the striking fact that indeterminate organisms can appear unified at the transitions of thought without the necessity of their being related to certain fundamental laws of logic. Hegel asks us to respect this new class of objects in transition: one whose ontic indeterminacy gives the objects in it a content that strains our most fundamental logical resources, yet each such object in transition is to be regarded by common sense as any other substantial, self-unified object. This would partly explain why so many astute commentators, such as Findlay, Inwood, McTaggart, Taylor, and others, have taken issue with the derivation of Becoming. This indicates, not so much a failing on their part as inherent barriers to conceptualizing living structures in a way that takes us beyond purely discursive thought proceeding in accordance with the classical laws of logic. Finding the ground of this "reflected unity" (PhG §172) will require coming to grips with the peculiar ontological status of this nonactual object in transition: an object that has to be regarded by common sense as any other substantial object, whose parts are known to be in an inseparable organic unity, but whose ontic indeterminacy throws into crisis our attempts to capture that unity.

We need new conditions for cognizing organic unity that take us beyond purely discursive thought. Since logical principles apply to what we would call *conceptual* content, this would seem to imply that our consciousness of organic unity falls in between purely discursive and nondiscursive thought. Accordingly, rather than use conceptual phrases, Hegel discards the kind of discursive language that pulls apart an object in reflection and instead uses pictorial language reminiscent of Goethe's botanical idiom: The flower "bursts forth" from the bud, "bends back into itself," and "recoils upon itself." Buds "force out" their flowers at the nodes. The seed spontaneously "passes over immediately" into a seed-leaf. New nodes form by a process of "internal self-repulsion," by a "self-repelling movement," in a kind of "repulsion which immediately takes itself back into itself." Hegel's visual organic model reflects our aspiration to "see" the contradictions that show, exhibit, or present themselves at the transitions. While the third middle term Becoming conceptually connects Being and Non-Being, a logical connecting middle is not something one can see. Hegel's imagery of "self-repulsion" implies inconsistent visualization of two incompatible images, a hypothetical state which reflects the fact that natural contradictions can't be logically mediated.

This doesn't make Hegel's way of speaking loose and irrational, versus the more rigorous way in which logicians talk about formal contradictions. Without appealing to the pure intuition *(Anschauung)* of romantic *Naturphilosophie*, he conveys rather through kinetic imagery that the changes at the transitions occur instantaneously and spontaneously and there can be no mediation of thought at the transitions, specifically, of the purely discursive kind requiring the mediation of logical principles. Without lapsing into vagueness, the sharp pictorial quality of his images has a determinacy and specificity that points us toward a new condition for seeing what's happening at the invisible thought transitions: one that recovers the whole progression of parts *in concreto* and in terms of the whole, through a spontaneous, creative faculty of intuiting Being and Non-Being in some streamlined sense that mediates between discursive and nondiscursive thought.

2.3 Perceiving Living Substances

This leaves us with only one alternative on a traditional metaphysics: to capture our consciousness of unity in Becoming in *phenomenal*, not logical, terms. I'll explore this second alternative in connection with Hegel's analogous critique of Perception in the *Phenomenology* for systematic reasons having to do with one-to-one correspondences between the logical categories and the shapes of consciousness (SL 28).[8] The problem in Perception speaks directly to our problem of how to understand the category of Becoming by perceiving substances a posteriori: that is, how do we recognize a thing as unified if the way it presents itself to perception is as a thing of multiple, diverse properties, where this diversity contradicts its unity? The best available representative of the kind of commonsense perceptual realism that Hegel has in mind in Perception (PhG §131) is none other than Goethe himself, whose strong empiricist commitments led him to try to account for our inarticulable awareness of what's happening at the transitions from within ordinary perception alone.

In "Perception," Hegel starts from a commonsense realist theory of perception. When he says a flower "bursts forth" spontaneously from a bud, or the seed "passes over immediately" into a leaf, or the buds "force out" their flowers at the nodes, the kind of spontaneity implied in his pictorial idiom doesn't imply an absence of event-causation or prior causal determination at the level of nature. The bud is the causal antecedent

---

[8] I'm roughly following Michael Forster's one-to-one mapping of the correspondences between the logical categories and the shapes of consciousness. See Michael N. Forster, *Hegel's Idea of a Phenomenology of Spirit* (Chicago: University of Chicago Press, 1998), chap. 15, "The Underlying Logic of the *Phenomenology*," 511–535, 524). In the preface to the first edition of the larger *Logic*, Hegel describes the *Logic* as a "sequel" to the *Phenomenology*, in which the dialectical progressions of the *Phenomenology* are grounded in the *Logic* and the logical concepts underpin the shapes of consciousness (SL 28). To avoid overschematization, I think one has to allow for some flexibility and differences in detail as to how the mapping goes: roughly, I'm following a one-to-one mapping of Being onto Sense-Certainty (PhG §91) and Becoming onto Perception.

of the flower. In nature, the transition to a plant's flowering phase may be relatively rapid or slow, but it takes place gradually and uninterruptedly over time. As Goethe observes, "[A]s abrupt as the transition from corolla to staminal organ is in some plants, we nevertheless observe that Nature cannot always traverse this distance in *one* stride."[9] Nature leaves no "time gaps."

Problems only arise, Goethe observes, because the changes take place abruptly in our *phenomenal* awareness. According to common sense, when the jasmine flower "bursts forth" spontaneously from the cluster of nodes, a visual thing still turns up at the transition. Something persists through the change in becoming.[10] But we can't literally see with bare perception, with our physical eye, strongly exclusionary phenomena in the gaps as the plant undergoes metamorphosis as both a bud and not a bud (but becoming a flower). Seeing the blossoming flower as the negation or "contradiction" of the bud, standing to its previous form in a relation of conceptual incompatibility, would involve simultaneously seeing two conceptually exclusionary phenomena. This we can't do, and the nonactual object "falls apart" in transition. But the aporetic crisis that occurs in reflection—as the object unravels in consciousness—doesn't correspond to a similar crisis at the level of natural causation. The feature of spontaneity to be accounted for describes rather the *phenomenal* quality of our experience of the time gap. What is plausible *phenomenologically* is that the constituent parts stand to one another in a relation of mutual incompatibility, instantly and abruptly displacing one another in our *phenomenal* awareness. From the *phenomenological* point of view, the transition

---

[9] Johann Wolfgang von Goethe, "On Morphology," in *Goethe's Botanical Writings*, trans. Bertha Mueller (Woodbridge, CT: Ox Bow Press, 1989), 48, 42.

[10] In our phenomenal awareness, we can reidentify the plant as the same plant from one moment to the next. Even after its metamorphosis we say, "the plant changes." Philosophically speaking, however, the problem with saying that A changes to B is that some features of the plant can't change without the thing ceasing to be what it is essentially. For if A changes to B, then it can no longer be A, because our perception of A, regarded as the cause of a change in part B, can never recur and be identical with our perception of what it was before. We are saying A is both itself and not itself. The problem of contradiction, considered as a general problem concerning change, arises as well for the concept of cause in nature, not just for the way we use words and propositions. Changes affecting the essential identity of a thing underlie the problem of cause and effect, particularly in the case of simultaneous causation, where the experience involves the simultaneous occurrence of parts instantaneously passing away and coming to be.

feels instantaneous, indivisible, and unmediated. While the object unraveling in conscious reflection poses no threat at the level of natural causation, it produces an aporetic crisis in our *phenomenal* awareness.

We might wonder, anachronistically, whether Hegel and Goethe might have responded differently had they had access to a plant's growth recorded by a slow-speed camera. Speeding up the film would seamlessly incorporate all phases of the plant's growth and show nature "filling in" the gaps without any glitches. But this would be of no help since with common sense we never doubted that a unified plant persists through the time gaps in our perception. We don't learn anything new through the mechanism's eyes about our consciousness of organic unity given in the temporal order of *our* perceptions. What we see through mechanical eyes, filtered to us through a distorting lens in accelerated, unreal time, can't meet our aspiration to "see" the parts carried across the gaps. Our experience is qualified by whoever is controlling the camera. Who is manipulating the speed of the camera? Who is controlling the distortion?

To account for our recognition of organic unity in relevant *phenomenal* terms, Goethe goes beyond brute perception and invokes a spontaneous, creative intuitive mental operation that he calls "intuitive perception": a psychological state that involves perceiving *oneself* as one actively "fills in" the gaps between the parts, until the parts blend into a seamless unity.[11] As the seed undergoes a gradual process of expansion into a seed-leaf, we reproduce in thought analogous movements of expansion and contraction that occur in nature. Intuitive perception gives us a composite perception of the plant's parts as a complete, regularly connected sequence. This state still occurs within perception and involves perceiving *ourselves* as we actively and nonmechanically fill in the gaps. When we do this, we observe what we do—not with our physical eye, but with our "mind's eye." In doing this, we become like nature. For the mental activity that carries us over the gaps is analogous to the living motion of nature.

Goethe himself seemed to realize that there has to be more to the story than this. Intuitive perception can give us a composite perception

---

[11] Eckart Förster argues that Goethe's notion of intuitive perception is reminiscent of Kant's Intellectus Archetypus in the third *Critique*. Förster, "On the Importance of §§76–77 in Kant's *Critique of Judgment* on the Development of Post-Kantian Philosophy," *Zeitschrift für philosophischen Forschung* 56, no. 2 (2002): 169–190.

of the plant's parts as a complete, regularly connected sequence only on the supposition that some underlying substrate persists throughout the plant's metamorphosis, to which the parts owe their unity. Without this underlying unifying substratum, the sequence of parts amounts to nothing more than a series of indifferently related parts. Goethe's way of accounting for our intuitive recognition of unity still from within perception is to invoke an "*Urphenomenon*" or "Archetype," which transmutes itself, by means of vital forces of expansion and contraction into every one of the plant's diverse forms and appearances. All of the plant's parts are to be understood as developing out of this single underlying structure. The blossoming flower is derived from the shoot with foliage of the same origin as the stem, and so on. All variations in form express this inner, essential vital force, which underlies and unifies all the inessential variations and permutations to which it gives rise. Our intuitive recognition of unity stays within intuitive perception, for, as Goethe claims, the *idea* of an Archetype and *perception* coincide. We perceive the idea in the organism through intuitive perception.

But can Goethe have everything he wants? Goethe's perceptual model undermines itself, Hegel claims, when its strict empiricist and essentialist commitments come into conflict: "[I]t is really the *essential* property of the Thing that is its undoing" (PhG §125/ *Werke* 3:103; italics added). By fixing an Archetype as the essential, primary point of reference, the *terminus a quo et terminus ad quem*, Goethe tries to assign strictly within perception alone a primary role to the essential underlying core of the plant and then cast its inessential, derived forms in a secondary role. The secondary properties function in a subsidiary role to merely qualify the primary object under consideration. But the very distinction between what is primary and what is secondary is arbitrary. To separate off in perception an essential core, the idea of an Archetype, from its inessential manifestations, presupposes the very distinction between what is essential and inessential that it was meant to demonstrate. The very distinction conflicts with Goethe's holistic commitments, which, recall, require that both primary and secondary parts be inseparably related to the unified whole, and on an equal footing in terms of giving us the identity of the thing. According to methodological holism, we can't know the Archetype as the primary fixed point of departure and point of return independently of the very nexus of inferential and exclusionary relations that we rely on holistically to give us the thing's primary, essential identity. Thus, by the model's own lights, Goethe's idea of an

Archetype must draw on an idea outside experience. With this illicit move, Hegel concludes that "Perception" thereby refutes itself. This conclusion should put us in mind of Schiller's remark to Goethe: "That is not an observation from experience. That is an *idea.*"[12]

But if neither logic nor perception can provide the basis for our intuitive consciousness of unity in becoming, then we've exhausted both ways on a traditional metaphysics of coming to know the unity of living organisms: Either by the way the object is in logical terms known a priori or by the way the organism presents itself to consciousness through perception a posteriori. To escape the "fork" of traditional metaphysics, Hegel leaves open the possibility at the end of "Perception" that the basis of our recognition of unity lies in a conscious, purposeful, living self: "Quite rightly," he says, "*consciousness* makes itself responsible for the oneness [unity]" (PhG §121/*Werke* 3:101). With Goethe, Hegel thinks there is something lawlike in natural organisms, which doesn't correspond to known perceptual or logical relations but to something unknown in the subject: the unknown unity of the living self. Even if we can't say in logical or perceptual terms how our concepts refer determinately to objects exhibiting unities and regularities, we still have to take responsibility for our commitments to conceptually determinate content. If something independent of the self is not responsible for a thing's unity in becoming, then the unifying medium has to be something supplied by us. I'll end this chapter with a brief sketch of the sense in which Hegel thinks living concepts and living selves are related in an important way.

2.4 Becoming a Living Subject

The living quality that a thing has for us is intelligible only on the hypothesis that we can undergo a process of self-reflection that will make our thought more appropriately receptive to nature. I began this chapter by distancing Hegel from the assumption that the relation between nature and our cognitive faculties starts out as appropriate, or that our minds are

---

[12] Goethe, "Fortunate Encounter," in *Scientific Studies*, ed. Douglas Miller (New York: Suhrkamp, 1988), 20. Hegel made a similar observation about Cuvier's claim to be able to infer from a bone alone the whole shape to which it belonged: "It is not a *perception* which prevails in this method, but a universal guiding *thought*" (VA 127).

so prestructured as to read into or impose onto natural objects a unity and purpose. Hegel's early model in these matters, Goethe himself, writes, "If we wish to arrive at some living perception [*lebendige Anschauung*], of nature, we ourselves must remain as quick and flexible as nature and follow the example she gives."[13] Nature manifests how we ought to be, or are meant to be, not how nature should be perceived and conceptualized by our concepts and categories. For our concepts to adequately capture the living essences of nature, in accord with which they move, our attitude toward living concepts and nature ought to exemplify the attitude that we ought to take toward ourselves. To study how concepts are living is to study how our relation to ourselves ought to be. Rather than model concepts on the unity and structure of living selves, we must model human consciousness on the *objectively* living exemplars in nature. We must become living subjects.

But if life in its human form is something essentially linked to desire and self-consciousness, as it is in the dialectic that unfolds in the self-consciousness chapter of Hegel's *Phenomenology*, then, like self-consciousness, becoming a living subject is something that must be achieved. That's why Hegel thinks it's not an empty tautology to refer to the achievement of "Life as a *living* thing" ("*Leben als Lebendiges*," PhG §171/*Werke* 3:141). For life, in this specifically mediated sense exists only in an individual's subjective awareness of himself *as* a living being, as expressed in the sentence "Life is only now actual as individual living subject" (AT 122). Just as self-consciousness can only be strenuously achieved through the recognition of another self-consciousness, only a living consciousness, which has achieved a *known* living relation to itself, can recognize another living thing in a way which belongs to a knower, and can only belong to a living knower. To recognize life in an object requires a form of cognition with the same living structure as that object. It takes life to recognize life.

In principle, anyone who is minimally alive can adopt this enlightened perspective on nature. But it doesn't follow that any unreflective, un-*Hegelian* person will see that all of the important structural features in Becoming are internal to their thought. One has to acquire an awareness of oneself as something possessing that very structure by acquiring a reflective, mediated awareness of one's own living nature becoming animated through appearances. We won't be appropriately receptive to

---

[13] Goethe, "On Morphology," 64.

the living currents of nature unless we change our modes of thinking and accept a new way of relating to ourselves as living objects. Hegel's revisionary logic of organic wholes demands this new way of thinking about nature. Although one can recognize one's living nature in an original immediate unity, the reflective process by which one becomes a living subject has to involve a higher kind of unity—not an immediate unity, but one which parallels the steps of reflection we passed through in the move from the static concept Being toward the dynamism of Becoming.

Following a similar series of steps, the self initially starts out regarding itself as a static fixed substance. "The self produces itself as an object," as Hegel puts it rather unappetizingly, and "The self becomes a *thing*." The self is initially indifferent to itself, even opposed to itself, as an inert, inanimate substance. To bring consciousness into more meaningful contact with itself as living, thought can't be directed at a static, dead substance. In the preface to the *Phenomenology*, Hegel emphasizes that to give up the "fixity" of the Ego, consciousness can't stand by as a passive spectator witnessing the parade of living concepts unfold in consciousness: "Thoughts become fluid when pure thinking . . . recognizes itself as a moment . . . —*not by leaving itself out, or setting itself aside*, but by giving up the *fixity* of its self-positing" (PhG §33/*Werke* 3:37, italics added). To move spontaneously in accord with nature, the self requires a form of cognition with the same dynamic structure as living objects: a subjective awareness of itself *becoming* a living subject through animated appearances. We need a concrete representation that will mirror the structure of ourselves as living, capturing only that content that is relevant to adequately mirroring the structure of living exemplars. Some of the content of consciousness will be indifferent to that structure—what Hegel calls its "indifferent diversity." The part of the self that is relevant to mirroring the motion of living exemplars involves a self-disrupting, self-correcting motion of reflection that moves in a contradictory way more characteristic of life. The relevant aspect of consciousness needed to grasp life is structurally more like the consciousness of *becoming* a living subject than like the consciousness of *being* a substance. Becoming a subject involves restructuring the self's understanding of itself as a fixed, static ego, standing to itself in an abstract relation of immediate self-unity, which overcomes the indifferent relation between itself as subject and object. This produces a third entity, a mediated unity, a reflected unity of the self: the self becoming a living subject.

2.5 Organic Concepts: Platonic or Historical Reading?

But if there is a deep aspect of empirical nature that has at its basis neither empirical nor logical features, but rather humanly constructed features, doesn't this throw us all the way back to the Kantian strategy I rejected at the beginning? Doesn't this mean that concepts are living only in our subjective way of reflecting about them or by analogy with our human faculties? How does Hegel avoid animistically attributing to nature concepts and categories appropriate only to a human consciousness?

There is a peculiar double sense in which living concepts depend on consciously designing agents in history and yet stand outside time.[14] Concepts depend on human consciousness to the extent that they can't be comprehended as unified and self-moving in an unmediated way. For, to repeat, there is no such thing for Hegel as unmediated knowledge of an immediate unity prior to a living consciousness providing the element of mediation needed to grasp its living unity. But concepts that depend on my consciousness in this sense don't make me the exclusive owner of them in any significant way. Being comprehended by human consciousness doesn't mark them with an idiosyncratic, subjective content,

---

[14] The divergence in historicist and Platonic readings reflects, not so much a misunderstanding on commentators' part, as a deep ambivalence in Hegel's own texts. There is a textual basis for both readings. On the one hand, the Platonic sense in which the Concept (sometimes called the Absolute, God, or Spirit) is atemporal and eternal is reinforced in the *Encyclopedia*, where Hegel writes that time has no power over the Concept because "it is not *in* time that everything comes to be and passes away, rather time itself is the becoming" (EG §258R). Whether the Concept in the form of Spirit stands outside time, Hegel similarly writes that Spirit is not in time, but belongs to eternity. Actual instantiations or historical appearances of Spirit pass away, and the passing away is at the same time the arising of a new appearance. Time (in the form of history) is merely the finite or temporal particular form in which Spirit or the Concept appears. What comes into being and passes away in time are particular finite appearances or new forms of Spirit (the Concept), but not Spirit itself. On the other hand, the historicist reading is also right to insist that human shapes of consciousness develop in temporal succession and human thought is what is responsible for the appearance of a new form of Spirit (cf. PhG §29, §46, §78, §295, §679). Therefore, to give a narrative of the development of concepts, one must give a *history* of Spirit or human thought: "[T]he World-Spirit itself, has had the patience to pass through these shapes over the long passage of time, and to take upon itself the enormous labor of world-history" (PhG, Preface §29). Thanks to Allen Wood and Sally Sedgwick for helpful comments on this issue.

which would identify them only with occurrent mental episodes of my consciousness. Although there is some active, productive ingredient in human consciousness that is essential to *comprehending* concepts, this doesn't mean that human consciousness is privileged on Hegel's view as being the primary originary source.

Rather, there is a second sense in which concepts move themselves because nature itself is prior to human consciousness and is self-moving. This sense in which concepts exist prior to nature and human history gets reflected in Hegel's general principle underlying the tripartite ordering of the main parts of his System: *Logic, Naturphilosophie,* and *Philosophy of Spirit.*[15] The triadic progression moves us from the most abstract presentation of concepts in atemporal, logical space in the *Logic,* where they exist independently of, and conceptually prior to, time and human consciousness, to their more concrete instantiation in empirical determinations in the *Naturphilosophie,* and, finally, to achieving their most concrete shape in spiritual life-forms in history in the *Philosophy of Spirit.* Beginning with the *Logic,* Hegel tells the story of how the concepts unfold independently of, and prior to, nature and human consciousness. In this respect, the logical concepts unfold and develop "behind the back" of the shapes of consciousness. The fact that the *Logic* precedes the *Naturphilosophie* in his System indicates that concepts possess an objective unity and organization temporally prior to, and independently of, nature and human consciousness. Hence, the concepts exist in some peculiar abstract sense prior to their appearances in life, nature, and history. Hegel further reinforces this claim about the conceptual priority of the logical concepts in the *Phenomenology:* "In the Concept [*Begriff*] that knows itself as Concept, the moments thus appear *earlier* than the filled [or fulfilled] whole whose coming-to-be is the movement of those moments. In *consciousness,* on the other hand, the whole, *though uncomprehended,* is *prior to* the moments" (PhG §801/ *Werke* 3:584, italics added). By implication, human self-consciousness, being the last to arrive on the scene, no more supplies the living motion in concepts than the living motion in nature is one that we latecomers have produced in our subjective reflection. Human self-consciousness may be at the pinnacle of nature—on a temporal, historicist interpretation of nature—but as Frederick Beiser points out rightly, "The organic whole is also *outside*

---

[15] For an account of the objectivist-realist side of Hegel's *Naturphilosophie,* see Findlay, *Hegel: A Re-Examination,* 22, 152–153.

consciousness, because human consciousness is only one part of nature which exists *apart from and prior to us.*"[16]

How then can we reconcile an atemporal reading of the concepts with an historicist, empirical reading? First, one has to see Hegel approaching a treatment of the same subject matter in a twofold manner: both in a purely logical manner at a high level of abstractness and in a historicist, empirical manner. This dual strategy gives rise to a split between the logical and historical versions of the story. One strategy is a "timeless," ahistorical treatment of the living motion of concepts, but not timeless in the sense of being Platonic, a priori, and standing outside time—that wouldn't make sense in a temporal concept like Becoming. A purely transcendent Platonic reading of concepts implies that thought is "eternal" in the sense that everything is settled from the very start, apart from the way concepts unfold dynamically in life, nature, and history. On such a dualistic separation of humanity from nature, there would be nothing up for revision. This would be to suggest wrongly that the a priori character of concepts in the *Logic* precludes appealing to dialectical experience as the catalyst for revision. Yet we know that nature exhibits its dialectical structures only in *interaction* with human consciousness. Rather, the logical determinations are "timeless" in the sense that accidental, empirical contingencies, which are subject to arbitrary changes in time, cease to count at the highest levels of generality at which the *Logic* operates.[17] On the second version of the story, human consciousness is responsible for completing and realizing the appearance of new forms of thought: "[T]he series of configurations [concepts] which consciousness goes through . . . is, in reality, the detailed *history* of the *education* of consciousness itself to the standpoint of Science" (PhG §78). Without human consciousness to provide the necessary element of mediation, the series of concepts couldn't achieve a completely realized, organized, and determinate nature. If nature already had a completed, self-sufficient status apart from our human awareness of it, this would wrongly make the progression a dyadic, not triadic, movement, stopping short of the transition to a *Philosophy of Spirit*. The fact that the triadic movement ends with the *Philosophy of Spirit*, tallying the contribution that human consciousness

[16] Frederick C. Beiser, *The Romantic Imperative* (Cambridge: Harvard University Press, 2003), 149; cf. 145–146.

[17] On the issue of necessity and contingency in Hegel's *Logic*, see George di Giovanni, "The Category of Contingency in the Hegelian Logic," in *Art and Logic in Hegel's Philosophy* (Atlantic Highlands, NJ: Humanities Press, 1980).

makes to this completion, suggests that the third part is the most "concrete" part because it completes the system and thus enjoys conceptual, but not chronological, priority over the *Logic* and *Naturphilosophie.*

How then are we supposed to relate ourselves to concepts as living? We grasp concepts as living as we strive to become living subjects ourselves. In strenuously taking on ourselves the motion of the whole concept, we participate in the powerful currents of nature. I grasp the rhythm of the organic whole; in staying with its movement, in working from life, this affects my mental states. I am changed by its living content. I feel my life. I feel my life as a unity and my unity with my life. I am becoming a living subject. But it's hard to take on this effort without falseness, without allowing one's ego to intrude. That's why we should take as our prime directive: Don't think, look—with wonder! Look, but don't disturb! Look and learn how to live. And when you look, observe what you do. What you do will be alive.

3

Formal and Natural Contradictions

3.1 Two Misreadings

The single most hated and reviled aspect of Hegel's System, which has led to the most violent misreadings and virulent attacks on it, is his doctrine of contradiction. Contradiction, he affirmed sweepingly and unequivocally, is an inescapable phenomenon of all natural and social forms of life: "Everything stands in opposition," he insisted boldly. "It is contradiction that makes the world, and it is ridiculous to say that contradiction cannot be thought" (EL §119Z2). Contradiction is a deeply embedded feature of Hegel's organic holism, with roots digging down deeply into his dialectical method and spreading to all parts of his System. What he calls his "Organic System," or the "Organic Totality," is built up out of a succession of concepts and categories, within which relations develop through the dialectical working out of contradictions.

For his heresy, his critics have heaped terms of abuse on him, such as, "anarchistic," "obscurantist," "absurd," "irrational," and "incredible"! Bertrand Russell castigates Hegel's doctrine of contradiction as "an example of how, for lack of care at the start, vast and imposing systems of philosophy are built upon stupid and trivial confusions, which, but for the almost incredible fact that they are unintentional, one would be tempted to characterize as puns."[1] Karl Popper reduces such heresy to

---

[1] Bertrand Russell, "Logic as the Essence of Philosophy," in, *Readings on Logic*, ed. I. M. Copi and J. A. Gould (New York: Macmillan, 1972), 78, and "On Denoting," in *Essays in Analysis* (New York: George Braziller, 1973), 110.

further absurdity: "If a theory contains a contradiction, then it entails everything, and therefore, indeed, nothing."[2] From such a heretical theory, Popper goes on to predict apocalyptically, will come the end of all criticism, rational argumentation, the collapse of scientific method, and all rational thought in general.

One reason for inquiring into the status of contradiction in Hegel's thought, beyond arcane and technical issues in logic, is that he assigns a preeminent role to contradictions in his dialectical method. The very term he uses to denote a dialectical transformation, *Aufhebung*, runs together two opposed senses that mean both to preserve and destroy. To the extent that dialectical method systematically informs the interconnected parts of his System, contradictions don't occur as local anomalies but appear throughout the levels of his System in such a way that they can't be totally eliminated. Contradictions penetrate down to the most mundane details of plant and animal experience. Even at the highest conceptual levels, we need contradictions of the fertile, generative kind that are productive of dynamic, progressive movement in thought (SL 440). This makes Hegel's views on contradiction more radical than modern paralogics, paraconsistent logics, or so-called fuzzy logics, which, as far as I understand them, can tolerate local contradictions because they don't have systematic connections that could threaten to spread and infect a system globally.[3] Given the far-reaching, global ramifications of contradiction throughout Hegel's System, we may thus ask the question: What is the status of the law of contradiction in Hegel's thought?

Detractors and defenders alike are deeply divided about this controversial aspect of Hegel's System. In the majority are influential and vocal commentators such as Bertrand Russell, Karl Popper, Marx, Engels, Lenin, Lucio Colletti, and Eduard von Hartmann,[4] who claim that Hegel

[2] Karl Popper, "What Is Dialectic?" in *Conjectures and Refutations* (London: Routledge and Kegan Paul, 1963), 317–319, 322.

[3] To make the very distinction between the benign kind of contradiction that stays local and the bad kind that spreads and infects a system globally, paralogics must be implicitly drawing on the law of contradiction. In order for the bad kind of contradiction to count as "bad" in the first place, there must be something wrong with a contradiction, and the law of contradiction is what one would have to invoke to ground what counts as the bad kind of contradiction, in contrast to the more benign kind.

[4] Russell, "Logic as the Essence of Philosophy," 78. By affirming contradictions, Karl Popper thinks Hegel is denying the law of contradiction; see Popper, "What Is Dialectic?" 316, 327–329. Among the Hegelian-Marxists, see Friedrich Engels,

affirms the existence of contradictions in a way that is incompatible with the law of contradiction. Among these commentators, notice, are some Marxists who have actually read Hegel. The Marxist dialecticians who portray Hegel as rejecting the law of contradiction don't necessarily regard this as an indictment of him.[5] But the rest of the critics in this class do. For the law of contradiction is the most fundamental logical law said to be at the basis of all intelligible speech, thought, argumentative practice, and action, without which all speech and thought would disintegrate into unstable, incoherent, nonsensical verbal constructions (cf. Aristotle, *Metaphysics*, K 1062a12–1062b10–11). Moreover, since Hegel intends his logical revisions not to remain local, but to spread and inform ordinary logic, the very logic for ordinary cognition that makes action and agency possible, affirming contradictions in this offensive sense would seem to have disturbing implications for his theory of action and moral agency.

But this first class of commentary gives an implausible and, in some cases, even a willful, misreading of Hegel. Hegel can't be affirming contradictions in a way that is incompatible with the law of contradiction because dialectical practice sees itself in the business of *removing* contradictions. Dialectical practice involves the acceptance of holistic method, as I've argued, which brings in a network of inferences and beliefs with systematic connections to other beliefs. By the very act of asserting certain propositions, we incur commitments and responsibilities about how we're going to think about other propositions. Propositions must figure in inferential structures because argumentative practice is marked by a permanent feature: Any statement with an assertoric structure asserts

---

Herr Eugen Dühring's Revolution in Science (Anti-Dühring), trans. Emile Burns (London, 1939), 132; Lenin, "On the Question of Dialectics," in *Philosophical Notebooks*, 359–360; Lucio Colletti, *Marxism and Hegel* (London: Lowe and Brydon, 1979), 9, 21; Eduard von Hartmann, *Über die dialektische Methode* (Bad Sachsa, 1910), 37ff.

[5] Instead of reconciling dialectical thought with classical principles of logic, Sean Sayers, for example, implausibly discards the law of contradiction as a necessary principle of rational thought, so that "it does not constitute an insuperable objection to dialectics." Sean Sayers, "Contradiction and Dialectic in the Development of Science," *Science and Society* 45, no. 4 (Winter 1981–1982): 410, 421, 425, 427. See also Anthony Smith on the Marxist, Colletti, who accepts that Hegel affirms contradictions in a way that requires the abandonment of the law of contradiction. "Hegelianism and Marx: A Reply to Lucio Colletti, *Science and Society* 1, no. 2 (Summer 1986): 153, 163.

something whose determinate content has to be defined in terms of opposite meanings, which it excludes. Thus, what allows speculative propositions to figure in dialectical argumentative structures in the first place is that they have a structure which permits negation. By the very act of engaging in argumentative dialectical practice, the point of which is to negate or remove contradictions, Hegel is making explicit certain inferential moves that implicitly draw on logical rules deeply embedded in the argumentative practice that he's engaged in. By participating in dialectical practice, he's making explicit his commitments to the law of contradiction, not necessarily to its analytic form as we'll see, but to the content of the law as it gets expressed nonpropositionally in the form of what he *does*. What he *does* in dialectical practice is to retain the psychological force of our negative reactive attitudes toward contradictions by enlisting them to *remove* contradictions. From this, it does not necessarily follow that Hegel affirms contradictions in a way that is in compliance with the law of contradiction. To reject something is not necessarily to accept its negation.

By contrast, there is a second class of commentators, who argue more charitably that Hegel affirms, or rather, in more cautious language, "does not deny" the law of contradiction. This class includes John McTaggart, G. R. G. Mure, Thomas Bole, Richard Norman, Charles Taylor, and, more recently, Robert Brandom.[6] Within this class is a further subclass of commentators, who argue sympathetically that Hegel is not using the term "contradiction" literally, but rather, in a weaker sense that falls short of real, full-blooded contradictions. This subclass portrays Hegel as weakly affirming "conflicts" or "oppositions"—be they between concepts or ontological parts—in a way that excludes all but the weakest forms of inconsistency that are still compatible with laws as understood by ordinary logic. Richard Norman argues that, notwithstanding Hegel's use of the term "contradiction," the term refers to a weaker relation between concepts: to inconsistencies and conflicts between opposed but interdependent concepts and beliefs applied to the same thing.[7] Norman discounts Hegel's examples of organisms as "minor illustrations," not as evidence

---

[6] John McTaggart, *Commentary on Hegel's Logic* (Cambridge: University Press, 1910); G. R. G. Mure, in *A Study of Hegel's Logic* (Oxford: Clarendon Press, 1950), 102–105; Thomas J. Bole, "Contradiction in Hegel's Science of Logic," *Review of Metaphysics* (March 1987): 526–527, 531. Richard Norman, *Hegel, Marx, and Dialectic: A Debate* (Brighton, Sussex: Harvester Press; Atlantic Highlands, NJ: Humanities Press, 1980).

[7] Norman, *Hegel, Marx, and Dialectic*, 31, 49, 160–161.

that his term applies to stronger ontological contradictions in nature.[8] Charles Taylor also draws on finer distinctions within the cluster of concepts surrounding contradiction, such as inconsistency, opposition, and conflict. The word does not refer, he maintains, to strong ontological *contradictions*, but, rather, to weaker relations of "ontological *conflict*." By which Taylor means: When one tries to assert the unity of a thing, differences or conflicts among the parts emerge which contradict the unity of the whole in the sense of the *incompleteness* attaching to our attempt to grasp the identity of the whole in terms of its parts. Thus, to fall into "contradiction" in Taylor's more charitable sense of the word means to rest content with a view that captures only partial, perspectival aspects of the totality.[9]

As well intentioned as this second class of commentary may be, it is in discord with what Hegel said. What he said, to repeat, was that "Everything is inherently contradictory" (SL 439). From the beginning of his university career right up to his later *Logic*, he tried to revive as a plausible and respectable element of German Idealism a thesis with remote origins in the classical tradition beginning with Heraclitus: "Contradictio est regula veri, non contradictio, false" ("Contradiction is the rule for the truth, noncontradiction for falsehood" (*Habilitationsthese* I). From there on in, he confirmed this unequivocally in his approval of the Heraclitean thesis, "Everything flows" (*panta hrei*): "There is no proposition of Heraclitus which I have not adapted in my Logic" (cf. SL 83; EL §88Z).[10] He said it in his larger *Logic*: "Every determination, every concrete thing, every Concept . . . [must] pass over into contradictory moments" (SL 442). He said it in his shorter logic: "Everything stands in opposition" (EL §119 Z2). He affirmed boldly and repeatedly everywhere: "Speculative thinking consists solely in the fact that thought holds fast contradiction" (SL 440). He said it; he meant it.

Thus, the second class of commentary does violence to what Hegel said by portraying him as affirming weaker inconsistencies and oppositions in a sanitized sense that falls short of full-blooded contradictions. A more adequate account must provide Hegel with a sufficient motivation for critically revising the form of principles and laws of what he calls

---

[8] Ibid., 162.

[9] Charles Taylor, *Hegel* (Cambridge: Cambridge University Press, 1975), 55, 105–107; cf. 229–230.

[10] G. W. F. Hegel, *Lectures on the History of Philosophy*, vol. 1, *Greek Philosophy to Plato*, trans. E. S. Haldane (Lincoln: University of Nebraska Press, 1995), 279.

"common logic" (also "formal logic" and "ordinary logic"), including the law of contradiction. For dialectical logic doesn't leave the laws of logic unquestioned and unrevised, but gives a radically reconstructive critique (*Rekonstrucktion*) in a properly speculative logic of matters already apprehended in ordinary, common logic (SL 39–40). Thus, a sanitized approach to contradiction can't do justice to the radicalness of Hegel's revisionary logic and metaphysics. For sanitized conflicts, being weakly in compliance with orthodox forms of logical judgment, are too weak to present a formidable challenge to these barriers. Any unthinking, unquestioned acceptance of the barriers that the traditional form of judgments sets up for thought, he thinks, is an obstacle to properly appreciating dialectical logic.

Therefore, I have conceived my task very differently from either class of commentary. I don't wish to portray Hegel as offering a philosophical position that either affirms or denies the law of contradiction. This would seem to exhaust all logical possibilities, at least on a classical bivalent logic. But Hegel's logic is not a classical bivalent logic. This he makes abundantly clear in his denunciation of bivalence between the true and the false, good and evil, virtue and vice, and other pairs of what he considers to be false opposites. He rejects as a "prejudice of ordinary thinking" the two false choices he is presented with on a bivalent logic: Either he must affirm contradictions, but they are of the barren variety that fatally reduces contradiction to an error that ought not to happen— hence, he loses contradiction as the positive, dynamic force that propels dialectical revisions forward—or he must endorse a watered-down version involving conflicts and inconsistencies, which falls short of affirming strong, full-blooded contradictions—hence, he loses his motivation for revising traditional forms of logical judgments. Hegel dismisses this either/or as artificial because it doesn't begin to exhaust the richness of possibilities that can arise on a radically revised speculative logic.

There is yet a third class of commentators, a minority, who rightly reject this false either/or. Among this class I include George di Giovanni, Robert Pippin, and Robert Hanna.[11] Di Giovanni correctly portrays Hegel

[11] George di Giovanni, "Reflection and Contradiction: A Commentary on Some Passages of Hegel's Science of Logic," *Hegel-Studien,* Band 8, 1973, 132; Robert Pippin, "Hegel's Metaphysics and the Problem of Contradiction," *Journal of the History of Philosophy* 26, no. 3 (July 1978); Robert Hanna, "From an Ontological Point of View: Hegel's Critique of the Common Logic," *Review of Metaphysics* 40 (December 1986): 309.

as neither denying the law of contradiction nor affirming it, but "radically qualifying" it.[12] According to Pippin, Hegel "*heartily embraces*" a way of characterizing the logical relation (between essence and appearance in the context being discussed) in a way that is simply a (true) contradiction.[13] Hanna portrays Hegel as revealing ontological biases packed into the form of ordinary concepts and laws as understood by common logic, which fail to adequately capture the contradictory ontology of reality.[14] Hegel then stretches the meaning of concepts and laws beyond common logic over a wider field of meanings in a way that preserves some of their initial meanings yet are not simply reducible to it.

While this third class of commentary is headed in the right direction, when it comes to answering what I take to be the fundamental question, "What is the status of the law of contradiction in Hegel's thought," these authors are vague, mysterious, or inscrutably silent. While they call for a "radical reconstruction" to "resituate," "reformulate," and "radically qualify" the law,[15] no details as to how this radical reconstruction is to go are forthcoming. The problem is how to talk about contradictions in a way that somehow takes us beyond the law of contradiction, yet in a logically non-contradictory way that still respects our rational aversion to genuine contradictions. They tend to resort to the visual, metaphorical language that Hegel himself uses. Di Giovanni says that the element of contradiction "lingers as a disappearing show." Hanna himself admits, "This aspect of contradiction may seem intolerably metaphorical; and indeed from a restricted common-logical point of view it *is* vague and unsatisfactory."[16]

Hanna tries to clarify further the relationship between philosophical reflection and ordinary understanding, through a conceptual shift that separates two levels at which dialectical logic and ordinary formal logic operate. He supports a two-tiered approach to logic: a formal logic that retains the law of contradiction, indispensable for analyzing bodies at rest, and a dialectical logic, indispensable for analyzing conflicted

---

[12] Di Giovanni, "Reflection and Contradiction," 132.

[13] Pippin, "Hegel's Metaphysics and the Problem of Contradiction," 308, cf. 310–311.

[14] Hanna, "From an Ontological Point of View," 309.

[15] Di Giovanni, "Reflection and Contradiction," 143; Hanna, "From an Ontological Point of View," 309, 337.

[16] Di Giovanni, "Reflection and Contradiction," 141; Hanna, "Hegel's Critique of the Common Logic," 337.

movement in becoming, without denying the efficiency of concepts or laws of common logic at their own level. At the level of ordinary logic, the law of contradiction is still in force, and Hegel does not deny it. Thus, dialectical principles involved in contradictions need not compete with ordinary logical principles when taken on their own terms and confined to their own level.

But the problem is how to reconcile the two standpoints in a way that could invite fair comparison to the law's form and function in common ordinary logic. If the law of contradiction operates differently from the standpoint of dialectic than from the standpoint of ordinary logic—hence the need to "resituate" it and purge it of ontological biases—does that mean the law is sometimes in force—namely, in an analysis of bodies at rest from the standpoint of common logic—but sometimes not—in the analysis of movement in becoming from the perspective of dialectical logic? Is the result that the two levels are not visibly connected at all? If the law has universal validity, then either it is fully in force—not just in degrees—at all times with no exceptions, or it isn't. How can an objective logical principle be in force from one "point of view" but not from another without undermining its claim to strict universality? And if the law doesn't hold with strict universality then in what sense are we still talking about the same law?

My strategy will be to reject the false either/or we are presented with on a bivalent logic along the lines of the third commentary, but without revising the law beyond recognition. Instead, I take as my starting point the need to resituate Hegel's views in relation to an ancient tradition with respectable origins in Pyrrhonian skepticism. Consistent with the Pyrrhonian skeptics' claim not to commit to any beliefs, they were careful in their language to say they did not affirm the law of contradiction; from which it did not necessarily follow that they denied it.[17] While the ancient skeptics were prepared to question or suspend judgment about almost everything else, curiously the law of contradiction was immune to suspended judgment. All assertion and refutation can take place only with the assertion of another proposition incompatible with the first. Thus, if the ancient skeptics were denying or suspending the law of contradiction, this would render all skeptical argument and refutation meaningless. While their

[17] On this matter in relation to Sextus Empiricus, see Richard Bett, "Rationality and Happiness in the Greek Skeptical Traditions," in *Rationality and Happiness: From the Ancient to the Early Medievals*, ed. Jiyuan Yu and Jorge Gracia (Rochester: University of Rochester Press, 2004), 109–134, esp. 121–222.

attitude was neither to affirm nor deny the law of contradiction, a tacit affirmation of the law of contradiction was implied in what they *did* in their method of equipollence. What justifies the move from the indeterminacy thesis about reality to suspension of judgment must be an implicit affirmation of the law of contradiction because that's the law that tells you there is something wrong with a conflict of appearances in the first place. If the law weren't being pragmatically employed in one form or another, there would be nothing wrong with a conflict of appearances to require one to roll back to a stance of suspended judgment.

I take Hegel's strong affinities with this skeptical stance as my jumping-off point: I regard him as neither affirming nor denying the law of contradiction but pragmatically employing it in what he *does* in dialectical practice. To complete what I think is missing in the third account, I supply an analysis of what specific form—if not its orthodox form—Hegel thinks the law of contradiction must take in argumentative practice. To reconstruct Hegel's revision of the law will require delving again into his logic of organic wholes and extending his organic model to logical principles. From this, it will emerge there are two kinds of contradiction: a fatal, formal kind versus a natural, organic kind. When Hegel affirms contradictions of reality, I'll argue, he's affirming the healthier, organic variety, not the toxic, fatal kind. Thus, we need not saddle him with an implausible denial of the law of contradiction. As to whether Hegelian contradictions of the natural kind can be employed alongside formal principles of logic without chaos, I'll argue that the two senses of contradiction can be held apart in reflection at least long enough to show that they can. But the two kinds of contradiction inevitably fall back together when we try to articulate the natural variety in discursive judgments and logical laws. My account of what motivated Hegel to radically revise our ordinary understanding of the *form* of the law of contradiction will turn on our inability to "speak" a contradiction using ordinary concepts and logical judgments.

3.2 Formal Contradictions

To avoid certain common misunderstandings, it's important to clarify first that Hegel's speculative logic was not intended to be formal. He makes this abundantly clear by including in it such "unlogical" matter as the ontological categories of "Life," "Teleology," "Organics," "Being," and "Becoming." No doubt, he himself fuels many misunderstandings by calling his analysis of reflection a "Logic." But one has to remember that in Hegel's time, and even much later, logic was described as a theory of thinking or reasoning, and, accordingly, the laws of logic were called "laws of *thought*."[18] As I emphasized in Chapter 1, Hegel's "logic" brings in psychological processes and reflection, which set it at some distance from modern formal logic. Thus, any attempts to formalize his logic, despite his protestations to the contrary, are flatly at variance with his repeated insistence to the effect that his speculative logic is not reducible to ordinary formal logic.[19]

In fact, the way contradiction is understood within formal logic is precisely what Hegel's doctrine of contradiction is meant to revise. As we'll see, he will question whether there is a coherent, unified understanding of the law of contradiction within formal logic even by those who defend it. Ignoring these concerns for now, let's look at the way that formal logic from Aristotle to Kant basically understands the law of contradiction. It is expressed by Aristotle in *Metaphysics* Gamma as: "It is impossible for the same thing at the same time to belong and not to belong to the same thing and in the same respect" (*Metaphysics*, Gamma, 4, 1005b18–20; cf. Kappa, 1062a). Here, "thing" designates propositions, as in, "Two contradictory *propositions* about the same subject are a sign of error." Aristotle also puts the same point in terms of predication: "It is impossible for one and the same thing to possess two contradictory *predicates*," and "This particular *predicate* does and does not belong to a thing." The law in its Aristotelian form maintains that a contradiction consists in the assertion of P and not-P of the same thing at the same time and in the same respect, where P consists of a self-contradictory proposition, predicate, or pair of contradictory statements conjoined together. Aristotle further understands the principle of contradiction as a principle of *thought*, such that formal contradictions would involve attributing contrary *beliefs or*

[18] Popper, *The Open Society and Its Enemies* (New York: Harper and Row, 1962), 2:328.

[19] See Michael Kosok's attempt nevertheless to formalize Hegel's logic in "The Formalization of Hegel's Dialectical Logic," in *Hegel: A Collection of Critical Essays*, ed. A. MacIntyre (New York: Doubleday, 1972), and Clark Butler's interesting attempt in "Hegel's Dialectic of the Organic Whole as a Particular Application of Formal Logic," in *Art and Logic in Hegel's Philosophy*, ed. Warren Steinkraus and Kenneth Schmitz (Atlantic Highlands, NJ: Humanities Press, 1980), 221, 226–231.

opinions to someone: "It is evidently impossible for the same man at the same time to *believe* the same thing to be and not to be" (*Metaphysics* Gamma, 4, 1005b29–30).[20]

Kant's understanding is Aristotelian to the extent that he understands a formal contradiction to be the knowing assertion of contradictions in subjective reflection or thought, through the use of contradictory *concepts* or *predicates,* as in: "The proposition that no *predicate* contradictory of a thing can belong to it, is entitled the principle of contradiction" (CPR A151; A273/B329). Kant's conception of general ("formal") logic gave rise to an organizing scheme, which deals with nothing but the pure analytic form of judgment alone, in general and abstracted from its empirical content (CPR B170; A55/B79). This formal notion of contradiction does not apply to processes of nature, he makes clear. A logical contradiction for Kant consists then of a relation between terms, sentences, and concepts, such that one can know that a self-contradictory assertion, like "square-circle," can never hold of one and the same thing on purely logical grounds. The fact that Kant defined analytic judgments as those statements whose validity can be established by either logical analysis of the meanings of the concepts involved alone, or whose denial yields a contradiction—means that he explained analyticity through the concept of contradiction. Kant's test for analyticity—whether the denial of a judgment yields a contradiction (CPR A151/B191)—was problematic to Hegel, and I will return to this issue shortly.

Now Hegel understands formal contradiction along these Aristotelian-Kantian lines: namely, as something "shifted into subjective reflection by which it is first posited in the process of relating and comparing [terms]" (SL 439–440). Hegel willingly admits that when contradictions occur as such—as a relation between sentences and predicates, in thought or belief, abstract proofs, or deductive arguments in this formal sense—they signify only error and ought to be avoided. For the kind of error at stake is so egregious as to lead Popper to maintain that if one were to accept a theory that involves a contradiction (or two contradictory statements),

---

[20] Cf. Jonathan Barnes, "The Law of Contradiction," *Philosophical Quarterly* 19, no. 77 (Oct. 1969): 302–309. On the differences among three formulations of the law of contradiction, which designate different objects (ontological objects, propositions, and beliefs), see Jan Lukasiewicz, "On the Principle of Contradiction in Aristotle," *Review of Metaphysics* 24 (1970–1971): 488–489.

then anything whatever would follow from it.[21] As Hegel is the first to admit, affirming contradictions in this formal sense amounts to absurdly applying contradictory predicates to one and the same thing in the same respect through illogical forms of judgment (SL 835). This absurd sense involves concepts, predicates, or propositions which appear weakly in conflict or opposition but which can be reformulated so as not to express a genuinely contradictory statement. This formal sense is clearly not the sense in which he sees himself to be affirming contradictions. For by Hegel's own lights, formal contradictions as such could never be productive of the kind of directed, fertile movement characteristic of dialectical thought.

But not all contradictions are of the fatal, formal variety that leads only to error. Hegel's concept of contradiction does not apply equally to things and to propositions. He rejects as a "prejudice" of ordinary thinking the assumption that every form of contradiction is "an error that ought not to happen" and "a subjective mistake" (SL 436). Michael Wolff has argued rightly that examples from Hegel's texts, his terminology, and consequently his empirical investigations and observations show that he never uses the expression "contradiction" to apply formally as a label for relations between sentences, predicates or terms.[22] Wolff argues that Hegel's linguistic usage of universally quantified existential statements indicates that he affirms more strongly that ontic contradictions exist in nature: "*There is* a host of contradictory things, contradictory arrangements, whose contradiction exists not merely in an external reflection but *in themselves*" (SL 440); "All things are *in themselves* contradictory" (SL 439), he insists. "Everything is *inherently* contradictory and in the sense that this law in contrast to the others expresses rather the truth and the essential nature of things" (SL 439). "Nature [is] the unresolved contradiction" (EN §248R). To find the positive contribution

---

[21] Popper, "What Is Dialectic?" 317. For the formal proof for Aristotle's assertion that from any proposition of the form p, not-p, any proposition whatever, q, may follow, see Clarence Irving Lewis and Cooper Harold Langford, *Symbolic Logic* (New York: Dover Publications, 1959), 250–251. See also Clarence Irving Lewis, *Mind and the World Order* (New York: Dover Publications, 1929), 207–208.

[22] Michael Wolff, *Der Begriff des Widerspruchs: Eine Studie zur Dialektik Kants und Hegels* (Königstein/Ts.: Anton Hain Verlag, 1981), 18. John Findlay argued this earlier in *Hegel: A Re-Examination* (London: George Allen & Unwin, 1958), 64–65. On this issue of whether Hegel affirms contradictions that are ontic, not just epistemic, see also Dieter Henrich, Otto Pöggeler, and Charles Taylor.

that contradiction makes to dialectical thought we must leave the realm of formal logic altogether.

3.3 Natural Contradictions

Rather than locate contradictions merely in subjective reflection, involving logically incorrect relations between propositions and predicates, Hegel locates them in ontological organisms undergoing change in becoming. As I have already demonstrated in Chapters 1 and 2, by assembling organic exemplars of his concept of contradiction from his *Naturphilosophie*, Hegel gives contradiction a naturalized, not formal, meaning in connection with life.[23] Starting empirically from nature, he takes nature on its own terms and accepts its basic structure. Throughout his corpus, Hegel asserts the stronger, ontological, claim that nature really is inherently contradictory in a way which resists domestication by our discursive concepts and logical laws.

One encounters contradictions of the strong ontological, not weak epistemic, variety, throughout Hegel's practical dealings as well as in his theoretical investigations. Strong ontological contradictions exist in human practices in the ethical-social world as well as in natural processes. Life is also present in self-conscious desiring animals such as ourselves, in the form of contradictory urges, desires, instincts, and appetites (SL 440; PhG §167). Hegel's practical contradictions have to do with irreconcilable conflicts of duty, which manifest themselves in conflicting desires that produce internally disrupted actions. His practical examples involve conflicted behavior, where we can't connect the expressions of such value conflicts with rational laws and moral imperatives that are constrained by principles of consistency. For, he writes, "*Virtue* too is not without conflict; rather is it the supreme, finished conflict. . . . [I]t is virtue, not only in comparison with vice, but is *in its own self* opposition and conflict" (SL 437). In the final chapters on ethics, I will extend Hegel's concept of

[23] EN §§343–349; SL 54, 94, 415, 438–439, 459, 527; PhG §12, §246; *System of Ethical Life*, 108–109. Additionally, as examples of contradiction, he cites: opposed natural forces, which possess unity and interdependence within their mutual exclusion; the structure of polarity in positive and negative electric forces; forces of attraction and repulsion; reproduction and annihilation, generation and destruction; irritability and sensibility; rest and locomotion; the centrifugal force in the motion of planets around the sun (SL 458–459).

contradiction to morals. There, we'll see him run together contradictory moral terms as in "Conscience is both good and evil" and "Evil consists in being self-poised in opposition to the good; it is a positive negativity" (SL 437). As we'll see, contradictions in morals are never understood by him as logically incorrect relations between statements or judgments in a way that violates logical laws.

Now when Hegel affirms contradictions in this strong ontological sense, notice that contradictions aren't just a wider application of Kant's antinomies or dialectical illusions, involving concepts in conflict in our understanding, where we may dispel the illusion by discarding our false concepts about reality. While Hegel praises Kant for showing that thought can develop in contradictory ways and that such "antinomies" are somehow essential and necessary, he thinks Kant should have extended his antinomies further to attributes of things, not just to misguided thoughts and principles. Naturalized contradictions for Hegel have to do not with relations between predicates and terms weakly in "conflict," but rather with "real opposition" (*Widerstreit*), to borrow a phrase from Kant himself who discusses it, "where two [positive] realities combined in one subject cancel one another's effects" (CPR A273/B329). "Real oppositions," Kant tells us, don't occur between a concept and merely its privation or lack (e.g., the subject and predicate terms in "A bachelor is married" aren't in "real" opposition since the concept "unmarried" implied in the subject term indicates merely a privation or lack of the concept implicit in the predicate term).

Hegel takes Kant's insights about real oppositions as far as he thought Kant should have: Hegel affirms more strongly that ontic contradictions exist in natural processes and human practices by which he means: two realities combined in one subject in a relation of strong mutual exclusion (not merely "incompletion") obliterate each other's effects, such that we can't reconcile strongly irreconcilable contradictions without giving up both parts at the existing level. The two realities combined in one subject cancel out each other's effects, such that the two sides can't coexist within a unity at the existing level. This relation is a pure transition (PhG §279; EL §119), which we must consider as an object in its own right, as an "einfacher Begriff," to use Hegel's phrase. Being rational, the presence of contradiction must force us to a higher level of reflection at which we grasp the organic unity of these opposites in a relation where no such distinctions or oppositions are implied in a third connecting middle.

Notice further, that real oppositions and real contradictions for Hegel aren't mere indeterminate *potentialities* and, hence, aren't reducible to Aristotle's notion of living substances. As Jan Lukasiewicz points out, Aristotle limits the range of the law of contradiction to actual existing things.[24] Thus, affirming the law didn't prevent Aristotle from losing sight of how life unfolds in organic unities undergoing change through a dynamic series of potentiality and actuality. In fact, Aristotle himself describes substance in the *Physics* as "that which is capable of receiving *contraries*"—though contraries are not full-blooded contradictories or oppositions. Aristotle invokes a further time condition that would seem to allow for the kind of change required to represent life as living in the contradictory sense sought by Hegel. Aristotle concedes that the sensibly perceptible world, conceived as becoming and passing away, can contain contradictions as strict potentialities: "For 'being' means two things; there is one way in which something can come to be out of non-being, and another way in which it cannot, so that the same thing can at the same time be a being and a non-being—but not in the same respect: for the same thing can at the same time possess *potentially* contraries, but not *actually*" (*Metaphysics,* Gamma 4, 1009a32–37). If two contrary properties in a plant originate from one and the same source, such that the plant *potentially* possesses both contraries equally, then Aristotle would allow that contradictions can coexist within a unity in this weaker sense in the form of indeterminate potentialities.

So to distinguish the contradictory operation implied in Hegel's characterization of living organic wholes from Aristotle's indeterminate potentialities, we must clarify that by "real opposition," Hegel doesn't merely mean two contradictory or opposite tendencies that *potentially* originate from one and the same unified source. Rather, "real contradictions" understood in his strong ontological sense, occur not merely *in potentia,* but exist in actuality between two real constituent parts or opposite tendencies originating from the same source, in such a way that the two realities combined in the same subject can't coexist stably in a unity, but must cancel out each other's effects.

So far, I've tried to make Hegel's organic view of contradiction a plausible and respectable thesis by arguing that when he affirms strong contradictions reality and nature, he's not falling into the egregious

[24] Jan Lukasiewicz, "On the Principle of Contradiction in Aristotle," *Review of Metaphysics* 24 (1970–71): 501

error of committing formal contradictions. By holding apart the two senses of contradiction, formal and natural, I've argued that Hegel's stronger, ontological claim—that nature *really is* inherently contradictory, in a way that resists domestication by our discursive concepts and logical laws—doesn't pose a threat to the Kantian-Aristotelian concept of contradiction. Where exactly does Hegel's strong ontological thesis run afoul of Kant, if Kant restricts formal contradictions to an epistemological claim about inadequate concepts, predicates, or beliefs, which merely appear in "conflict" or "opposition" but which must be reformulated so as not to express genuinely contradictory statements? Why not leave it open whether a concept of contradiction could apply to nature on Kant's view in just the way envisioned by Hegel?

Kant's Subjective Idealism forecloses on this possibility because nature on this view must be thought of as structured in a way that can be captured by our discursive speech forms and logical laws. To preserve a "fit" between thought and reality, the conditions restricting the possible features of reality are supplied by features of thought. Reality can't be contradictory because Kant forbids contradictory statements and propositions. Thus, formal contradictions of the Kantian-Aristotelian variety inevitably have a bearing on natural contradictions. For when we try to speak of or represent natural contradictions in traditional judgments and discursive thought-forms, we find we can't connect the way these naturalized contradictions get embodied in nature with our formal speech and discursive thought patterns that forbid the expression of contradictions. Given our discursive limitations, things can't be seen by us through our concepts, predicates, and statements as contradictory without falling into error. We have no alternative but to look at and speak about a Kantian world in such a way as to *eliminate* contradictions.

Whereas Hegel's metaphysical monism collapses the distinction between thought and nature. We can't hold formal and naturalized contradictions apart any longer on his view because he demands that we reconcile our speech and thought-forms with the way natural contradictions get embodied nonpropositionally in nature. Thought processes for Hegel are read *out of* (not *into* or *projected onto*) nature. We must bring the way we speak about unity and contradiction in our concepts closer to reflecting the way nature really is. He preserves contradictions in nature at the expense of losing a "fit" between forms of judgment and reality. For we can't get an accurate representation of the way the world really is, in all its contradictory phenomena, he thinks, if we don't revise our ordinary habits of thinking, concepts, logical principles, and judgments.[25] Hegel's demand for a radically revised logic folds readily into the picture at this point. For it is specifically the business of his *Logic* to revise our speech forms and thought tendencies to reflect the naturally embodied contradictory tendencies in nature by making our concepts living.

3.4 Identity and Contradiction

The locus classicus of Hegel's discussion of contradiction occurs in his "Doctrine of Essence [*Wesen*]" (SL 409–443).[26] This passage was preceded by the first phase of the *Logic,* the "Doctrine of Being," where we encountered the general problem of phenomenal change as it was discussed in connection with the categories of Being and Becoming. The need to distinguish between the essence of a thing and its appearances arose when we inquired into the underlying substrate unifying a thing's changing appearances in Perception, the phenomenal correlate of Becoming. Now, in "Essence," Hegel considers further the essential/inessential distinction as a way of reconstructing the cluster of basic concepts, principles, and logical forms of judgment relevant to his doctrine of contradiction.

It's significant that Hegel begins the passage on contradiction with an analysis of Identity, Difference (*Unterschied*) and related concepts since he treats unity and contradiction, and their expression in the law of identity and the law of contradiction, as negative equivalents (SL 409, 416; EL §115R). This can't be a strict equivalence since "pure" Identity is initially understood as involving an unmediated notion of self-sameness that excludes an element of negation. But when understood more reflectively, Identity will be shown to have implied within it a concept of negation because taken as a whole, each law is already a reflection of the whole and, as such, contains within itself a relation to other laws.

[25] See Rolf-Peter Horstmann, "What Is Hegel's Legacy and What Should We Do with It?" *European Journal of Philosophy* 7, no. 2 (1999).

[26] Hegel's accounts in the early logics (1802, 1804–5) and *Encyclopedia Logic* (EL §§115–120) are much more abbreviated and condensed (sometimes to a single paragraph) than the stretch of text I have in mind in Book 2 of the "Objective Logic" in the *Science of Logic* [*Wissenschaft der Logik*] of 1812–1816.

Now Identity, Difference, and Diversity are shown eventually to lead to the concepts Opposition and Contradiction, which finally culminate in Ground. To arrive at a revisionary reconstruction of the concept of identity, and associated principles and laws, Hegel will make explicit what we are really doing in deeper reflection when we holistically understand the internal linkages and inferences among this complex network of concepts and laws. Since Hegel accepts a basic equivalence of the laws of identity and contradiction, let us understand his revision in the way he does: first by way of his revision of the law of Identity.

Like Aristotle, Hegel emphasizes that there are simpler first principles which hold good prior to the law of contradiction. The "first law of thought" gets expressed in the form of the judgment "A is A"—that is, everything in its beginning is in an immediate identity with itself. Alternatively, we may reformulate the law of Identity using the concept of negation as the principle of double negation: "A is not not-A." From this, we may derive the law of contradiction as its negative equivalent: "Something cannot at the same time be both A and not-A" (at the same time and in the same respect). Of the two logical laws, Hegel thinks the law of contradiction is the more fundamental (SL 439). But the law of identity makes a simpler, more presuppositionless starting point since its form doesn't need recourse to the concepts of negation, logical multiplication, and the added temporal concept "at the same time" (SL 416; 1802 *Logic*, 13). In fact, the law of identity has as rightful a claim to be a presuppositionless starting point in the realm of Essence as Being had in the Doctrine of Being (EL §115Z).

Hegel's general strategy is to give a critique of the way these concepts and laws are apprehended by common consciousness as immediately self-evident, analytic, and without need of proof. His particular revision of A is A is aimed at our ordinary understanding of the bare analytic form of judgment as self-evident and requiring no proof or demonstration of its validity. On our ordinary understanding, the analytic form of judgment alone is a "formal and empty" assertion of immediate identity. By this, he doesn't mean to deny or reject "A is A" wholesale.[27] But

---

[27] It's important to see that Hegel is not rejecting or denying the meaningfulness of Identity statements in an ethical context, where he gives as a meaningful instance of A is A "It is right because it is what is right" (PhG 437). The point is that the analytic, tautologous form of this identity statement is not what gets you to its significance: namely, an immediate and unreflective trust and acceptance

rather, he rejects an intellectualist construal of its analytic form that he associates with a claim of Kant's logic: namely, that nothing but the pure analytic form of the judgment abstracted from the empirical content of the object need be involved in our recognition of the self-unity of a thing (CPR B170). In proper dialectical fashion, Hegel generates his criticism from within the analytic form of the judgment itself. The traditional subject-predicate form—"God is God" (SL 415), "A tree is a tree" (SL 414), and "The plant is the plant" (SL 414–415), to take some of his examples—leads us to expect that the two terms or concepts will pick out two different substantive attributes of the same thing, the first occurrence of A picking out a substantive predicate different from the second occurrence (SL 416; EL §115R). But the law of identity identifies objects in an absolute identity by means of a predicate that picks out the same object referred to by the same subject term. The two relata, picked out by means of the same subject and predicate terms, are construed, not as the same in some substantive respects yet different in others, but as empty and tautologously related. Our expectations are cheated, so Hegel's criticism goes, because almost nothing seems to be said by an exact repetition of the first term. A monadic concept of self-relatedness can't provide the implied relation of difference that would meaningfully allow the two relata to be the same in some respects yet different in other substantive respects.

From the standpoint of reflection, Hegel concludes, "[I]t is evident that the law of Identity itself, and still more the law of contradiction, is not merely of analytic but of *synthetic* nature" (SL 416). His revision involves stretching the concept of Identity over a wider field of meanings to include within it a nexus of more complex inferences and articulations, including the incompatibility relation, a relation of mediation, and a notion of determinate negation. He conceives of the concepts of Identity and Difference, not monadically as isolated concepts, but as relational and inseparably bound together as a correlated pair of concepts. Each opposite is related to its other in a mediating relation of exclusion of what it is not. Reflectively understood, this deeper, synthetic interpretation of

---

of ones community's canon of ethical norms. Other identity statements also contain a tautological, but meaningful, truth: for instance, "He's a he," disambiguates gender in a nonvacuous way in a context where a person's gender is ambiguous. The tautological truth in "Boys will be boys" is precisely the point since the two relata do not refer to two different occurrences of "boys."

identity has to be expressed in an alternative *form* of judgment that will adequately reflect our experience of unity in living, changing organisms: the identity-in-difference principle.

3.5 Paradox of the Law of Contradiction as Ground

In a parallel revision, Hegel radically revises our understanding of the law of contradiction, the negative equivalent of the law of identity, as analytically self-evident. Again, his dialectical strategy is to generate a paradox from within the analytic form of judgment alone. Similarly, he critiques the intellectualist claim, which he associates with Kant and Aristotle, that the form of judgment is analytically self-evident requiring no proof of its demonstration. Aristotle regards the law as the ultimate, final law to which all other axioms return (*Metaphysics* Gamma 4, 1005b33–35). Like Aristotle, Kant understands the law as so central to any conceptual system that it is a "universal and completely sufficient principle of *all analytic knowledge* but beyond the sphere of analytic knowledge it has, as a sufficient criterion of truth, no authority and no field of application" (CPR B191/A152). Kant's concept of analyticity is of interest here insofar as it points us toward difficulties Hegel has with Kant's understanding of the analytic form of the judgment in which the law of contradiction gets expressed. Hegel specifically targets for revision Kant's claim of analyticity, which he thinks generates as many difficulties as it rescues in the concept of contradiction.[28] Since the law of contradiction itself is a logical judgment, and the paradigm for analyticity just is such a principle of logic, it's natural to take the form of judgment itself as analytically valid (CPR B191). For Kant writes in the *Prolegomena* that he understands the law as the most foundational principle grounding all analytic judgments: "The Common Principle of all Analytic Judgments is the Law of Contradiction—All analytical judgments depend wholly on the law of Contradiction, and are in their nature a priori cognitions" (*Prolegomena*, 15). Since Kant defined analytical judgments as those statements whose validity can

---

[28] On this issue, Michael Wolff explains that, "Quite rightly, it was assessed to this extent by Quine, that Kant's definition of analyticity explains 'little' because here the concept of contradiction in the senses used is necessarily in as much need of clarification as the concept of analyticity itself. Both concepts, Quine said, are two faces of the same doubtful coin (medal)." Wolff, *Der Begriff des Widerspruchs*, 16.

be established either by logical analysis of the meanings of the concepts involved alone, or whose denial yields a contradiction, his concept of contradiction leads us toward the concept of analyticity.

Hegel's argument for revising the analytic form of the law of contradiction occurs in the section titled "Ground" (SL 446–456), although his explicit mention of the law precedes the category Ground.[29] By Ground, Hegel has in mind a conceptual derivation of the law of contradiction from Leibniz's principle of sufficient reason (SL 446, EL §121Z). The latter is not itself a logical principle, but Hegel treats it as the expression of a logical law in the form of a principle: "For everything, there is a reason [ratio, condition, ground] why it exists, rather than not [existing]." The conceptual connection between the law of contradiction and Leibniz's principle of sufficient reason follows Wolff's and Leibniz's conceptions of the law of contradiction as being derivable from the principle of sufficient reason.

Now it is in "Ground" where Hegel questions Kant's claim that the law of contradiction provides the foundation or ground for all analytic principles in its function to ground, guide, condition, explain, or provide a sufficient reason for something being the way it is. Hegel generates a paradox concerning Kant's analytic conception of the law of contradiction: If the law were valid by virtue of the concepts involved or by logical principles alone, then by Kant's test for analyticity, asserting its denial should lead to a contradiction. But a formal demonstration of the law's analyticity must be constrained by considerations of consistency. Thus, a proof of analyticity must tacitly invoke consistency as a constraint on what would count as a valid proof. Inconsistency is bad only on the assumption that the law of contradiction, the very thing in need of grounding, is valid. This makes Kant's test of analyticity circular by the very structure it itself sets up. In order for the law of contradiction to ground thought— to tell us there is something wrong with a contradiction—it must itself be subject to its own conditions of consistency. This leaves the law itself in need of being grounded or demonstrated; and it becomes one of its

[29] The category of Ground in the Jena logic turns into his identity-in-difference principle. Textually, this transition is strongly marked in EL: after opposition and polar opposition, the transition in EL goes straight to Ground. Contradiction there is not a concept or category, notice, but a *transition* leading to Ground. Sublated contradiction "falls to the ground," as Hegel puns (SL 437). That is, it is the proper ground, which contains within itself both Identity and Difference, that is sublated.

own determinations which it itself must support (ground). Thus, any proof or demonstration of its analyticity in terms of logical principles alone involves a *petitio principii* by drawing on implicit premisses that involve already having accepted the conclusion. Of this circular reasoning, Hegel concludes, "One finds oneself in a kind of witches' circle in which determinations of real being and determinations of reflection, ground and grounded, phenomena and phantoms, run riot in indiscriminate company and enjoy equal rank with one another" (SL 461).

By themselves, circularity or the absence of proof are not necessarily problematic. There are other marks of the a priori, namely, necessity and universality. Kant himself admits that conceptual proof is absent in meaningful judgments of taste. Aristotle, for that matter, denied that you can give a proof or demonstration of the law of contradiction and yet maintained that the law is so fundamental to the practice of arguing and communicative practice that it must be in force at all times to guide and constrain argumentative practice. Hegel himself allows that the development of Spirit takes a circular structure.

What is disturbing about the paradox can be brought out by comparing it to Wittgenstein's remarks about the standard meter of Paris. In a series of parallel moves, Wittgenstein argues that we have no proof or demonstration of the standard meter as an arbiter of length: "What does it mean to say that we can attribute neither being nor non-being to elements? . . . There is one thing of which one can say neither that it is one metre long, nor that it is not one metre long, and that is the standard metre in Paris."[30] For the physical measuring rod to constrain, guide, ground, or place a check on what is to count standardly as one meter, the actual stick must instantiate the very property being represented—the length of one meter. But the measuring rod in its role of ground is supposed to be distinct from what it grounds. If the physical rod must instantiate the very property being represented, in order to serve in its role as absolute arbiter of length, then we run into paradox. For to claim to know that the rod instantiates the very property it was designed to measure, we have to illicitly smuggle in the very standard in question to get a quantitative value of one meter. Instead of discovering the value existing independently, the standard itself seems to be creating this value by

[30] Ludwig Wittgenstein, *Philosophical Investigations* (New York: Macmillan, 1953), §50.

bringing into existence the very length being measured. This makes the check an uncheckable check, the ground ground*less* relative to itself.

Analogously, what makes Hegel's paradox about the logical measuring rod troubling is that the same logical law that is both grounding or providing the foundation of all thought is simultaneously itself in need of grounding. We can't appeal to the analyticity of the law as its ground without invoking a *petitio principii*. If we identify the law of contradiction, the thing doing the grounding, as the same as the token instantiation of the particular law in need of grounding, then the law is cast into a dual role as both the thing doing the grounding and what is also in need of being grounded (SL 447). To get an independent grip on the thing being grounded, Hegel insists, "we really demand that the content of the ground be a different determination from that of the phenomenon whose ground we are seeking" (SL 462). Thus, the principle doing the grounding, explaining, constraining, guiding, or providing a sufficient reason for something being the way it is, has to have a status independent of the thing being grounded.[31]

We are now in a position to take this paradox back into our main question: What is the status of the law of contradiction in Hegel's thought? The paradox arising on an intellectualist construal of the law indicates that our ordinary understanding of the law falls into disunity. For if ground can't be the same as what is grounded, then the logical measuring rod splits into two roles: (1) the analytic form of the law of contradiction, known as an absolute unconditional ground that constrains and guides all thought; and (2) its conditional, contingent content as a particular principle itself in need of being grounded. Paradoxically, the law grounds our thought, yet the ground itself is something in need of grounding. In performing dual functions, as both ground and what is grounded, the law is shown to be disunified, "self-repelling," at odds with itself, and, as he likes to put it ironically, falls into "contradiction" with itself. Hegel concludes then that there is no satisfactory way to deal with this paradox on Kant's transcendental logic because the law is anomalous with respect to itself. Therefore, since this logical principle is not coherently unified on an intellectualist construal of it, our ordinary analytic understanding of the law needs revision.

---

[31] Thanks to Béatrice Longuenesse for drawing my attention to the dual status of Ground, particularly as it bears on the law of contradiction.

More reflectively understood, the law has a deeper interpretation in which it is not formal or analytic, but synthetic (SL 416). Not synthetic in the sense that he thinks the axioms and theorems of geometry are synthetic a priori, but in the sense that we need a synthesis or unifying understanding of its form and content to deploy coherently in argumentative practice. As with Identity judgments, Hegel demands a revision of the traditional form it takes in the abstract understanding as an analytic principle whose form is split off from its empirical content. He employs a synthetic, unified understanding of the law of contradiction in the form of dialectical principles that hold opposites together by forcing one to think of their interpenetration: for example, the determinate negation principle and the identity-in-difference principle.

Notice, finally, that Hegel's revision doesn't call for a wholesale rejection or denial of the law any more than Wittgenstein's paradox leads to abandoning the measuring rod as an arbiter of length. Clearly Hegel doesn't abandon the law's meaningful employment in dialectical practice. For to assert anything meaningful at all one must tacitly invoke the law, since, to repeat, every positive assertion has determinate meaning only insofar as it is defined against that which it excludes. If the law weren't still in force, all argument and positive statements would be rendered meaningless—including the very statements that Hegel uses to state the paradox. Just to assert that "Ground is distinct from what is grounded" requires him to draw pragmatically on the very law whose coherence and unity is being called into question.

Let us leave the matter here as Hegel does: "[C]ontradiction is not the end of the matter but cancels itself out" (SL 433). The role of anomalies, antinomies, and contradictions within the theory is to create a source of tension within our ordinary understanding that serves as a positive catalyst for revision. If dialectic mirrors the natural form that contradiction takes in nature, as I've argued in previous chapters that it does, then contradictory principles and laws, like natural contradictions, can't be dismissed as "false" and self-canceling, but are accepted within the theory. If these paradoxes, anomalies, antinomies, and contradictions within the movement of reflection follow the pattern of dialectic, then our contradictory, disunified understanding should resolve itself (SL 433–434). Following the self-resolving motion of natural organisms, the disruption in our unified understanding of the law undergoes a self-correcting, self-resolving synthesis.

The desire for unity that drives our restless striving after a healing synthesis is a sign of life itself. The steps of reflection that we have just passed through—Identity, Difference, Opposition, Contradiction, finally, toward conceptual resolution in Ground—are the higher privilege of living human beings (VA, Intro., 97). And whosoever has lost their desire for this restless striving has already made a pact with death.

PART II

AESTHETIC HOLISM AND INDISCURSIVITY

4

Life's Beautiful Form

In the second main part of this book, I extend Hegel's organic conceptual scheme to how we speak of organic totalities in connection with judgments of beauty. Aesthetics provided Hegel with a rich field for discovering a kind of intuitive knowledge, which mediates between discursive and nondiscursive knowledge through judgments about beauty. If becoming a living subject is a necessary condition for grasping concepts as living, then any indication by which our living nature can be known is of paramount importance. Nature in its beauty, Hegel thinks, discloses to us the idea of life and by doing so gives us a clue into the workings of our own living nature.

Hegel's ideas about the freedom and independence of life as it appears in the beauty of nature take up Kant's idea that our interest in natural beauty points to something relevant for philosophical reflection on morals. Nature "speaks to us" by giving us intimations of the prerequisite conditions that make morality possible. By opening up a vision of independence and freedom in nature, the beauty of nature reveals itself as constituted in such a way so as not to be indifferent to the realizability of our moral ends. In apprehending life in its beautiful form, we feel ourselves enlivened as living subjects. We may thus look to life's beautiful form for the hints it can give us about our own spiritual animation in its freedom.

The problem of aesthetic holism folds readily into the set of interlocking problems that we encountered in the preceding chapters. Chapter 1 introduced the problem of how living organisms can possess mutually exclusive contradictory parts while undergoing change, yet somehow display a harmonious unity and continuity. Chapter 2 developed this problem further in connection with how we express contradictory tendencies in nature in common speech and thought-forms. In Chapter 3, we saw the disruptive tendencies that arise within organic wholes expose features of reality that we can't articulate using traditional logical concepts and their expression in logical laws. In this chapter, I demonstrate how Hegel adapted Kant's organic terminology from the third *Critique* as a springboard for understanding a sense in which life is aesthetic in nature.

The subjective, emotivist aspect of Kant's aesthetics can appear to put Hegel out of sync with Kant's larger epistemological project, even out of sync with the conditions that Kant himself places on knowledge in his first *Critique*. That Kant has placed aesthetic judgments in a precognitive, preconceptual sphere that go beyond the conditions for knowledge established in the first *Critique* have led some critics to dismiss the epistemological significance of judgments of taste.[1] In Chapter 1, we saw undeniably important differences between Hegel's approach and the a priori approach of Kant's first *Critique*. There, I characterized the Goethe-Hegel connection in terms of a sharp *contrast* with Kant's theory of concepts.

But to portray Hegel as merely criticizing the "excessively subjective" aspects of Kant's emotivist aesthetics, as some commentators have done, would obscure the extent to which Hegel incorporates many of these subjective elements into his own aesthetics. Kant is an important and unrecognized precursor of Goethe in this tradition of using the idea of life as a central aesthetic category.[2] Hegel speaks approvingly of Kant's idea of life, especially as it relates to his concept of internal purposiveness (EL §204R). References to Kant's idea of life are conspicuously absent from the secondary literature on Hegel's aesthetics, but without them, one loses the vital connection to Kant's organic terminology from the third

---

[1] Donald Crawford, *Kant's Aesthetic Theory* (Madison: University of Wisconsin Press, 1974), 78; Mary Gregor, "Aesthetic Form and Sensory Content in the *Critique of Judgment:* Can Kant's 'Critique of Aesthetic Judgment' Provide a Philosophical Basis for Modern Formalism?" in *The Philosophy of Immanuel Kant,* ed. Richard Kennington (Washington, DC: Catholic University of America Press, 1985), 189, 191.

[2] Cf. Rudolf Makkreel, "The Feeling of Life: Some Kantian Sources of Life-Philosophy," *Dilthey-Jahrbuch für Philosophie und Geschichte der Geisteswissenschaften,* Herausgegeben von Frithjof Rodi, Band 3 (1985): 86.

Critique, which provided Hegel with a springboard for his own aesthetic holism. In *Faith and Knowledge,* Hegel credits the power of imagination in Kant's third *Critique* as one of the most interesting points of the Kantian System (GW 70–73). Far from thinking the subjectivism of Kant's aesthetic imagination makes it an inferior mode of knowledge, I'll argue that it was specifically in the subjective, intuitive aspects of Kant's aesthetics that Hegel detected our access to the deeper, partial knowledge of totalities that he was trying to define in his own aesthetics. By retaining holistic links between the faculties of the imagination, understanding, and desire, Kant makes it clear that to place aesthetic imagination in the preconceptual sphere does not demote it to an inferior mode of knowledge with no epistemological significance. Through an analysis of Hegel's appropriation of the most radically subjective aspects of Kant's aesthetics, I mean indirectly to bring out the epistemological significance of Kant's third *Critique.*

4.1 Hierarchy of Life

Hegel opens his *Lectures on Fine Art* by appropriating Kant's idea of life as a central aesthetic category.[3] On Kant's organic concept of life, a single living force courses throughout all of nature so that all the different species of minerals, plants, and animals—even lifeless inorganic matter—are a manifestation in different degrees of nature's organization and development.[4] Similarly, in Hegel's hierarchy of life, a living

---

[3] Hereafter, references to Hegel's *Vorlesungen über die Ästhetik* (VA) will be from the T. M. Knox translation, which is based on Hotho's edition. Hegel's lectures on fine art were a compilation of students' transcripts, and the usual caveats hold about using Hotho's edition. On the issue about whether the editor, Hotho, distorts Hegel's views by adding onto the stratified text a further interpretive layer, A. Gethmann-Siefert observes, "The 'aesthetician' Hotho still continues . . . to exert an influence upon contemporary philosophical discussions in the field of aesthetics" ("H. G. Hotho," *Hegel-Studien,* Beiheft 22 (1983): 23). References to Kant's *Critique of Judgment* are from the Guyer translation and will be abbreviated (CJ). References to Kant's *Lectures on Metaphysics,* translated and edited by Karl Ameriks and Steve Naragon (Cambridge: Cambridge University Press, 1997), will be abbreviated (LM). The German Akademie edition will be cited using the abbreviation Ak. followed by the volume and page number.

[4] Frederick Beiser, *The Romantic Imperative* (Cambridge: Harvard University Press, 2003), 138, 170.

force manifests itself as a force of nature in the earliest, simplest forms of matter and mineral life, and then progresses through the more complex forms of plant, vegetable, and animal life, finally culminating in the most complex forms of human life. In the second chapter, "Naturschöne," Hegel catalogues his hierarchy of life-forms according to a principle of purposeful organization, which rises continuously from the inert and mechanical toward the organic and purposively organized as a necessary step to achieving life at the highest levels of self-conscious rationality. All life-forms are ranked in terms of their degree of adequacy for embodying what he variously calls the "Idea of life" (also "Concept of life" and sometimes the "Universal Concept").

At the bottom of the hierarchy, Kant and Hegel extend the term "life" to things that are not alive in a literal, mundane sense. This doesn't so much reflect a tendency of eighteenth-century natural science not to distinguish between living and nonliving nature. For Kant all material bodies are lifeless, and he allows the term a broader application to things that are strictly speaking lifeless (LM 28:285, 29:913, 28:594, 28:762). Life is present in such lifeless matter in a sense that can't come from matter alone but from an internally active principle of life, which, in its connection with matter, is not reducible to lifeless matter (LM 28:275). Life goes undefined in Kant's aesthetics, but he gives a metaphysical definition of life in the *Metaphysical Foundations of Natural Science* as the capacity of a substance to determine itself, by bringing about a change through motion.[5] He equates life with the power of a self-moving organism to actively contribute something to what it is essentially through a change through motion. Even minerals and geological formations have a capacity to be self-determining (i.e., have a felt purposiveness), which Kant extends by analogy to the kind of conscious creation occurring in manmade art (CJ §58/Ak. 5:349). Crystals count as alive for Hegel, too, in the similar sense that they possess a capacity to determine themselves to motion by means of an inner "vocation" (VA 130, 136). Even lifeless geological formations and the solar system count as living in this sense, he thinks, since they exhibit their regularities and symmetries by a "free force of their own" (VA 130, 136; EN §341).

Matter in motion is not by itself sufficient to characterize animate life. For when a block of ice melts from a solid to a liquid, to take Aristotle's

[5] Kant, *Metaphysical Foundations of Natural Science*, ed. Michael Friedman, trans. Ellington (Cambridge: Cambridge University Press, 2004), 105.

example, the ice undergoing motion satisfies this condition and is still not alive. Since the movement of the ice originates from an external source—the sun warming the ice or heat emanating from a stove—the melting ice is passive with respect to its own movement. The ice contributes nothing, and once the ice dissolves into a liquid, it can't repair itself back into a solid. Since Kant and Hegel seek to identify life with an internally active principle, which, in its connection with matter, is not reducible to lifeless matter (LM 28:275), life in their special sense must involve the further activity of *determining oneself* through motion. For the limited sense in which inorganic matter can grow, as in the formation of crystals, merely involves growth on the outside with the successive repetition of the crystal's initial form (EN §341). Only where the generative activity of a thing is determined from within, where the interior organization of the thing isn't a mechanical repetition of a preformed mold, can the thing be considered living. Hegel thus ranks living things above inanimate, inorganic forms because they are better at embodying Kant's Idea of life: "Only the *living* thing is Idea" (VA 119).

Now what's distinctive about living things gets particularly reflected in the part/whole relation. The stones that make up a hearth can be taken apart, moved, and reassembled in a different home. The stones retain their character even when detached from the hearth because the parts determine the whole and there is nothing in the hearth that is not reducible to stone and mortar (VA 121; SL 515). But structures and permanence don't get us to the distinction between organic and inorganic matter. While the stones are organized according to some arrangement, the difference between the merely organized and "organic" gets reflected in living things in the internal arrangement of their vitally functioning parts to the whole. Dismember an animal and reduce it to a heap of parts and nothing of the animated whole remains over to put back together. Sever a hand from a body and once deprived of the sustenance it gains from its attachment to the whole organism, the hand loses its size, agility, and complexion; it shrivels, decomposes, and perishes altogether (VA 121). Once dismembered, you can't put the body parts back together like a clockwork mechanism. External relations among the lifeless parts can't account for the living principle unifying the parts.

The capacity of animals to determine themselves to motion sets animal life above mineral, vegetable, and plant life (VA 122–123, 136–137). The principle of life is not immediately visible, except in the visible traces it leaves on the animal's outer form: It pulsates at every point on the surface of the body: in the rhythm of the breathing of the animal and in the grace of its movements. It shines through the look in the animal's eyes and the glossiness of its coat. The principle is alive in the expressiveness of the animal's voice. The principle of life permeates throughout the parts of the body as an "animating soul" (*Geist*), which organizes the parts and holds them together in an animated unity. Nothing happens in the parts that is not affected by the whole. The parts are reciprocally interdependent and have their identity only in relation to the whole.

But life's beautiful form in Hegel's Kantian sense has to involve more than the activity of determining oneself through motion. A writhing mass of maggots on a decaying corpse feeds in a frenzy of self-determining motion. But the sight is ugly and causes revulsion, not the enlivening feelings of pleasure that come from seeing one's living status reflected in life's beautiful form. Organic nature in the form of plant and animal life is shown to be inadequate, restricted as it is by contingencies and ugly imperfections (EN §248R, §250R). Kant and Hegel allow that animals have souls or an inner life, but referring to the souls of animals doesn't solve the problem of living unity because an animal's soul can't be known from careful observation and perception.[6] At this brute, physical level of nature, Hegel writes, "What we now see before us in the life of an animal organism is not this point of unity of life, but only the variety of organs." He describes this lack of self-consciousness in an animal as "a cloudy appearance of a soul as the breath and fragrance which is diffused over the whole" (VA 132). For animals don't have the capacity to register their consciousness of being alive. And where there is no inner consciousness of one's own agency there can be no Idea of life.

Hegel follows Kant in seeking to remedy the deficiencies of unconscious brute nature in the human form (cf. CJ §17). Hegel places a further condition on life that a living thing must be able to relate to itself as living. Hegel raises the beauty of the human form to the status of

---

[6] Where, for instance, does the soul of an animal exist in those animals, such as crabs and salamanders, which can regenerate missing claws and tails. If the animal can regenerate its parts, it was thought that the soul or organizing principle must have also existed in the parts that were regenerated. In animals of the lowest forms, such as polyps and worms, which can regenerate their parts, sometimes even the entire animal, it was thought the properties of life in the animal were distributed throughout the matter. Thomas L. Hankins, *Science and the Enlightenment* (Cambridge: Cambridge University Press, 1985), 132–133.

"the living work of art" (PhG §§720–726). In his art-historical narrative, he ranks the human form and actions, as rendered at the height of their perfection in Classical Art, sculpture, poetry, and literature, higher than life as it appears in unconscious nature in the plant and animal forms of Symbolic Art. The human spirit, he thinks, finds the whole concept of natural life completely actualized in its own bodily organism, so that, in comparison, animal life appears imperfect and hardly living at all (VA 150).

What makes the human body a more adequate embodiment of the principle of life than plant and animals is that the inner principle of life animating the whole now registers as a pleasurable *feeling* of life (*Lebensgefühl,* VA 126). Only human subjects are capable of registering their self-conscious awareness of themselves as living organisms through this pleasurable "swelling of life" (*turgor vitae*), which shows itself over the entire surface of the human body: in the beating of the heart and the pulsation of blood that penetrates throughout every member as an expression of its animating soul. Like the pulsating heart that shows itself all over the surface of the skin, the pleasure of life permeates the body by means of the "inner senses" without being limited to a specific organ. We see before us the point of unity of life in the animating soul, as it gets displayed visibly throughout all of the body's parts.

But even the human form at the height of its perfection possesses deficiencies that make it inadequate to embody life in Hegel's very highest sense. You don't get a perfect interpenetration between inner and outer in the human body, he thinks, because the feeling of life isn't manifested in every organ. Among the variety of organs, some of the organs are said to be the seat of the soul, its feelings and passions. Other organs are devoted to lowly animal functions. To express the unification of inner and outer, the feeling of life must retain a physical aspect (as in pleasurable sensations, tremors, shivers, goose pimples, convulsive movements in the diaphragm brought on by laughter, etc.). But while the feeling of life retains a physiological component, sensing life can't depend only on the outer senses that are limited to specific, isolated organs. He seeks a more unified form of expression and feeling in life-forms that can relate to themselves as living: one which is inseparable from the body thus making it observable, yet not limited to a specific organ.

To satisfy this condition, Hegel looks specifically to human life-forms that can cultivate a *self-conscious* awareness of how they relate to themselves as free and independent. The "free beauty" of plants and animals could embody this idea of freedom and independence only in the form of "hints" and "foreshadowings." But Hegel's idea of life presupposes certain human psychological traits that could be present only in a human will. To the extent that nature is not linked to the will of an agent, it can't embody an idea of freedom as obeying one's will and not being subject to another's will. Like Kant, Hegel thinks our interest in beauty is that it gives us intimations of the prerequisite conditions that make morality possible: namely, a kind of freedom that depends on human recognition of our purposive agency through self-conscious modes of feeling and expression.

But not just any human life-form has this self-conscious awareness of its life as free and independent. The passages on life and desire in the Self-consciousness chapter of the *Phenomenology* precede a degenerate stage of unfreedom in which a slave's unfree, degraded mode of existence stands as a warning that not just any human life-form can reflect back at us our self-conscious awareness of our free and independent status. Although very much alive in a natural, brute sense, slaves don't have the capacity to determine themselves to motion since their mode of existence is driven by an external, coercive source. To capture the look of our freedom and independence—the very prerequisites to morality that are conspicuously missing in a slave—Hegel seeks a more unified form of feeling and expression in spiritual life-forms that are capable of recognizing themselves as living through self-conscious modes of feeling and expression (VA 126). He looks specifically to expressions of life in what Kant calls the "self-conscious soul" of a spiritual subject (CJ §29, §119), namely, the rational mind in the production of aesthetic ideas.

4.2 Aesthetic Ideas versus Concepts

Hegel's hierarchy of life culminates with his recognition that human expression at the highest levels of art and culture are the most adequate embodiments of the Idea of life. Having passed through mineral and crystal forms, plant and animal life, Hegel now looks specifically to the rational human mind producing aesthetic ideas to express its living nature. At the highest level of rational human thought, "ensouled organisms" experience life in a self-conscious way through a faculty of presenting aesthetic ideas that Kant calls "Geist"—the animating principle of the mind (CJ §49.2–3, §29). In this connection, Hegel famously claimed that art reached its zenith in the production of aesthetic ideas: "Born of the spirit [*Geist*] and received by the spirit" (VA 2). To avoid attributing to natural beauty certain ideas that could have arisen only from the products of a rational consciousness, Hegel ranks the rational mind in its production of aesthetic ideas as the highest point of organization and development: "God is more honoured by what the spirit makes, than by the productions and formations of nature" (VA 30; cf. EN §248R). He even claims hyperbolically that "even a useless notion that enters a man's head is higher than any product of nature"—that is, if there was a clear conscious agency animating its production (VA 2).

This does not so much indicate a departure from Kant's emphasis on natural beauty, as many commentators have thought. Kant's *Critique of Teleological Judgment* provided Hegel with a precedent for bringing artistic activity and nature under a unitary scheme of organic purposiveness. Kant gives Hegel a way to avoid a dualistic way of thinking about aesthetic ideas as the production of mind/spirit in intellectual abstraction from nature. Since the factors present in natural processes are salient in artistic production, Kant extends the expression of aesthetic ideas to natural beauty (CJ §51.1/Ak. 5:320). For Kant allows that the function of beauty, whether natural or manmade, is to express aesthetic ideas. Genius, in particular, he thinks, shows itself through *Geist*, and in raising aesthetic experience to the level of *Geist* producing aesthetic ideas, Kant regards the products of genius as the *mediation* between nature and mind. Thus, even the "highest point" of spiritual organization and development still occurs continuously within nature.

So far I've argued that Kant's organic scheme allowed Hegel to accentuate the fundamental continuity between the organic scheme he worked out for plants and animals and human activities, by extending the principle of "inner purposiveness" that Kant worked out for nature to human processes and artistic activities. Hegel's remarks about the "living work of art" depend for their significance, not by excluding, but by analogy with, the idea of life as it appears in living works of nature. Since the principle of life extends continuously throughout all of nature as a whole, from the simplest rock and crystal formations to the highest forms of self-conscious, spiritual expression, Hegel carries over this principle from the realm of natural explanation to the human domain of the mind in its production of aesthetic ideas.

This is not to say that Hegel adopted Kant's aesthetics wholesale. Paul Guyer detects a difference between Hegel and Kant on the relationship of aesthetic ideas to concepts. Hegel thinks concepts, even those gener-ated by the imagination, are not yet ideas until they represent something concretely embodied or actualized in objects (VA 106). Guyer thinks this difference indicates a shift away from the general nonconceptual frame-work set up by Kant.[7] For Kant denies that beautiful objects have any con-ceptualizable content at all, let alone one inseparable from their form (CJ §49). Whereas, an aesthetic Idea for Hegel is something concretely em-bodied "in" its object in the sense that its content can't be abstractly con-sidered and detached from the form in which it gets concretely expressed. Embodiment or "manifestation" refers to the adequacy of the media to represent the idea being communicated, in particular, to those features of the sensuous medium that are relevant to the idea being communicated. On Hegel's view, all there is by way of a significant meaning is the sensu-ously embodied form in which it gets expressed, such that the content is undetachable from the form in which it gets expressed.[8] Thus, Guyer con-cludes that Hegel's claim that the Idea or Concept is *adequately* embodied in its object clashes with Kant's claim that no concept can be adequate to capture the object.[9]

But beneath this surface conflict, I think there runs a deeper cur-rent of continuity. The sense for Hegel in which aesthetic ideas can't be exhausted by concepts is perfectly consistent with Kant's claim that no concept is fully adequate to capture aesthetic ideas. An aesthetic Idea for Hegel is higher than a determinate empirical or logical concept since the meaning of an Idea is not exhausted by something available to

[7] Guyer cites Kant's remark that "the freedom of the imagination consists in the fact that it schematizes *without a concept*[;] the judgment of taste must rest on a mere sensation of the mutually enlivening imagination of its freedom and understanding with its lawfulness" (CJ §35/Ak. 5:287, also Introduction, sec-tion VII/ Ak. 5:190, and §9/Ak. 5:217, 219). Paul Guyer, "Hegel on Kant's Aes-thetics: Necessity and Contingency in Beauty and Art," in *Hegel und die "Kritik der Urteilskraft*," ed. Hans-Friedrich Fulda and Rolf-Peter Horstmann (Stuttgart: Klett-Cotta, 1990).

[8] Aesthetic ideas are a sensuous rather than intellectualist way of talking about a complete interpenetration of form and content. Neither form nor content is primary in what Hegel calls an "Idea" of the living work of art. Rather than dis-tinguish between the content of a thing and its mode of presentation, the inner animating Idea is embodied in its outer appearance in such a way that the outer form completely manifests the inner essence or content. On Hegel's monistic way of conceiving the relationship between form and content, all there is by way of a meaning is the concretely embodied expression.

[9] Guyer, "Hegel on Kant's Aesthetics," 84–85.

perception. This is evident especially in his primary example, the Idea of life, which is something that can be embodied in aesthetic form, yet is not reducible to it. For he thinks we can't articulate the Idea of life through determinate conceptual judgments in precisely the Kantian sense that no concept can give the rule for judgment. While it's true that Hegel insists that an animating Idea must be concretely embodied in the sense of manifesting itself as visible appearance displayed equally throughout all parts of a thing, the relevant content being embodied is not the Idea as it appears *in toto*. It would be impossible to observe or perceive the Idea of Life as it appears as a totality embodied in a finite concrete form. Only a partial aspect of the Idea gets embodied, namely, that fragment of the whole that is relevant to reflecting something essential about the totality. For whatever is being comprehended in aesthetic experience as a totality merely through partial totalities can't be fully represented in an image, conceptualized in a concept, or made intelligible in language.

Quite the opposite of shifting away from Kant, Hegel falls right into step with him in this regard. For Kant stresses that representations of the imagination, what he calls "ideas," are opposed to concepts for the reason that an idea can't be fully represented to sense perception or to the imagination in images.[10] Aesthetic ideas for Hegel are similarly something that can't be fully represented to sense perception in images, representations, and concepts; yet, they are inseparably connected to the aesthetic whole in which they get embodied. In our primary example, the mind's production of aesthetic ideas lends itself to a preconceptual representation of life in its totality in a way that goes beyond what can be made intelligible in discursive concepts. This gives Hegel's untranslatability thesis concerning the radical indeterminacy of aesthetic ideas

---

[10] On the relation between Kant's aesthetic ideas to the rational ideas of God, freedom, and soul, Crawford writes that for Kant, "aesthetical ideas are characterized as specific images or representations of the imagination, which manifest ideas, such as love or envy in the case of poetry, which occasion much thought, yet without the possibility of any definite concept being adequate to it. It consequently, cannot be completely compassed and made intelligible by language" (CJ §49/Ak. 5:314). In this respect, Hegel's aesthetic Ideas resemble Kant's theoretical ideas of God, freedom, and the soul, which aren't products of the imagination that can be completely realized in sensuous form (SL 755–756). In fact, Kant's point was precisely that rational ideas can't be represented sensuously. Like rational ideas, aesthetic ideas strive after something which lies beyond the bounds of possible experience. Donald Crawford, *Kant's Aesthetic Theory* (Madison: University of Wisconsin Press, 1974), 120–122.

a sense perfectly consistent with Kant's claim that no concept is fully adequate to capture aesthetic ideas. Ultimately, Guyer himself gestures toward this deeper affinity between Kant and Hegel in connection with Kant's solution to the antinomy of taste. Our response to beauty involves, not just our faculties, but reference to a special indeterminate "concept," the supersensible substrate, which Kant uses differently than determinate concepts and about which, he himself admits, he knows nothing. Guyer conjectures rightly that Hegel "replaces this vague notion (of the supersensible substrate) with the sensuous embodiment of the metaphysical concept that he calls the "Idea" or the "concrete concept."[11]

4.3 Indiscursivity of Aesthetic Wholes

So far we've seen that through his critical engagement with Kant's aesthetics, Hegel appropriated an aesthetic medium that could represent the totality of life through life's beautiful form. The aesthetic imagination in its epistemological role of producing aesthetic ideas gives us a glimpse of something deeper about life in its totality. Both Kant and Hegel take it as primitive that we are ever striving to impose unity and coherence onto nature in a way that tries to make sense of its unmanageable complexity. But we can only approximate but never quite reach our rational goal. While we desire to attain something which we don't fully have—a rational grasp of that which defies rational comprehension—the fact that we have this urge to subsume the greatest complexities in nature under the simplest unities indicates that we are rational. Even the striving of our powers to comprehend the limitless power and magnitude of the sublime discloses to us a power of reason in us. And we find this experience of our essentially rational nature in connection with aesthetic experience *pleasing.* Although very subjective, Hegel regards this feeling of pleasure associated with the "rational totality of the concrete concept" (VA 134) as a *rationalized* feeling. "In this satisfaction," he writes, "there lies the *rational* element, the fact that sense is gratified only by the totality, and indeed by the totality of differences demanded by the essence of the thing. Yet once again the connection remains as a secret bond, which for the spectator is partly something to which he is accustomed, partly the foreshadowing of

[11] Guyer, "Hegel on Kant's Aesthetics," 88.

something deeper" (VA 138). In striving to impose simple unity and coherence onto nature, Hegel thinks we're unconsciously striving toward
knowledge of this deeper bond.

But at the crossroads where Kant and Hegel say *how* we gain knowledge
of this deeper bond, they head down separate paths. In sections §§76–77
of the third *Critique*, Kant sets up a contrast between our discursive intellect and an intuitive intellect as a framework for helping us comprehend
why it is the discursive "peculiarity" of our understanding that gives us a
problem with grasping organic wholes. The problem of the part/whole
relation led Kant to hypothesize a second standpoint, a different intuitive
understanding with knowledge of a higher, privileged kind, which tran-
scends the limiting conditions placed on knowledge in the *first Critique*:
namely, a divine intuitive intellect that doesn't move from the parts to the
whole. Given our discursive limitations, we can never grasp the unities
that organic wholes display in mechanically explicable terms that move
us from the parts to the whole. For in mechanical terms, the complexity
of the whole outweighs the simplicity of the parts. Since our discursive understanding goes from the parts to the whole, we can't grasp the complexity of an infinite totality taken as a whole, where the maximal complexity
of the whole somehow precedes its simpler parts. Finite discursive minds
such as our own can only entertain the idea of knowledge of this higher,
privileged kind by analogy with this divine intuitive intellect. We can only
strive toward this deeper knowledge, but never possess it.

Béatrice Longuenesse has argued persuasively that Kant deserves
some credit for Hegel's somehow finding within this framework a way to
reach this higher kind of intuitive knowledge.[12] Kant's analysis of aesthetic
judgments is where we have the choice of remaining strictly within the
discursive point of view, Longuenesse argues, or somehow finding within
this point of view a way to reach a higher intuitive kind of knowledge. But
Hegel thinks Kant spoiled his own insight by drawing the wrong conclusion: namely, that the divine intuitive intellect is not our human point of
view. In pointing out the necessity of a nondiscursive intellect in connection with our experience of the beautiful, Hegel writes, "Kant should have
kept his eye on his own Idea of the unity of an intuitive intellect in which
concept and intuition, possibility and actuality are one" (GW 91). Kant

[19] Béatrice Longuenesse, "Point of View of Man or Knowledge of God: Kant
and Hegel on Concept, Judgment, and Reason," in *The Reception of Kant's Critical
Philosophy*, ed. Sally Sedgwick (Cambridge: Cambridge University Press, 2000).

has put us in touch with another kind of knowledge, not a hypothetical kind of knowledge, and he's given us a very vivid description of it. Hegel takes the intriguing exit from the limitations of discursive knowledge left open by Kant, according to Longuenesse, and builds on Kant's idea that our apprehension of nature in its beauty reveals something peculiar about our faculties that allows us to detect special principles governing nature's unity.

At this juncture, Hegel swerves away from Kant's two-standpoint view in an original and important way. The question for Hegel is not "*Do* we attain knowledge of these living unities?" but rather "*How* do we do what we do?" Hegel adopts Kant's idea of the organic unity of an intuitive intellect in §§76–77 as a description of the way we do in fact cognize organic unities. Given our discursive limitations, we can't grasp the unity and coherence of the whole if the maximal complexity of the whole precedes the simpler parts. For our discursive minds are not so structured as to be able to take in maximal complexity, moving as they do from simpler parts to the whole. If we can't explain our knowledge of organic totalities using a purely discursive intellect that moves from the parts to the whole and yet it is a *peculiarity* of our intellects that we do in fact grasp these unities, then we must come by our totalistic knowledge of living unities in a way that is not subject to the conditions of finite conceptualizability and discursivity.

Far from being "exotic" and requiring a God-like point of view, Hegel de-exoticizes this intuitive, nondiscursive standpoint by redescribing its epistemic conditions in a way that makes it possible for ordinary subjects such as ourselves to occupy it. The imagination's production of aesthetic ideas provides the peculiar epistemic conditions that make it possible for us to catch a glimpse of the super-complex whole as a simple unity—albeit a unity with an internally differentiated structure—but not in a maximally complex way that would require an exotic, God-like point of view. Aesthetic Ideas constitute a form of imaginative expression on a continuum with nature's principle of life. As Hegel writes, the "soul-laden unity of an organic whole embodies this secret harmony, an inner bond grounded in the special animating principle of nature" (VA 984, 982–985). Just as the principle of nature permeates throughout all the parts of an organism and manifests itself as visible appearance displayed equally throughout all the parts, an aesthetic Idea permeates all the parts of the aesthetic whole, animates it from within, and manifests itself visibly throughout all the parts. As Hegel writes, "[T]his totality is not determined from without and alterable; it shapes itself outwardly from within" (VA 122). Our knowledge of the "secret harmony" of the whole can't be given through an experience of maximal complexity; rather it must be "revealed" to us intuitively through traces, hints, fragments, and partial totalities in aesthetic experience. Although the complexity of the whole outweighs the simplicity of the parts in mechanically explicable terms, in sensuous imaginative perception our experience of the simplicity and unity of the totality has primacy for us over the unmanageable complexity of the infinite totality. We subsume the greatest complexities under the simplest unities by means of aesthetic ideas embodied in fragments of the whole and glimpse aesthetic unities noncognitively through these *partial totalities*. Although aesthetic ideas capture only one small part or aspect of the totality, partial knowledge on Hegel's aesthetic holism can meet his demand to "tell the truth" about the whole without requiring exact verisimilitude to nature. For on his organic-holism, a mere fragment can give us insight into the essence of the whole without being identical to it. By pointing beyond itself, it captures what is essential about the totality, not as a pale imitation testifying falsely about its original, but as a part inseparably and organically related to the whole.[13]

4.4 Pleasure as Expressive of Agency

Let's return now to marking the significant respects in which the radically subjective elements of Kant's aesthetics influenced Hegel's Idea of life as aesthetic in nature. Hegel follows Kant's subjective turn to the

[13] Hegel devotes a long section in the introduction to his *Lectures on Fine Art* to discrediting Plato's attack on imitative art and artists (VA 29–32, 155). Plato's Socrates trivializes the imitative artist as someone who, instantly and without effort, duplicates appearances of nature in a flash like a person holding up a mirror to nature (*Republic* 596d9–13), implying that the standard of truth requires exact verisimilitude with nature. Due to limitations of the artistic media, mimetic art falls short of this standard because it captures only a small part or aspect of the original; hence, it can't impart knowledge about the essential nature of the original. But unlike photorealistic copies that conceal their artifice by naturalistic illusions, there is no pretense that the parts of artistic representation that Hegel is concerned with—namely, an animating aesthetic Idea as it manifests itself as visible appearance—are identical with the original whole. The parts in which the aesthetic Idea gets concretely embodied stand to the thing being represented, not as copy to original, but as part to organic whole.

body and its feelings to explain our peculiar intuitive responsiveness to living unities. Pleasure and pain are deeply rooted in Hegel's aesthetic conception of life and play a significant preconceptual, precognitive role in his larger epistemological project in conveying precognitive knowledge of living unities. For the life of Spirit conveys itself as a unity through bodily feelings, and there can be no feeling of life apart from bodily feeling.

These strong interconnections among pleasure, turgor vitae, and desire are all prefigured in Kant's aesthetics. What keeps Kant's aesthetics from becoming overly intellectualist is that he thinks our access to organic life is through bodily feelings, pleasure and pain. Significantly, in the opening section of the third *Critique*, Kant connects the bodily sensations of pleasure and pain to the feeling of life itself. A representation is aesthetic, he writes, when "the representation is related entirely to the subject, indeed to its feeling of life [*Lebensgefühl*], under the name of the feeling of pleasure or displeasure" (CJ §1/Ak. 5:204; cf. §23/Ak. 5:245). Pleasure for Kant is something connected with the feeling of the furtherance of life (LM 28:247, 28:586). The feeling or an awareness of the enhancement of life attending the beautiful gives pleasure [*Lust*]. And this pleasure just is an awareness of the feeling of life, or something that encourages the awareness of life. Displeasure [*Unlust*] is named as well as an intuitive mode of apprehending life, as we'll see in connection with the sublime.

This connection between life and subjective pleasure need not imply that our preconceptual knowledge of living unities, either for Kant or Hegel, stays confined to subjective, idiosyncratic feelings with only a fleeting, unsharable content. What invests pleasure of the distinctively aesthetic kind with a greater significance that takes us beyond mere bodily sensation is the ultimate ground of this pleasure. It takes life to recognize life, and the ground of this pleasure must spring from a living source: namely, the mental life of a subject (LM 28:246)—in fact, the vitality of the subject's *whole* powers of judgment. The methodological significance of Kant's holism is that receptivity to what promotes life involves the power of your *whole* mind, both the imagination and the understanding, where the ground of this pleasure is found in the harmony of an object with the *mutual relations* of the cognitive faculties. Thus, Kant grounds this pleasure in the feeling of enhanced vitality of "the mind in its *entirety*" by establishing holistic links to the understanding, imagination, and the faculty of desire. When you feel the power of your whole mind working in its entirety as a unity, the resulting pleasure gives you an awareness that manifests directly the indeterminacy of life itself. For this quickening and *enlivening* of all your cognitive powers produce the pleasure that involves the active responsiveness of life itself. In feeling an increase of life, we are apprehending ourselves as living beings. We are becoming living subjects (LM 28:247, 28:586).

Even when the understanding and the imagination are in conflict, as in response to the sublime, the simultaneous feelings of pleasure and pain are said to enliven one's faculties to be receptive to what promotes life. While pain or displeasure is the feeling of a hindrance to life, Kant allows that both pleasure and pain exist simultaneously in response to the sublime. This duality of feeling he characterizes as an "Erschütter-ing," or a convulsive movement or violent feeling that shakes us (CJ §27/Ak. 5:257), which produces an overall effect that he calls "negative pleasure." Even in the quasi life-threatening experience of the sublime, the element of pain can enliven and enhance our sense of ourselves as alive. For the imagination recognizes that we have a need to strive to comprehend the limitless power of nature but that our finite rational powers are inadequate to comprehend it in its infinite magnitude. Putting the imagination and reason in conflict in this way produces the negative pleasure associated with life itself at its purest—as purely disinterested mental spontaneity—because it discloses to us our peculiarly rational strivings and powers. Rather than produce the kind of pain associated with hindering life, the negative pleasure conveys a feeling of the furtherance of life insofar as this recognition reflects our power of reason.

The methodological significance of Kant's subjective turn, then, is to accentuate the active contribution that all our mental faculties, with our *whole* mind, make to aesthetic experience. Kant needs to retain significant holistic links to the cognitive faculty of the understanding for aesthetic experience to refer to the vitality of the subject's *whole* powers of judgment. He's constrained by the need to demonstrate the universality of judgments of taste, which implies that something is shared. For, as he writes, "Nothing can be universally communicated except cognition and representation so far as it belongs to *cognition*" (CJ §9/Ak. 5:217). No publicly sharable content can be communicated through a subjective feeling alone, for a feeling of pleasure—understood now as promoting an active awareness of life—refers only to the vitality of the subject (Intro. VIII/Ak. 5:190). But although aesthetic judgments are not discursive judgments in the sense of disclosing knowledge about an object,[14] still they must conform minimally to the lawful conditions that make conceptualizability possible. In fact, what is so vivifying for Kant just lies in the lawfulness and freedom of this experience, in the imagination's free conformity to law and "its conformity to law without a law." While the play of the imagination is said to be free, in the sense of being free from constraint from rules as if it were a product of nature, still, the imagination doesn't exhibit *limitless* freedom.[15] Makkreel writes, "[T]he imagination may project only within the limits of human possibility. This experience of (indeterminate unity) relates back to the unity of our own life."[16] By grounding our intuitive apprehension of life in the feeling of enhanced vitality in the cognitive faculties shared by all, Kant has given it a structure that permits it to communicate something sharable and reproducible in anyone with the relevant cognitive faculties.

One overlooked aspect of Kant's holistic aim of bringing into active play all our cognitive powers as a *whole* is that the faculty of judgment retains its links to the faculty of *desire*. This link between pleasurable feelings of life and desire follows naturally from Kant's practical definition of life in the *Lectures on Metaphysics*: "Living beings have a

---

[14] Although aesthetic judgments have a traditional subject-predicate form, "X is beautiful," they don't count as judgments in the proper sense of the predicate disclosing something objective about the subject term. Rather, a judgment of taste is a disguised way of saying that a reliable causal connection exists between the beautiful form and a living mind with the power to be enlivened by what promotes life.

[15] As Makkreel rightly observes, our aesthetic experience is not chaotic, irrational, and lawless. While the faculty of imagination is the power of *Darstellung* (presentation, exhibition) that gives rise to new representations for the understanding and which gives rise to new concepts, it still must be law-governed in the sense of being subject to certain rational conditions of conceptualization. That is, the imagination involves "free play" in accordance with lawfulness of what is conceptualizable. The kind of purposiveness felt in both natural and manmade beauty refers to the overall order, not chaos, of our experience. The regularities in nature are not random or produced out of chaos; it is "as if" nature were following some blueprint or purpose which contributes to bringing about that very effect, and, as such, may be regarded regulatively as the cause or explanation for the way organisms are (ought to be). And although we can't account for these regularities of nature in terms of the mechanical laws, we still take their regularities and unities as exhibiting and conforming to certain lawlike regularities and patterns. Rudolf Makkreel, *Imagination and Interpretation in Kant* (Chicago: University of Chicago Press, 1990), 63.

[16] Ibid., 47.

faculty of desire; one can make this into a definition of living beings" (LM 28:587). Pleasure (Lust) is felt with the satisfaction of desire; displeasure is felt whenever desires are hindered or left unsatisfied. If desire involves feeling the causal power of your inner representations to effect an alteration in your movements, then a pleasurable surge of life involves feeling the power of your own agency in attaining what you desire (by choice). Where there is no consciousness of your active agency, there can be no experience of life: "A thing lives if it has a faculty to move itself by its choice. Life is thus the faculty for acting according to choice or one's desires" (LM 29:894).

By linking aesthetic pleasure to a faculty that promotes an active awareness of life, in contrast to a passive cognitive relationship to an object, Kant gives aesthetic pleasure the more active, dynamic aspect that it needs. Because desires are motivating, they can be adduced to explain why the kind of pleasure involved in aesthetic experience involves wanting to *continue* in the state that is giving one pleasure (CJ §10/Ak. 5:220). For Kant attributes to aesthetic pleasure a kind of internal causality which drives one to preserve a *continuance* of the state of representation and active engagement of those cognitive powers that are producing pleasure (CJ §12/Ak. 5:222).

We get a prime illustration of this in the very way we try to cognize living unities in nature. In apprehending living forms in nature, we glimpse "hints" or "presentiments" of differences unified and associated in their incompleteness, and yet still we are satisfied. We desire to subsume the greatest complexities in nature under the simplest unities. In striving rationally to impose unity and coherence onto nature, but never quite reaching our goal, we learn that our rational capacity is prior to our *desiring* faculty. The very act of striving provides the understanding with this insight. The fact that rational satisfaction consists in merely approximating—but never fully satisfying—the desired goal allows aesthetic pleasure to retain an element of desire without making pleasure-based judgments of taste impure. The fact that we still derive pleasure from merely approximating, though never reaching, the goal, makes this experience of our essentially rational nature pleasing in a way that meets the conditions of properly disinterested contemplation.[17]

---

[17] Properly disinterested conditions of aesthetic judgment (CJ §2)—namely, a contemplation of the beautiful that puts us out of gear with all practical considerations about the object for the purpose of satisfying our practical desires—don't rule out an element of desire in aesthetic pleasure. Retaining

In this chapter I've tried to show that Kant and Hegel had kindred ways of subjectively accounting for our preconceptual, noncognitive knowledge of living unities through life's beautiful form. Far from rejecting Kant's radical subjectivism, by building on Kant's work, Hegel was led to a form of intuitive comprehension that allows us to glimpse organic unities noncognitively through partial totalities. His account of how we acquire partial or "half" knowledge through noncognitive traces, hints, and fragments of the whole came directly out of the teleological explanation developed by Kant for organic life in the third *Critique.* The epistemological significance of this "partial knowledge" for Hegel, I've argued, was that it provides us with precognitive knowledge, a kind of "half knowledge" of organic totalities, falling halfway in between intuition and rational knowledge. In the next chapter, I explore the extent to which Hegel gives this partial knowledge a paradoxical construal: calling it both "perfect, ideal, and harmonious" and yet "limited, half-knowledge" because it falls short of full-blooded, conceptual knowledge (VA 101).

---

this element of desire gives aesthetic pleasure a striving active element of a kind that need not depend for its satisfaction on actually obtaining the object of desire. Just as one can feel analogues of the emotions pity and fear in the theater, minus certain behavioral components that would, say, lead a philistine to jump on stage to save the heroine or flee the villain, one might say we can experience an *analogue* of desire in response to the beautiful, minus the practical, impure component requiring satisfaction with the real existing object.

5

On Saying and Showing

Knowledge for Hegel is holistic, in the sense that it is something grasped, not in isolation, but in relation to pictorial forms of thought, out of which it emerges in the long historical process leading natural consciousness to conceptual knowledge, as represented by the progression of shapes of consciousness in the *Phenomenology*. Hegel's discussion of classical Greek art and religion, in particular, raises a crucial issue concerning the *Aufhebung*[1] that pictorial thought undergoes in relation to conceptual thought. On the positive side of the *Aufhebung*, Hegel locates our first intuition of Spirit in early Greek religious art and mythology, whose prerational, deeper, archaic nature enabled the early Greeks to represent to themselves truths about Spirit (God or the "Absolute") in imaginative, mythical, and poetic terms that transcended conceptual articulation. With an eye to distilling the speculative content of this intuitive, immediate form of knowledge, Hegel's philosophy tries to articulate, with systematicity and rigor, the *same* truths which the Greeks had grasped enigmatically and obscurely in their religious mythology. On the negative side of the *Aufhebung*, the Greeks' grasp of these truths was so unreflective and inarticulate as to make it necessary for them to be superseded in form by the clearer conceptual type of thought exemplified in Hegel's

[1] *Aufhebung* is Hegel's term of art denoting a dialectical transformation, meaning: (1) to lift up, (2) destroy, and (3) preserve a form of thought at a higher level. In this respect, the term *Aufhebung* resembles the Latin *tollere*, which also runs together two opposed senses "to preserve" and "to destroy."

philosophy. Both the preservation and supersession of these truths are absolutely fundamental to Hegel's thought and cannot, I maintain, be rightly understood or appreciated in isolation from the aesthetico-mythic-religious-historical context from which they originated.

My first task in this chapter is to point out an apparent contradiction implicit in Hegel's claim on the positive side, that this artistic mode of cognition or "picture-thinking" (*das vorstellende Denken*) and "picture-thoughts" (*Vorstellungen*), as he calls it, yields a kind of knowledge.[2] My strategy for bringing out this incoherence is to draw a sharp contrast between artistically embodied truths of the Greek variety and propositional truths of the linguistic variety that Hegel puts such a premium on. I conclude, provisionally, that when "picture-thinking" is essentially defined in terms of a contrast with propositional knowledge and held to a standard appropriate for propositional knowledge, this invidious contrast points to a contradiction in calling pictorial thought "knowledge," as Hegel does. Moreover, as I'll argue in the later chapters on ethics, this contradiction would seem to point to a deep incoherence in Hegel's thought, since it also generalizes to the mode of ethical thought that he thinks underlies the Greek's ethical actions. Ultimately, my aim is to use this purely negative conclusion as the means to accomplish a positive end.

My second task is to argue, sympathetically, that this contradiction within pictorial-artistic thought was not a symptom of a confused or split mind, but was one of which Hegel was well aware and which he purposely generated. Far from undermining his claims about artistic knowledge, these contradictory aspects, I argue, are what makes it possible for pictorial thought to undergo the negative and positive sides of the *Aufhebung*. There is a tendency among commentators, however, to emphasize one-sidedly the perfection or defects of artistic thought, or to force together these contradictory aspects in disregard of the fact that

---

[2] Cf. PhG §60, §197, §678, §729. Picture-thinking is Hegel's term used in connection with art and natural beauty to depict an activity of the imagination involving concrete thinking in pictures, visual representations, and pictorial figures. In PhG §60, in the choice between *Vorstellungen* and *Denken*, Hegel contrasts picture-thinking (*Vorstellungen*) with the Speculative *Satz*, or what can be expressed in discursive propositions. His use of *Vorstellungen*, here, is not to be confused with *Vorstellung* as representation, because he speaks of art, not as *Vorstellung* (representation), but as *Darstellung* (presentation) or *Schein* (appearance), as in "das sinnliche Scheinen der Idee."

their contradictory meanings are intended to exclude one another.[3] But Hegel's strong affinity for the Greeks makes his characterization of their artistic thought as both "perfect" and "limited" (PhG §476, §701), a prime manifestation of a shape of consciousness containing a balance of truths and defects. This makes it a better-suited candidate than, say, the earliest shape of consciousness, Sense Certainty, for bringing out both positive and negative sides of the *Aufhebung*. At the end of this chapter, I specu-late as to the deeper motivation driving Hegel to accomplish the positive and negative sides at the same time, in particular, the negative task of superseding this aesthetic ideal for which he had a strong affinity. I argue that his motivations can only be rightly understood by connecting them to tensions inherent in the historicist-interpretive practice in which he is engaged.

Hegel's views on the truth content of artistic representation remain remarkably intact across his corpus as a whole. The pre-*Phenomenology* Jena writings emphasize language, especially oral speech, as the high-est medium for self-conscious expression.[4] The *Phenomenology* retains this emphasis on the superiority of signs over symbols, in the remarks on the relation of language to pictorial, religious expression in the Religion chapter. These remarks represent Hegel's mature reflections on art and provide the basis for my interpretation. Whatever evolution occurred in his views in the later works, in my view, amounts to clarifying and

---

[3] An example of someone who one-sidedly emphasizes the perfection of classi-cal art over its defects is Johann Joachim Winckelmann, who nostalgically longs to return to the perfection of the Greek aesthetic ideal (*Reflections on the Imitation of Greek Works in Painting and Sculpture* [La Salle, IL: Open Court Classics, 1987]). By contrast, examples of commentators who one-sidedly emphasize the defects of ineffable knowledge are Charles Taylor, in connection with Hegel's discussion of classical art and religion and thought in general (*Hegel* [Cambridge: Cambridge University Press, 1975] and "Hegel's Philosophy of Mind," in *Hegel's Philosophy of Action*, edited by Lawrence Stepelevich and David Lamb [Atlantic Highlands, NJ: Humanities Press, 1983], 84; Jean Hyppolite, "The Ineffable," chap. 1 of *Logic and Existence* [New York: State University of New York Press, 1997], 11, 12; and Robert Wicks, "Hegel's Aesthetics: An Overview," in *The Cambridge Companion to Hegel* [Cambridge: Cambridge University Press, 1983]. Wicks sometimes runs to-gether the negative and positive aspects of Hegel's views, although these aspects mutually exclude one another, and concludes that Hegel's attitude toward art in general is "thus mixed" (358). He thereby implies that Hegel's attitude toward art was ambivalent, hesitant, and tentative, and that he did not have a full aware-ness of his own attitude toward the role of art.

[4] *First Philosophy of Spirit* (1803/4), in *System of Ethical Life* (1802/3).

expanding the cryptic and extremely compressed aphorisms in the Religion chapter, some of which are abbreviated nearly beyond the point of comprehension. I'll draw on corresponding passages from the *Lectures on Fine Art*, the *Encyclopedia*, and the two preceding parts of the *Phenomenology* to generate supplementary material to fill out the remarks.[5] Admittedly, there's a notable shift in the later *Lectures on Fine Art* in emphasis away from language toward an emphasis on self-conscious reflection. But this should not be regarded as a fundamental shift in attitude or a sign that Hegel later discredited what he wrote in the *Phenomenology*.[6] His account in the Berlin *Lectures* (1823–1829), delivered almost sixteen years later, remains faithful in spirit to his original insights in the *Phenomenology* (1807). The connection between reflection and language still implicit in the *Lectures* is restored explicitly in the passages on language and the ineffable in the *Encyclopedia*.

My references to artistic thought and its representations are to be understood as relativized to a particular historical epoch, namely, early Greek culture.[7] I'll focus on the Greeks' sensuous mode of understanding truths about Spirit that Hegel thinks were expressed in their nonlinguistic art

[5] I'll be relying on correspondences among the Consciousness, Spirit, and Religion chapters, first noticed by Georg Lukács and subsequently mapped out in painstaking detail by Michael N. Forster in *Hegel's Idea of a Phenomenology of Spirit* (Chicago: University of Chicago Press, 1998).

[6] One reason, I would speculate, that explicit references to language drop out entirely in the *Lectures on Fine Art* is that these later lectures, like the Berlin lectures on *Philosophy of Religion*, were given from a systematic, rather than a consciousness-oriented, phenomenological, point of view. Cf. Daniel Cook, "Language in the Philosophy of Hegel," *Janua Linguarum*, no. 135 (1973): 107. Michael Inwood's fine introduction to the *Lectures on Fine Art* successfully synthesizes, I think, Hegel's views on art from the *Phenomenology* with his later views on art in the later Berlin lectures.

[7] Hegel's reference to this specific period is not merely an *illustration* of the abstract phenomenon question, but rather this historical case *just is* the paradigm he is describing that is driving his argument. The actual historical period of early Greek culture that Hegel has in mind was only a sixty-year period lasting from the Median wars, 492 B.C., to the beginning of the Peloponnesian War, 431 B.C. ("The Greek World," in *Lectures on the Philosophy of History*, trans. J. Sibree [London: Colonial Press, 1900], 265, 268–271). Forster identifies the historical referent of the later stages of the Artificer moment with early Greek culture. Only the later forms of art in the Artificer moment are relevant for my purposes, not the Persian, Indian, and Egyptian art forms in the Religion chapter, which he argues, are "precursors" of the early Greek art forms (Forster, *Hegel's Idea of a Phenomenology of Spirit*).

forms (in the "Artificer" moment of Natural Religion, PhG §§691–698, and the most abstract art forms in "Art Religion," PhG §§699–709). Since Hegel thinks that the kind of spirituality that the Greeks were capable of expressing at this early stage was one that could be wholly displayed by the human body, I'll focus on sculpture of the human body. The paradigmatic artworks that he thinks conveyed this spirituality were sculpture of the Olympian Gods, larger-than-life heroes, and aristocratic-warrior athletes.[8] While Hegel applies the term "picture-thinking" more broadly to deeds, events, actions, and human feelings as they are rendered in poetry and classical art in general, in this chapter I'll bypass the specifically linguistic art forms that he also has in mind in order to avoid introducing complications too early on. He thinks tensions and contradictions in a culture begin to find their earliest and most primitive articulation already within a stage of artistic culture itself, namely, in the poetic language of epic and tragedy. He thinks the specifically linguistic art forms, unlike the visual arts, propagate ideas through concepts, and hence deal in a currency similar to that of philosophy; thus he assigns a pivotal role to epic and lyric poetry, Greek tragedy, and other literary art forms in leading to awareness of certain conceptual tensions and contradictions.

5.1 Art and Indiscursivity

We may begin by generating an apparent tension between Hegel's two primary claims about art and artistic thought, namely, that it was both "perfect" and "limited." On the surface, the tension is already built into the fact that the very meanings of the terms exclude each other. Classical art was "perfect" or "ideal," Hegel thinks, because it inchoately expressed deep speculative truths about Spirit, to which subjects are said to have had an "immediate" and "certain" access. Hegel writes approvingly of this form of artistic knowledge: "[Self-Consciousness], in the work, comes to know itself *as it is in its truth*" (PhG §693). That is, he thinks the Greeks represented themselves in their anthropomorphized gods and portrayed the gods as intimate and interactive with mortals and intelligible to them by virtue of their anthropomorphized traits. Through their human and mythical exemplars, the Greeks came to know the comforting

---

[8] VA, 79, 433–434, 435, 479; see also 490, 486, where he writes: "Amongst the particular arts, therefore, sculpture is above all adapted to represent the classical Ideal. . . ."

truth, he thinks, that the gods *just are* what is immanent in humanity's own inner impulses, passions, and powers.[9] Hegel thus exalts early Greek art, and this period of culture in general, as one of "beautiful harmony and tranquil equilibrium,"[10] during which religious art and culture flowered and reached their highest moment of perfection.[11] In particular, the early Greeks' religious art, he thinks, served as a vehicle for disclosing to them this knowledge ("a truth that is a knowing," PhG §720) that the divine and human are one.

However, what makes this naïve form of thought "limited," he thinks, is that the Greeks were expressing at the level of high culture ideas that they were incapable of expressing at the lower level of ordinary language. These were speculative ideas that they had never learned or reflected on, and which they could not, even, in principle, articulate. Although the Greeks had the concepts "God," "human," and the "is" of identity, nevertheless he thinks they couldn't string these concepts together to articulate the proposition "The divine and human are one" because this proposition wasn't a simple one to them. This proposition only appears trivially simple to our more advanced form of consciousness.[12] Hegel

[9] VA, 433–434, 479; cf. 486, 490.

[10] PhG §349, §476; also PhG §462, §463, §476, §700.

[11] Hegel's famous "end of art" thesis—that art reached a state of perfection in the classical, organic art of early Greece and that such perfection would never be attained again (PhG §753; VA, 10–11)—may seem to place him in a long line of thinkers who give accounts uniquely privileging certain epochs in the history of art to the exclusion of others. For instance, among many others, his commentator, Georg Lukács, cast a nostalgic glance backward and located this moment of perfection in the novels of Goethe, Balzac, and Stendhal. However, Hegel's theory of fine art contains an important departure from this tradition. Hegel denies that art objects have an absolute value independent of their role in transforming consciousness. His end of art thesis is not that artists will stop producing art or that people will stop appreciating it. Rather, now that Consciousness is transformed to the point where it no longer needs to grasp Spirit in sensuous terms, art has "come to an end" in the sense that it has ceased to possess the value it once had to Consciousness as the sole purveyor of truths about Spirit. That's why art and religion have been superseded in this role by philosophy.

[12] Cf. "[The divine Being's] universality at the same time *appears trivial to the progressively developing self-consciousness*" (PhG §711). The Greeks' utterances of the plain words "God" and "human" are a simplified version of the ultimate, more complicated truth of Hegel's System and "do not express what is contained in them" (PhG §20). Undergoing the dialectical process of the *Phenomenology* and the *Logic* is essential to fully articulating this truth that the Greeks could only begin to dimly express.

writes, "[T]he work at first constitutes only the abstract aspect of the activity of Spirit, *which does not yet know the content of this activity within itself,* but in its work, which is a Thing" (PhG §693). In his *Lectures on Fine Art,* he renders in richer detail the kind of unreflectiveness that he has in mind and the particular historical subject he has in mind. There, in a passage that I'll quote in full, he draws a parallel between the defects of picture-thinking and the conceptual limitations of the interlocutors in Plato's early Socratic dialogues:

> Thus this [artistic] activity has a spiritual content which yet it con-figurates sensuously because only in this sensuous guise can it gain knowledge of the content. This can be compared with the charac-teristic mentality of a man experienced in life, or even of a man of quick wit and ingenuity, who, although he knows perfectly well what matters in life, what in substance holds men together, what moves them, what power dominates them, *nevertheless has neither himself grasped this knowledge in general rules nor expounded it to others in general reflections. What fills his mind he just makes clear to himself and others in particular cases always, real or invented, in adequate examples,* and so forth; for in his ideas anything and everything is shaped into concrete pictures, determined in time and space, to which there may not be wanting names and all sorts of other external circum-stances. (VA, Intro., 40; italics added)

The mistake being referred to here, is that this naïve, prereflective per-son cited particular examples instead of giving an overarching, general, theoretical definition. The early Greeks, Hegel thinks, could not yet articulate their knowledge of this truth in propositional terms because their kind of knowledge was "preverbal," not in the sense that they lacked the gift of language, but rather in that they could only "point to" (using words) examples that captured their meaning sensuously, pictorially, and nondiscursively. Socrates' interlocutors generally met his requests for a unitary, essential definition with blank incomprehension because the altogether different form of language he demanded to repair their conceptual limitations, one capable of expressing higher essences, was different from the prosaic language with which they were accustomed to describing their ordinary thoughts and actions in everyday life.

But unlike Socrates, Hegel doesn't deny that persons possessing this kind of practical wisdom have knowledge, only true belief. He maintains only that they lacked the conceptual resources needed to formulate, expound, and explain what they know in a form which will satisfy Socrates' requests for a general, theoretical definition in his "What is X?" questions. As Hegel puts it, "they only half say it."[13] Just like practical, intuitive persons who can be said to *know* practical truths that matter in life, our artistic, intuitive types are said to *know*, with certainty and directness, some important truths. But their overall worldview precluded them from possessing the necessary concepts and higher conceptual language to expound what they know in a general propositional form.[14]

As I argued in Chapter 4, Hegel thinks that pictorial knowledge in connection with natural beauty is limited in the sense that Kant intends when he uses the word "Darstellung." As Kant says, natural beauty gives us an intuition or "clue" of the systematicity of nature, not in logical or cognitive judgments, but in a presentation or exhibition. Nature "foreshadows" or gives us a "divination" of the unity of this higher Concept (*Critique of Judgment, §49*). For Hegel, too, Nature doesn't bring the Idea of life explicitly into consciousness as full knowledge, but foreshadows or "hints" at it; the human spirit has only a "presentiment" of itself as a living thing in nature. Our intuitive glimpse or intimation of the Idea of life in beautiful form is limited since our nondiscursive intellect doesn't bring the Idea explicitly into consciousness as full knowledge, but stops short at giving us a "divination" of the Idea of life. The presentation of nature as beautiful goes no further than foreshadowing "life's true Concept" (VA, 130). Thus, we don't get the real, full-blooded Idea of life from natural beauty; nature discloses the harmony of living wholes to us nondiscursively only through "partial totalities."

And if unreflectiveness and conceptual unclarity are evils, as they are for Hegel, then the kind of picture-thinking that fosters in an individual

---

[13] Hegel, "First Philosophy of Spirit" (1803–1804), trans. H. S. Harris, 245.

[14] Kant anticipated this aspect of Hegel's aesthetic theory in his third *Critique*: "By an aesthetic idea, I mean that representation of the imagination which induces much thought, yet without the possibility of any definite thought whatever, i.e., concept, being adequate to it, and *which language, consequently, can never get quite on level terms with or render completely intelligible*" (*Critique of Judgment*, §49). In the previous chapter, I've noted the symmetries and marked some of the differences between Hegel's aesthetics and Kant's subjectivist, emotivist aesthetic theory. While Kant thought that there "can never" be any such concepts, Hegel thought that Consciousness was simply not developed enough *at that period in history* to possess the concepts and conceptual resources to represent these truths to itself in language.

only a dim, obscure, inarticulate "hint" or "presentiment" of the truth ("a truth that is a knowing") is not full knowledge ("still not the truth that is known"). Hegel himself indicates he is aware of this paradox when he writes, "That essence . . . which is immediately united with the self is in itself Spirit and the truth that is a knowing, though still not the truth that is known, or the truth that knows itself in the depths of its nature" (PhG §720; cf. VA, 104). In a reversal of our expectations, Hegel demotes this ideal form of artistic knowledge to something defective falling short of knowledge, and takes back with one hand what he gives with the other.

This paradoxical construal of nonpropositional truths poses a difficulty. These historical subjects are said to *know* in an intuitive sense something which they do not yet know in a discursive sense. This raises the same vexing concerns about artistic thought that Hegel raised about Sense Certainty, the first form of consciousness in the dialectical progression that similarly related nonpropositional thought and discursive thinking in a mutually exclusive way. If we followed the logic of Hegel's refutation of Sense Certainty, then we were led to the conclusion that such an immediate, nonpropositional form of cognition is not knowledge. This conclusion should generalize to all cognitive claims associated with nondiscursive meanings, including artistic meanings. I argue in what follows that the force of Hegel's own argument should lead him to embrace the conclusion that knowledge claims associated with pictorial thinking are vulnerable to a similar style of refutation.

First, a caveat about modeling an analysis of artistic knowledge on the dialectics of saying and showing in Sense Certainty.[15] At first, this undertaking seems fraught with hazards because Sense Certainty and artistic thought do not invite comparison in almost any respect. Clearly, Sense Certainty, being the most primitive form of consciousness, does not have the complex structure of artistic thought, which is a more developed shape of consciousness. However, since Hegel's System is a cumulative one, we can understand certain elements of later shapes in terms of

[15] Charles Taylor also finds a natural application of Wittgenstein's distinction between saying and showing to Hegel's views on artistic thought (see *Hegel*, 141–145, 471–473). Also, see Taylor's discussion of these affinities between Hegel and Wittgenstein on language and Sense Certainty in "The Opening Arguments of the Phenomenology," in *Hegel*, ed. Alasdair MacIntyre (Notre Dame: University of Notre Dame Press, 1976). Taylor doesn't make the connection that I do here, between the two forms of sensuous thought or the paradox that arises for Hegel's claims about artistic pictorial thought once this connection is made explicit.

elements of earlier ones because he insists that nothing of the contents of the earlier shapes is lost (PhG §167). Certainly, citing the cumulative structure of his System isn't sufficient, by itself, to justify an analogy of artistic thought to Sense Certainty. For this argument could be used to prove that every shape of consciousness can be reduced to, and understood in terms of, Sense Certainty. I certainly do not intend a reduction of all the shapes of consciousness to Sense Certainty. So to press home this analogy will require a justification specific to artistic thought.

An analogy to Sense Certainty will be a useful tool for understanding the particular aspect of picture-thinking we are focusing on, though the analogy is not expected to capture every aspect of the complex structure of picture-thinking. Not every aspect of an analogy can be expected to carry over coherently to the thing needing illumination; every analogy must break down at some point. The most relevant aspect of Sense Certainty that applies to artistic thought is its defect of indiscursivity. Although the Greeks had language, Hegel thinks they used their artworks to express what they could not express in language. Hence, following the cumulative principle that each shape of consciousness has preserved in it *all* the residual elements of the shapes of Consciousness from which it emerged, it is methodologically sound to trace back this defect of inarticulability in picture-thinking to an original kinship with its distant relative, its cruder cousin, Sense Certainty, in whom the trait of indiscursivity is most salient (cf. PhG §446).

5.2 On Saying

The chapter that opens the *Phenomenology* is structured around a dual perspective in which Philosophical Consciousness is "testing" Ordinary Consciousness's claims to knowledge, by invoking an ordinary, commonsense criterion of knowledge that should be familiar to, and derived from, ordinary cognition. Philosophical Consciousness undertakes to refute its interlocutor, Sense Certainty, in terms it must accept, since the standard for evaluating its claims is not something alien imported from the outside (PhG §82, §84). This criterion involves the presupposition that for something to count as knowledge, the content of this knowledge must be able to be formulated or stated independently in propositional terms (in general concepts or descriptive expressions, "spoken" or "written down"; cf. the first "dialectic of saying," PhG §§95–102), about which it makes sense to apply the terms "true" and "false."[16] Or if the object of knowledge is a purely contextual one, then the interlocutor must be able to point to (using demonstratives, ostensive expressions, or literally with gestures [cf. the second "dialectic of pointing," *Aufzeigen*], PhG §§105ff.) what its experience is of or about. In other words, the discursive standard requires it to formulate the content of its claim in terms that might lend credence to its claim to have a cognitive relation to objects which yields the richest form of knowledge.

Now Philosophical Consciousness employs this discursive standard to run a *reductio ad absurdum* style of argument against Sense Certainty's claim that a greater degree of certainty attaches to its judgments because they are based on an immediate, primordial mode of cognition that makes it receptive to a pure, unique, absolutely singular, and unmediated experience. Philosophical Consciousness doesn't *deny* that these singular objects and experiences exist, only that it can reduce *ad absurdum* Sense Certainty's *claim* that such objects can be known through this primordial form of cognition. Now Sense Certainty fails this standard when it tries to name its object or determinately to refer to its singular, absolutely individualized experience with expressions, like "this," "here," and "now." Even when it uses the most minimal demonstratives, it is using conceptually loaded universals, which implicitly introduce concepts, conceptual distinctions, and an element of mediation that aren't supposed to be involved in its pure, unmediated experience.

---

[16] On the criterion of knowledge in Sense Certainty being a discursive one, see Taylor, *Hegel*, 141–145. Another representative of the orthodox reading is Merold Westphal, who maintains that Hegel is committed unqualifiedly to a purely discursive, conceptual theory of knowledge. I glossed the issue of universals in its linguistic version in an earlier version of this chapter (*Journal of Value Inquiry* 28 [1994], reprinted in *Hegel and Modern Philosophy*, International Library of Critical Essays in the History of Philosophy, vol. 2, ed. David Lamb [New York: Croom Helm, 1987]). Hegel's own examples and wording initially suggested this exclusively linguistic interpretation. For example, he writes, "Sense Certainty does not *say* what it means, and in this it refutes itself." But here I do not mean to overemphasize the importance of linguistic concepts and expressibility for articulating propositional content. All that Hegel needs to appeal to as a criterion at this point is an expressive medium, be it linguistic or nonlinguistic, which can discursively convey this propositional content. One doesn't have to appeal to language exclusively in order to still press home the point about the private, *nonintersubjectivity* of Sense Certainty's experience and meanings, the point upon which the refutation of Sense Certainty turns.

Similarly, in the "dialectic of pointing" Hegel considers and explores the possibility that we can be *shown* the content (PhG §105). If what is being brought before our eyes is a content which is concretely embodied, then this unique particular defies universalization or generalization in words. We fail to indicate this unique particular by ostension because gesturing toward this content using demonstratives like "this" or "that" doesn't uniquely determine reference.[17] Thus, the dialectics of pointing shows that there can be no publicly accessible means of determinately referring to the object that Sense Certainty grasps.

While Nietzsche concludes from this that language can't reach this unique, original, absolutely individualized "unrepeatable x," and that all language and thought-forms *falsify* experience,[18] on the contrary for Hegel, language is the "truer," for he thinks that such sensuous objects beyond the reach of language have no truth:

> [I]f they wanted to *say* it, then this is impossible, because the sensuous This that is meant *cannot be reached* by language, which belongs to consciousness, i.e., to that which is inherently universal. In the actual attempt to say it, it would therefore crumble away; those who started to describe it would not be able to complete the description, but would be compelled . . . to speaking about something which is *not*. . . . Consequently, what is called the unutterable is nothing else than the untrue, the irrational, what is merely meant (but is not actually expressed). (PhG §110)

This discrepancy between Sense Certainty's ineffable claims to knowledge and its discursive criterion for evaluating such claims would seem to entail the skeptical conclusion that if our mode of knowing *were* of the kind that Sense Certainty claims it to be, then there would be no knowledge. Certainly Hegel doesn't intend to lead us to aporia. Instead, the absurdity of such a skeptical conclusion requires that this form of immediate cognition undergo the appropriate revision to remove the offending impurity that led to self-contradiction in the first place. Language gestures in the

---

[17] On this connection between Hegel's dialectic of pointing and Wittgenstein's remarks on ostension and reference, see Taylor, *Hegel*, 143.

[18] Friedrich Nietzsche, "On Truth and Lies in a Nonmoral Sense" (1873). In *Philosophy and Truth*, ed. and trans. Daniel Breazeale (Amherst, NY: Humanity Books, 1999), 179–180.

direction that such a revision should take by indicating that the real object Sense Certainty experiences is not something immediate, but something with the structure of a universal:

> But Language, as we see, is the more truthful; in it, we ourselves directly refute what we *mean* to say, and since the universal is the true [content] of Sense Certainty and Language expresses this true [content] alone, it is just not possible for us ever to say, or express in words, a sensuous being that we *mean*. (PhG §97)

The aspect of the analogy with Sense Certainty that carries over to pictorial thought is that holding artistic thought to this propositional standard leads to a similar refutation of its knowledge claims. Sense Certainty rules out anything that is not propositionally expressible; whereas artistically embodied knowledge is precisely something that is not linguistically expressible. For the deep connection at this stage of Consciousness's development between a sensuous object embodying a truth and linguistic inexpressibility rules out the possibility that subjects can articulate their knowledge of truths prior to their sensuous embodiment. Artistic activity for Hegel is not a matter of executing in marble or rendering in verse preconceived propositions or concepts, but is to be understood as a *process* in which a subject's experience is brought about simultaneously with its representation. Stone is altered by chiseling, chipping, and sanding; canvas is covered with pigment; sounds are strung together to form sense. A transformation altering the subject's inner thoughts occurs at the same time that mechanical transformations are performed on these external materials. Internal and external operations are mutually reciprocal, and in this interactive process, both thought and object acquire a form and content that they did not originally possess.[19] All there is by way of a meaning is the sensuously embodied expression, and such a meaning is undetachable from the unique, concrete, sensuous form in which that meaning got expressed. The statue of the Greek God, for instance, doesn't express any truth or meaning beyond what it transparently wears on its surface; as Hegel writes, "Hence, the special mode of mental being

---

[19] Hegel writes, "[T]he work comes closer to the self-consciousness performing it and . . . the latter, in the work, comes to know itself as it is in its truth. But in this way, the work at first constitutes only the abstract activity of Spirit" (PhG §693; cf. PhG §491; VA 39, 95).

is 'manifestation.' The spirit is not some one mode or meaning which finds utterance or externality only in a form distinct from *itself*: it does not manifest or reveal *something*, but its very mode and meaning is this revelation" (EG §383).[20]

The matter has been left something like this. Normally, if subjects claim to experience a meaning or to judge something in a certain way, then if their cognitive apparatus is sound and they are not trivially mistaken, insincere, or lying, then all there is to evaluate as true or false is what they *say*, and we can't penetrate beyond the surface of their words. But since Hegel thinks that this form of pictorial thought lacks the concepts and necessary mediation required to formulate its experiences in propositional terms, the truth of an artistic representation can't be constituted by the subject's assessment of its truth. Hence, the attempt to capture the distinction between true and false sensuous content at the level of subjects' grasping a normative rule, which they can represent to themselves in a verbal description, is out of place. It follows, he thinks, that what the Greeks "said" is irrelevant to describing and interpreting their artistic meanings.[21] And since what they "said" can't constitute a criterion for meaning and understanding, a Sense Certainty-style criterion that requires that the content of a knowledge claim be "said" fails. Thus, we must attempt to get behind the veil of words by adverting to a nonlinguistic criterion.

---

[20] This emphasis on the indiscursivity of art has the effect of repudiating a prominent modern approach to aesthetics, according to which artworks have meaning because the real core of that meaning can be reinterpreted in a linguistic medium. (See Cleanth Brooks, "The Heresy of Paraphrase," in *The Well Wrought Urn*, chap. 11.) The error of the "heresy of paraphrase"—the error of treating artworks as vehicles for communicating truths that are equally formulable in linguistic propositions, prosaic discourse, or theoretical doctrines—lay in regarding the sensuous aspect of artworks as something only contingently related to the content, as a kind of superfluous adornment that could be split off from the content and dispensed with in favor of a clearer, more direct means of reproducing the same content.

[21] Hegel shifts the locus of interpretation and description away from the subjective intentions of persons toward public, sharable meanings. This makes his view superior to another modern approach, the intentionalist view, according to which, to disambiguate the meaning of a work, we have to advert to the artist's own interpretation or what he "reports" as the last court of appeal. For a good representative of the intentionalist view, see E. D. Hirsch, "In Defense of the Author," in *Validity in Interpretation* (New Haven: Yale University Press, 1967).

5.3 On Showing

But when we turn to the alternative possibility that picture-thinking can meet the criterion in the dialectic of pointing, we also find that merely pointing to (literally, with demonstratives or ostensive expressions) the art object fails to uniquely determine the full meaning or content of the subject's experience. Again, Hegel's invidious contrast between sensuous representation and a linguistic medium points to the deficiencies of artistic representation over speech in communicating this speculative content. What the contrast between a "thing" ("substance") and language (a "subject") points to is the need for the subject to give a clearer rendering of the thing's meanings in speech:

> [T]he work [of sculpture] still lacks the shape and outer reality in which the self exists as self; it still does not in its own self proclaim that it includes within it an inner meaning, *it lacks speech*, the element in which the meaning filling it is itself present. (PhG §695)

Plastic art lacks the precision and articulability of language, which is what makes language a better form for capturing the specific speculative truths Hegel is interested in. Certain subtle nuances and shades of meaning may find a better articulation in the medium of sculpture than language. For instance, Laocoön's silent, anguished scream transfixed in stone is better at expressing his grief than words. But the complex propositions and meanings that Hegel is interested in, the kind that will actualize Spirit, require expression in a correspondingly complex, mentalistic medium. Cold, bloodless stone he thinks is too coarse to adequately fix one aspect of Spirit's essence: what is embodied in a living, flesh and blood human being with interior experiences and an emerging self-consciousness:

> [E]ven when it [the soul of the statue in human shape] is wholly purged of the animal element and wears only the shape of self-consciousness, it is still the soundless shape which needs the rays of the rising sun in order to have sound, which, generated by light, is even then merely noise and not speech, and reveals only an outer, not the inner, self. (PhG §695; cf. §697)

The anthropomorphic metaphor of a statue deprived of speech goes well beyond making the obvious point that static, inanimate objects lack the marvelous ability to speak on their own behalf. It makes the important point that in helpless silence their meanings are only half expressed and await clarification by a self-conscious speaking subject who can fully articulate them.[22] Hegel refers us to language as a medium that is specially tailored to capturing this inner, spiritual content, for, as he says, language just is the self-exteriority of thought.[23]

> This higher element is Language—an outer reality that is immediately self-conscious existence. Just as the individual self-consciousness is immediately present in Language, so it is also immediately present as a universal infection. . . . The god, therefore, who has language

[22] Plato's image of the "silent" statue continually persists throughout Natural Religion and Art Religion. Hegel puts it to the most intriguing use as the transitional art form between the symbolic art of Natural Religion and the classical art of Art Religion. The ambiguous, half-animal-half-human statue of the Sphinx near Cairo, Egypt, stands at the crossroads between the "speechless, dumb," instinctive, unconscious symbolic forms of Natural Religion and the self-conscious expression of Greek art religion (PhG §695). The Sphinx, with the natural body of an animal (a winged lion) and the self-conscious face of a man, has the gift of speech to a certain extent; but its speech is not rational, scrutable speech (the kind of speech which is essential to conveying the essence of self-consciousness or Spirit). Rather, its riddling speech marks the supersession of the natural religious art forms by the self-conscious art forms of Art Religion because it represents "the conscious wrestling with the non-conscious, the simple inner with the multiform outer, the darkness of thought mating with the clarity of utterance" (PhG §697). The end of this struggle between instinctive and self-conscious thought is marked by the myth of Oedipus, the Sphinx Slayer, whose solution to the riddle (and attempt to refute the oracle concerning his own fate) makes him a paradigm of a self-conscious, self-determining, rational agent. See also *Lectures on the Philosophy of Religion*, ed. Peter C. Hodgson (Berkeley: University of California Press, 1988), 327, in which Hegel makes explicit reference to this myth and fills in the details of this narrative in the *Phenomenology*. The clarity of Oedipus' rational thought and speech winning out against the riddling, ambiguous meanings of the Sphinx signifies the supersession of the unconscious, instinctive works of the Artificer by the rational, self-conscious religious expression of the Artist: "These monsters in shape, word, and deed are dissolved into spiritual shape" (PhG §698). The "Artisan" has become a self-conscious "Artist" (§698).

[23] In the *First Philosophy of Spirit* (1802–1803), Hegel appeals to language (especially oral speech) as the most perspicuous medium in which to reveal the conscious qualities of the life of Spirit. Language, there, is named as a superior medium for directly revealing one's inner thoughts and character because the sign has a greater capacity than the symbol for expressing the essential properties of one's inner intentions, wishes, desires, and conscious experiences.

for the element of his shape is the work of art that is in its own self inspired, that possesses immediately in its outer existence the pure activity which, when it existed as a Thing, was in contrast to it. (PhG §710)

We have come full circle. Hegel's insistence that this self-conscious content can *only* be expressed unambiguously in a linguistic form brings us back to the point where we began. We began our refutation of picture-thinking by applying the dialectic of saying to picture-thinking, and we saw that the content of representational truths can't be "said." When we inquired as to whether this content could be "shown," the dialectic of "pointing" returned us to our starting point. If we followed the logic of Sense Certainty, then the claim that artistic thought is a nonpropositional, pictorial form of knowledge should lead to a refutation of these historical subjects' knowledge claims. For this kind of talk cuts against a propositional standard of knowledge that refers to subjects' understanding and explanation as constituting a general norm for determining their meaning and experience. Therefore, the knowledge claims associated with pictorial artistic expression are shown to be as dubious as those of Sense Certainty, if we take as our standard a propositional one.

5.4 Paradox of Picture-Thinking

Thus, Hegel appears saddled with a contradiction. The contradiction is between his claim that artistic thought is a form of knowledge and his propositional criterion for evaluating sensuous forms of thought. We saw that Sense Certainty's failure to meet this criterion led to a refutation of its knowledge claims. Parallel difficulties in assessing the knowledge claims associated with Sense Certainty and pictorial thought demand that Hegel be evenhanded in applying his criterion of knowledge to both forms of sensuous thought. So to be evenhanded in applying to artistic thought the criterion to which he rigorously held Sense Certainty, Hegel should be led to refute representational, pictorial truths and to question the authenticity of an artistic, intuitive mode of grasping such truths. Thus, Hegel is stuck in the strange predicament that such ineffable knowledge does not qualify as knowledge *by his own lights!*

This threat of incoherence is potentially embarrassing. If Hegel's criterion of knowledge is sound, then his claim that artistic thought produces knowledge lapses into incoherency. But if artistic thought is genuinely a case of knowledge, then his criterion of knowledge had to have failed because it doesn't cover all the cases that he wants to count as knowledge. Furthermore, if a propositional standard is an inappropriate one to apply to picture-thinking, then we are left without a criterion for evaluating the correctness, efficacy, or truth of artistic representation. Some other criterion must be invoked, and we would like to know what that other criterion is.

This paradox would seem to point to a deep incoherence in Hegel's thought, as we'll see in the final chapters on ethics. For it would seem to apply with equal force to the Greeks' moral actions and, in narrower application, to their artistic representations. Hegel treats art in the Religion chapter, not as having a value *sui generis*, but as a concrete expression of a perfectly general mode of cognition that underlies all three characteristic features of Greek culture: ethics, art-religion, and nature. As he writes, "All issue in works of art" (PhG §750).[24] Just as he thinks that the Greeks' cognitive relation to the ideal content of art was "immediate," he similarly characterizes their relation to their community's ethical norms as immediate, unreflective, and trusting (PhG §737, §436, §437).[25] Hegel writes, "The *relationship* of self-consciousness to [the laws] is equally simple and clear. They *are*, and nothing more; this is what constitutes the awareness of its relationship to them" (PhG §437). In Chapter 6, "Value Conflicts and Belief Revision," I'll similarly point out a tension that arises with this immediate, intuitive form of thought in connection with ethics: namely, this unquestioning, automatic deference to community norms breaks down specifically under the strain of having to act in accordance with irresolvably conflicting laws.

This threat of incoherence in the general form of cognition underlying both artistic and ethical thought thus poses the following dilemma for Hegel. Either he must dispatch the threat by conceding that artistic thought is ineffable, and so fails to count as knowledge after all. In this case, nothing is wrong with a propositional standard, and it can remain fixed as the appropriate standard for evaluating knowledge. Or he must allow that artistic thought is genuine knowledge, and that individuals

[24] On this correspondence, see PhG §750: "The religion of art belongs to the ethical Spirit which we earlier saw perish in the condition of right or law."

[25] See Forster, *Hegel and Skepticism*, 57–58, 72, who characterizes this relation as one of unquestioning deference to communal consensus on all ethical matters.

don't quite succeed in expressing all that they mean. On occasion, they even point mysteriously beyond language to unsayables. If so, then our ordinary, propositional criterion requires revision because it fails to cover all the relevant cases.

Clearly Hegel rejects the first horn of the dilemma, the horn that denies there are certain truths that transcend conceptual articulation. This doesn't mean he embraced the prevailing Romantic Intuitionism of Jacobi and Schelling, according to which, infinite, divine meanings are conveyed through immediate feelings and intuitions, and are not teachable to the limited human understanding.[26] Hegel does not think this mismatch between inner experiences and the external expression of them is a sign that language is incapable of expressing all that consciousness grasps or that the truths of artistic-religious thought have the odd property of being utterly subjective, inherently interior, and unlearnable. Rather, he thinks that these truths *require* expression. Thus, Hegel's view of the role of language at the level of art is far from a simple interpretation that impales him on the first horn of the dilemma.

Is Hegel's other alternative more promising? The second horn of the dilemma claims that not all knowledge is effable, and, therefore, we ought to relax our criterion a bit and not rigidly hold all forms of knowledge to a strict, propositional standard. It is more tempting to take this way out of the dilemma. One might argue that we can't identify the criterion introduced by Philosophical Consciousness in Sense Certainty with a standard that Hegel endorses, i.e., the absolute standpoint of Science. While Science is supposed to provide such a criterion for testing knowledge claims, at this point Hegel can't help himself to it as a criterion because in the opening chapter of the *Phenomenology,* Science still requires proof that it is the sought-after criterion. Moreover, one might continue to argue, the principle of internal criticism requires that the standard for testing be given in terms accessible to the unregenerated form of consciousness under investigation. So, in fact, what we are getting in Sense Certainty is a standard that is taken from the shape of consciousness under scrutiny, not one that Hegel wholeheartedly endorses. Hegel is giving a history of consciousness, one could argue, and he's describing a standard of knowledge that covaries with the particular shape of consciousness he is describing at a particular point in history.

[26] PhG §6; cf. EG §446, §447, and Hegel, *Faith and Knowledge,* trans. Walter Cerf and H. S. Harris (Albany: State University of New York Press, 1977).

The standard introduced in Sense Certainty itself requires revision along with Sense Certainty's knowledge claims, and we should expect this standard to change in the process. So it might be argued that we should take a historical understanding of his criterion in Sense Certainty and recognize that we are not getting Hegel's endorsement of what a standard of knowledge, in all cases, ought to be.

But this can't be right. The progression of the shapes of consciousness was written from the standpoint of someone slotted at a later stage in history, at which consciousness has already passed through all of its stages. To such a person, the progression is dynamic, and a unitary grasp of all its stages represents a kind of organic synthesis of his education, the culmination of which can't adequately be expressed neatly in the extremely compressed form of a philosophical theory, but only in the form of a sprawling narrative of the whole history of consciousness. The twofold perspective of the dialogue between ordinary consciousness and Philosophical Consciousness in Sense Certainty was written from this wider-ranging viewpoint: from the point of view of natural consciousness undergoing the process of internal critique, leading it from natural consciousness to the absolute viewpoint, and from the standpoint of one who has already attained the absolute standpoint, who looks on this process and supplies "us" with richer remarks that are not directly available to ordinary consciousness. In this running commentary for "us," Philosophical Consciousness points out the distinction between the claims of its interlocutor, Consciousness, and what Consciousness is really doing in propounding its claims—and this is reflective activity not available to the form of Consciousness in question. This activity includes Consciousness' tacitly committing itself to a propositional standard for evaluating its claims. Now the mere fact that this propositional standard is one that is implicit in the interlocutor's way of thinking doesn't discredit it in Hegel's eyes because Consciousness is actually a richer entity than it knows itself to be. And its tacit standard for evaluating its knowledge is more than what it knows it to be. This tacit standard is adoptable by Hegel because, in a sense, the individual's form of knowledge *just is* Absolute Knowledge. That is, if Science's knowledge is "real," then it has to be identified with the knowledge of actual, existing beings, not imported into his philosophy ex nihilo. So if ordinary Consciousness' knowledge claims must be formulated in a linguistic form, then this is also, minimally, a standard for Science. Therefore, Hegel can't dissolve the tension by embracing the second horn of the dilemma, the horn that discards a propositional standard of knowledge.

5.5 Solution to the Paradox

So far, not so good. Can Hegel avoid the charge of internal inconsistency by threading a delicate middle course that jointly captures essential aspects of both horns, while denying that either one individually captures the whole truth? Certainly, he did not change or forget his own criterion to which he holds Sense Certainty by the time he wrote the Religion chapter. Certainly, he was explicitly aware of the contradiction in artistic thought. For he himself analyzes art on the model of language in the passages that I cited from "Art Religion," and he himself locates the specific defect of artistic cognition in how far pictorial, religious representations fall short of approximating an adequate speculative language.

The first step in resolving the dilemma is to avoid attributing to Hegel false premises that will entangle him in what he said in Sense Certainty. He was not presupposing that the Greeks possessed knowledge of the high-powered speculative truths they were expressing in their art. This should prevent Hegel from getting ensnared in his own propositional criterion. He allowed that certain truths could be inarticulable by the persons posing them and yet still count as a kind of "lesser" knowledge. Notice that in Sense Certainty, Hegel did not commit himself to the dubious premise that to count as knowledge propositions have to be fully articulable *by everyone at all times*, even to the persons holding them. Rather, he's committed to the more defensible premise that all knowledge, if it is to count as knowledge, is fully articulable in principle and, eventually, *by someone*, though perhaps not by the Greeks themselves.[27] This is perfectly consistent with Hegel's holding that these truths must eventually be fully articulable by those persons who aspire to give them the status of knowledge. The strict, rigorous, propositional criterion is the standard to which Hegel holds these persons for whom these truths are a kind of "greater" knowledge at the end of the process. He deliberately runs artistic cognition up against this standard that it cannot but fail to meet, in order to make the point that when measured against this strict standard, artistic cognition is not knowledge of the "greater," highly articulated, conceptual type available to someone at the end of the process. The looser criterion is the standard he employs before the process of arriving at this greater knowledge. Employing this looser standard allows him to show that the Greeks anticipated the speculative content of his System.

---

[27] Michael Forster made this point in discussion.

Nothing is inconsistent in Hegel's employing the strict, rigorous, propositional criterion of knowledge when he is engaged in the task of running artistic thought up against it to show the degrees of falseness in this mode of cognition which require revision. And there is no inconsistency in employing a looser criterion when he is accentuating the elements of truth in this lesser knowledge, which were present from the start and which merit preservation in his philosophy. By employing two different criteria to evaluate artistic cognition, a rigorous or looser one, depending on which of these tasks he is engaged in, Hegel is able to accomplish two things at once: One, to interpret Greek artistic culture charitably in order to justify preserving what truth content is in its prerational, religious, and mythical materials. Two, to show that this material contained contradictions that require it to be superseded by the clearer, conceptual medium of his own philosophy. To accomplish the first task, the positive one of showing that salvageable truths are to be excavated from the sediment of this ancient culture's nonconceptual materials, Hegel employs a weak, nonpropositional concept of knowledge by which this material may be said to yield truths "that are a knowing." To accomplish the second task, the negative one of showing that this material contained fatal contradictions ("truths that are still not yet a knowing"), he employs a stronger propositional standard.

Hegel's methodology, then, consisting of both negative and positive strategies, allows him to occupy a position that avoids a bona fide contradiction. By showing that he gracefully sidesteps the traditional concepts of truth and knowledge that would lead to the incoherence in the first place, our puzzlement over the incoherences is thus removed. Hegel's position is not an ordinary one of claiming that all knowledge rests on subjects' abilities to completely articulate, at all times, what they know in a form recognizable as knowledge. This is a criterion we might ascribe to Plato, but it is not one we should attribute to Hegel. Such a criterion is shown to be too strong because it excludes cases that Hegel wants to allow are knowledge. Like Nietzsche, Hegel denies a traditional, bivalent notion of truth, according to which something is either true or false, fully known or unknown, highly articulated propositional knowledge or not knowledge at all, all or nothing. This denial is what leads to the paradoxical consequence that artistic cognition occupies a "middle ground of beauty" (VA, 104), where this gray, shaded, middle ground is one between fully grasping truths and not grasping them at all, between "the truth that is a knowing, though still not the truth that is known."

My final point in this chapter is that Hegel's need to accomplish both tasks is connected to his response to tensions intrinsic to his role as interpreter of history and other cultures. I'll employ a modern theory concerning the threat of anteriority as a useful framework for trying to make sense of Hegel's dual strategy in his approach to classical art. Harold Bloom characterizes the struggle of the "strong" poet as one in which the poet resists the threat of mere emulation and discontinuity from the past, by actively redefining the tradition.[28] My application of Bloom's model is intended only to serve as a useful tool for explaining and understanding Hegel's strategy, not as psychobiography.

The first thing to say is that Hegel's remarks on classical art are intended as more than just a charitable interpretation that respects conceptual differences between us and the Greeks; they are a tribute to Greek art. In this sense, Hegel stands to the Greeks more in an unequal relation of debtor to creditor than in the relation of field anthropologist from an advanced culture to a more primitive culture, presumptuously trying to make sense of its practices. But his idealization of Greek culture amounts to more than just servile adulation. The images of passivity, dependence, and servility that encomium, eulogies, and praise call to mind are contradicted by Hegel's insistence, at every turn, on the importance of Science for giving us the correct standpoint from which to interpret the Greeks' achievements. Notwithstanding his pitch for Science, this task of idealizing, praising, and assimilating the classical ideals requires that he stand in a passive relation to the Greeks. For Hegel is a latecomer, in the sense that he comes chronologically after the primary artistic event. As a mere praiser and beneficiary of its accomplishments, he stands in a secondary and dependent relation to it, just as debtors stand in an unequal, passive relationship to their creditors. This threat of exclusion from participating in the impressive achievements of a bygone world historical community—just from the accident of having been born too late—is enhanced by the disturbing possibility that historical and cultural differences make human beings essentially inscrutable to one another, such that a true conception of an ancient culture's art, texts, and historical materials ultimately isn't available to us. This threatens to underscore the radical differences between us and this ancient culture, whose perfection

---

[28] Bloom applies considerations of influence only to modern poetry from Milton onward, whereas, I extend them to the classical poets. Harold Bloom, *A Map of Misreading* (Oxford: Oxford University Press, 1975).

and "beautiful harmony and tranquil equilibrium" stand in contrast to our present world, which is rife with dualisms that are tearing us apart.[29] For if such perfection is too remote in time and affinity from our actual world, it can offer us precious little comfort.[30]

Hegel overcomes the anxiety of standing in a secondary relationship to the Greeks by relating his philosophy in a mutually exclusive way to his Greek predecessors' art in the production of *truth*, reminiscent of Plato's preemptive solution in the *Republic* to the long-standing rivalry between philosophers and poets. In confronting and disarming the great rival poets, whom he revered, Plato makes the desperate move of divesting them of any creativity at all by reducing them to people who mindlessly copy appearances like a person holding up a mirror to nature. On an agonistic model, this would be regarded as a strategic response to the anxiety Plato feels toward the strong, creative, precursor poets whom he seeks to

[29] See Forster on these unhappy dualisms in modern culture, among which include dualisms between God and humans, between humans and nature, between individuals and their communities. But Hegel has a cure. One of the main tasks of the *Phenomenology*, Forster argues, is to provide a cure for these dualisms that are a prime manifestation of attitudes preventing a harmonious participation in nature and society. Forster describes some of the pedagogical techniques for overcoming these dualisms by which the *Phenomenology* restores to the reader a correct sense of his relation to reality, which as far as Hegel is concerned, is a prerequisite of mental freedom (Forster, *Hegel's Idea of a Phenomenology of Spirit*; see especially chap. 2 "Curing Modern Culture: The Pedagogical Tasks," 17–125).

[30] Hegel warns us against the desire to retreat to beautiful, but long-lost worlds in the past or to seek solace in future unrealizable utopias: "The logic of the absolute Identity theory requires that the philosopher should comprehend what *actually is*, not create a bridge between a lost world and a dream world of the future" (*System of Ethical Life*, trans. H. S. Harris, 86. Cf. *History of Philosophy*, 2:94–95).

In his entreaties to schoolboys to study classical languages, Hegel claims that studying foreign languages is the means of making what is foreign our own; for example, "This world (and language of the ancients) separates us from ourselves: we reconcile ourselves with it and thereby find ourselves again in it, but the self which we then find is the one which accords with the tone and universal essence of mind" ("On Classical Studies," *Early Theological Writings*, trans. T. M. Knox [Philadelphia: University of Pennsylvania Press, 1948], 328). Our intimate familiarity with our native language, he thinks, in some sense prevents us from having true knowledge of it. By providing a contrast to our own language, foreign languages lend to what is familiar a necessary element of mediation to enable us to consciously experience our own language in a richer way and, hence, "relearn" that which we already know.

usurp. By making the aggressive move of denying the poets any creativity at all and, thus eliminating them as rivals, Plato is vindicating the importance of philosophers against the suggestion that they are useless.

The sense in which Hegel is rivaling the Greeks in his philosophy is much more benign.[31] We get no such virulent attack on art based on a deliberately philistine misunderstanding of its nature. However, Hegel is prepared to push to aggressive extremes the principle that subjects only learn what they implicitly know subsequent to giving it a representation. He pushes it to the point of divesting the Greeks of any true understanding whatsoever of their own art, maintaining that the high-powered speculative truths that the Greeks embodied and experienced in their art were lost on them, the very consciousnesses producing them, and that we understand the meaning of their work better than the Greeks themselves.[32] Hegel's relationship to the Greeks was akin to his tragic schoolmate's, Hölderlin, in that he reluctantly and with great strain concedes that the perfection of classical Greece was a unique and unrepeatable event in the modern world and he did not long to revive its lost artistic, ethical, and political ideals.[33] In showing that Greek art

---

[31] Donald Davidson uses the term "benign" to describe literary critics' use of metaphors to describe, interpret, and evaluate art objects, in an attempt to create a distinct poetic moment which will artistically rival the original artistic object being criticized or praised, as in, "The critic is in *benign* competition with the metaphor maker," in "What Metaphors Mean," in *Inquiries into Truth and Interpretation* (Oxford: Oxford University Press, 1984), 264.

[32] Kant, Schleiermacher, and Nietzsche all made remarks to the same effect. Kant claimed that he understood Plato better than Plato understood himself, as in, "I shall not engage here in any literary inquiry into the meaning which this illustrious author [Plato] attached to the expression. I need only make the remark that it is by no means unusual, upon comparing the thoughts which an author has expressed in regard to his subject, whether in ordinary conversation or in writing, to find that we understand him better than he has understood himself" (*Critique of Pure Reason*, A314, B370). In a similar spirit, Schleiermacher maintained, in connection with his philological, hermeneutical work on classical texts, that we understand the Greeks better than they understand themselves. Nietzsche, too, said, "[T]he meaning of tragic myth set forth above never became clear in transparent concepts to the Greek poets, not to speak of the Greek philosophers. . . . The structure of the scenes and visual images reveal a deeper wisdom than the poet himself can put into words and concepts" (*Birth of Tragedy*, trans. Walter Kaufmann [New York: Random House, 1967], 105).

[33] In a letter to his friend Böhlendorff on December 4, 1801, Hölderlin wrote, "[I]t is also so dangerous to deduce the rules of art for oneself exclusively from

no longer transmits the highest truths that get transmitted through his philosophy, Hegel resists the suggestion that his philosophy stands in a secondary, superfluous relation to the closed perfection of the Greeks' achievements. At the level of his philosophy, Hegel is as much actively rivaling the Greeks as passively praising them and assimilating their virtues into his philosophy. Well aware of the dangers of presumption, he acknowledges on the positive side of his strategy his profound debt to, and dependence on, them. At the same time, on the negative side, Hegel is concerned to assert his System as providing the vital link in the chain of historical events, by presenting its truths as continuous with and necessary to realizing the Greek ideal.

Now we are in a position to understand why Hegel needed to employ both a loose criterion and a strict criterion of knowledge to accomplish both tasks that he seeks to accomplish. Certain tensions inherent in the role of historian and interpreter require him to stand in a relation of dependency to the perfection of Greek artistic culture and, at the same time, in a relationship of rivalry to the art objects of praise. These two tasks of praising and competitively rivaling the Greeks in his own philosophy is connected importantly to the two tasks mentioned above. What motivates him to undertake the first task of using a loose standard to show that early Greek cultural materials contained ideal truths that ought to be preserved and praised, is that Hegel is still beholden to the Greeks. What motivates the second task of employing a stricter standard to show that these truths are inferior to the clearer conceptual articulation of them in Science is Hegel's need to competitively rival their past accomplishments, as a way of ensuring a favorable reception of his present philosophy on the part of his contemporary community.

Greek excellence. I have labored long over this and know by now that, with the exception of what must be the highest for the Greeks and for us—namely, the living relationship and destiny—*we must not share anything identical with them*" (#236 [italics added], *Essays and Letters on Theory*, trans. Thomas Pfau [Albany: State University of New York Press, 1988]), 149–151. On this issue of whether the Greek aesthetic ideal was a normative ideal for Hegel and Hölderlin, see Georg Lukács, *The Young Hegel*, trans. Rodney Livingstone (Cambridge: MIT Press, 1966), 403–404; Walter Jaeschke, "Early German Idealist Reinterpretation of the Quarrel of the Ancients and Moderns," *CLIO* 12, no. 4 (1983); Peter Szondi, "Hölderlin's Overcoming of Classicism," *Comparative Criticism* 5 (1983); Dieter Henrich, "Hegel and Hölderlin," *Idealistic Studies* 2 (1972); and Christopher Jamme, "Hegel and Hölderlin," *CLIO* 15, no. 4 (1986).

Now we have a context in which to understand the meaning of Hegel's competitive remark that we understand the Greeks' art better than they understood it themselves. It is a strategic response to anxieties that as a latecomer he stands in a secondary, dependent position to the objects of praise. Second, it's a response to the threat that it might not be possible to reach a proper understanding of the Greeks' achievements (PhG §753).[34] Against this double threat of exclusion, Hegel's act of revision is to deny that objects have an absolute meaning detachable from the history of their reception by interpreters who come after them. Hegel exchanges a static emphasis on "silent" objects as perfect and complete artifacts with the more dynamic conception of emendable, fluid, oral speech, as representative of a self-conscious, speaking subject who is necessary to complete or interpret the "silent substance" on its behalf. This means that a historical object or event is incomplete, even well after the physical process ends. It depends on a more advanced consciousness than the one producing the object to excavate the deeper, hidden, unconscious meanings that were inaccessible even to the Greeks themselves. Far from being born too late, as ideal interpreter and receiver of what has come before, the latecomer is in a position to "reverse consciousness" of the object's old meaning and actively give it a new meaning. Only this later, more advanced standpoint puts Hegel in a position to actively alter and complete its meaning (complete it in the sense of bringing Consciousness to a proper reflective knowledge about it that reveals a deeper meaning than it had before it underwent this process). It is crucial for Hegel that as a result of this dialectical movement we get a "reversal of consciousness itself" (PhG §87). We get a new kind of knowledge and a new "object" to which that knowledge corresponds and a new set of standards for evaluating them (PhG §85, §86). The new standard for evaluating knowledge claims involves the "nothingness" of the original object of the previous form of consciousness:

> From the present viewpoint . . . the new object shows itself to have come about through a reversal of consciousness itself. This way of looking at the matter is something contributed by *us*, by means of

[34] On the problem of recovering a full understanding of an ancient culture, Hegel warns us that we cannot understand the ancient Greeks any more than "the perceptions of a dog" (Introduction to *Lectures on the Philosophy of World History*, trans. H. B. Nisbet [Cambridge: Cambridge University Press, 1975], 18).

which the succession of experiences through which consciousness passes is raised into a scientific progression—but it is not known to the consciousness that we are observing. (PhG §87)

"Seeing the new object arise from the old" is something only a more advanced form of consciousness overseeing the whole process through the filter of Science can contribute because it is not accessible to the historical consciousness under scrutiny. Paradoxically, in this sense of actively altering and "completing the meaning" of the art object, the latecomer is in a position to "come before it."[35] Thus, Hegel reverses the priority of the historical artifact over interpretation by recasting the interpreter's subordinate and possibly excluded role in relation to the object into a reciprocal role of mutual dependency. By building into his theory the notion that it required a lengthy historical process to complete the meaning of classical art, he vindicates the superiority of his later historical perspective against the suggestion that it is a superfluous, secondary event, irrelevant to the perfection and completion of the primary, artistic event. Ending the *Phenomenology* with a pitch for the preeminence of his own philosophy is more than a bit of swaggering, egomaniacal boasting. Hegel thinks he provides the only conditions under which we can appreciate and interpret rightly what the Greeks have accomplished, but only on condition that his own philosophy be accepted as integrated with, and indispensable to, interpreting these achievements—hence, linking ancient and modern, foreign and familiar, dead and living, distant and near. And if Hegel failed to show that his contribution is the continuation and crowning achievement of the Greek aesthetic ideal, then that perfection is a closed one and unhappy modern humanity is cut off from its own history's highest moments.

[35] This paradoxical phenomenon of "coming before" may be seen in the artistic process, as well as in the interpretive-critical process. When the influence of an artist's predecessor is so evident in his work that one may say with confidence that the antecedent artist would not have come into prominence after him, had the later, subsequent artist's work not come into prominence, then that subsequent artist has altered the course of art history and, in a sense, "comes before" that artist. Similarly, when one can point to an artist's champion, for instance, what Ruskin was to Turner, and say with confidence that Turner's paintings would not have come into prominence had Ruskin not existed, then such a critic and interpreter is inextricable from the history of that painter's work.

PART III

ORGANIC-HOLISTIC AGENCY

6

Value Conflicts and Belief Revision

In the third main part of this book, I begin the practical application of Hegel's organic model in order to explore the extent to which his revisionary logic informs his concept of ethical agency and action. What it means to conceive of actions holistically involves grasping purpose and result, means and ends, and intentions and consequences as organically unified parts of a living whole. To grasp the whole compass of a deed organically means that both inner and outer aspects of action must be viewed as possessing an essential organization and inseparable connection even when the diversity of its parts contradicts its unity. Morally ambiguous cases in particular will present a problem for conceiving of such actions holistically, yet in accord with a principle of moral bivalence, according to which, an act must be evil or innocent, but not both at the same time. Such actions conceived of holistically inevitably lead to the contradictory judgment that "Vice is virtue" (SL 437) and "Supreme guilt is compatible with supreme innocence" (ETW 236). In what follows, I argue that the contradictory structure of such cases plays a critical role in Hegel's explanation of what brings about revision in moral concepts at the moral thought transitions.

6.1 Intellectualist Interpretation

The pivotal transition from Consciousness to Self-consciousness in Hegel's *Phenomenology* is of such perplexing complexity that some of his detractors dismiss it as the confused product of a changed mind. The apparent shifts of interest at this important juncture of the dialectic, from intellectual issues to practical concerns about agency and action, led one commentator to conclude that "even those with a minimalist reading of the real or original core of the *Phenomenology* have no satisfactory account of it."[1] Even one of Hegel's sympathizers, who argues for the coherence of the overall design of the book, dismisses his account of the transition in the *Phenomenology* as "thin," "vague," and "unconvincing," and bypasses it in favor of his account in the later *History of Philosophy* and *Philosophy of History.*[2]

However, I will argue that, far from raising problems at the transition, Hegel's introduction of certain practical considerations of agents acting and their social experiences responds to some special nature of the transition. I'll sidestep Hegel's first and more famous account of the transition from Consciousness to Self-consciousness in "Lordship and Bondage" and instead focus exclusively on his second, less well-known version of it in "Ethical Action" (PhG §§464–483). I'm referring to his historical account in which he applies the general model of action and conflict from "Lordship and Bondage" to a moral context, explaining the transition from unreflective moral intentions to critical moral reflection. Hegel understands this transition as a particular historical development coming about in early Greek culture,[3] and arising out of specific historical circumstances; namely, out of a context of irresolvable value conflicts. My motivation for focusing on Hegel's historical account rather than on his arguably ahistorical account in "Lordship and Bondage" is to provide a concrete, historical framework within which the transition

---

[1] The apparent shift of interest, Robert Pippin maintains, "presents us with the most serious of the transition problems, the 'you can't get there from here' problems in the *Phenomenology*, so serious that even those with a minimalist reading of the real or original core of the *Phenomenology* have no satisfactory account of it" (Robert Pippin, "You Can't Get There from Here," in *The Cambridge Companion to Hegel* [Cambridge: Cambridge University Press, 1992], 58).

[2] Michael N. Forster, *Hegel and Skepticism* (Cambridge: Harvard University Press, 1989), 62–76.

[3] For specific historical referents of "Ethical Order" and "Ethical Action," I'm following Forster who names them, respectively, as the early Greek city-states at their height followed by their subsequent breakup in later Greco-Roman history Michael N. Forster, *Hegel's Idea of a Phenomenology of Spirit*, Part I: "History and Historicism in the Phenomenology" (Chicago: University of Chicago Press, 1998).

to Self-consciousness may be analyzed in sharper empirical detail than is usual in the secondary literature. The basic structure of irreconcilable value conflicts is anticipated in the model of mutually unsatisfiable desires in "Lordship and Bondage."[4] But "Ethical Action" has more of an explicit social content than "Lordship and Bondage," and provides a more filled-out account than the original core chapters, showing how Hegel intended the mechanism of irreconcilable conflict and contradiction in action to explain the transition. Moreover, I believe that what is puzzling about the transition comes out most vividly in an ethical context, in particular, a context of unresolvable value conflicts.

My first task in this chapter will be to motivate Hegel's practical account of the transition from Consciousness to Self-consciousness, which uses a model of action and conflict at its basis. My strategy will be to deny that an "intellectualist" account, as I'll call it, which explains this development apart from a context of action, can explain it with rigor and necessity. My first result will be the negative conclusion that we need an alternative account to explain and understand this special node of the dialectic. My second, positive task is to argue that Hegel's practical, action-based account was designed to avoid precisely the difficulties that I allude to in a purely intellectualist account, and to meet his own requirements of philosophical rigor. The morals I will derive are local and are not intended to generalize to every node in the dialectical process. But my elaboration of this single link will point to an important philosophical argument in its own right, independent of the plausibility of the ongoing dialectical process taken as a whole.

We may begin by dispatching the dominant explanation of the transition, what I'll call the intellectualist view. I'll restrict my criticisms to narrower versions that prevail in the literature, in which a diagnosis of some intellectual defect in the early Greeks' form of thought is all that figures in elaborating the conditions that caused them to adopt a more reflective stance toward their norms and values. My criticisms are not aimed at broader, more defensible versions in the minority, which supplement this account with additional socioeconomic and political

---

[4] Prima facie, the concept of value conflicts in "Ethical Action" looks incompatible with the concepts of desire and recognition in "Lordship and Bondage." I argue that the two accounts can be seen to complement each other, in "Desire and Necessity in Lordship and Bondage," *Papers of the 18th International Wittgenstein Symposium*, ed. Kjell Johannessen and Tore Nordenstam (Kirchberg am Wechsel, 1995), 334–340.

factors.[5] A good representative of the narrower intellectualist account is Charles Taylor, who dismisses Hegel's practical account of the collapse of Hellenistic thought as sketchy, vague, and incomplete.[6] Instead, Taylor invokes Hegel's later Berlin account involving the intellectual, philosophical movement of the Sophists and Socrates. Hegel characterizes the general mode of thought underlying the Greeks' relation to their community's ethical and political norms as one of trusting deference to, and immediate, unreflective identification with, its norms and practices, which, of course, included slavery (PhG §448, §476). As Hegel writes, "[T]he law of his own heart is the law of all hearts" (PhG §461). On an intellectualist account, it was the Sophists and Socrates who led to the collapse of this trusting, unreflective acceptance because the Sophists advised that everything before considered right by the community— its customs, maxims, rituals, duties, laws, and institutions—should be tested against each individual's internal convictions. The criticism of the old ethical order implicit in this advice was that there was something wrong with taking their absolute rightness on blind trust. The specific defect of Greek ethical life, Taylor writes, was that, "In the Greek polis, men identified themselves with its public life. . . . But the public life of each of these poleis was narrow and parochial. It was not in conformity with universal reason. With Socrates arises the challenge of a man who cannot agree to base his life on the parochial, on the merely given, but requires a foundation in universal reason."[7] Thus, according to this intellectual diagnosis, what caused the Greeks to abandon their uncritical acceptance of the principles and begin to reflect on reasons grounding them was this defect of parochialism.

My objection to these intellectualist accounts involving the Sophists, and other intellectual factors, is not that such accounts have no place

---

[5] Michael Forster's intellectualist account in *Hegel and Skepticism* is an example of the broader version I have in mind.

[6] Charles Taylor, *Hegel* (Cambridge: Cambridge University Press, 1975), 176–177. Such criticisms are more appropriately aimed at *interpreters* of Hegel's account, like Jean Hyppolite. His practical account of how tragic conflicts led to the decline and collapse of Greek ethical life is more richly suggestive and impressionistic than explanatory and systematic. See Jean Hyppolite, *Genesis and Structure of Hegel's Phenomenology of Spirit* (Chicago: Northwestern University Press, 1974), 336–364.

[7] Charles Taylor, "Hegel's Sittlichkeit and the Crisis of Representative Institutions," in *Philosophy of History and Action*, ed. Yirmiahu Yovel (Dordrecht: D. Reidel, 1978), 142–143.

within an explanation of the collapse of Consciousness.[8] For undeniably Hegel himself says, "It was the Sophists . . . who first introduced subjective reflection and the new doctrine that each man should act according to his own conviction."[9] Rather, my objection is that to bring to bear this "story" of the Sophists to explain this point of the dialectic in the *Phenomenology* is out of place. It is out of place on two counts. My first objection is that there's no textual basis for it in the *Phenomenology*. Indeed, quite the opposite of criticizing the Greeks for their "parochialism," Hegel praises them for their "universalism" (PhG §451, §457, §461–462). It is no accident that Hegel's account involving the Sophists and Socrates appears in the later Berlin lectures, which, unlike the *Phenomenology*, is not meant to depict the event from the phenomenological perspective of Consciousness.

My second objection is that even if Hegel had wanted to take this position in the *Phenomenology*, he couldn't have because it is inconsistent with his official methodology. The internal critique of each shape of consciousness has to proceed in terms accessible to the unregenerated form of consciousness under scrutiny. Hegel's official methodology prohibits him from editorializing in his own voice from within the ongoing dialectic about the values he assigns to the progressing shapes of thought. Strictly speaking, from within this point of the dialectic, there is nothing intrinsically defective, contradictory, or false about this "innocent, perfect form of knowledge," as the young Hegel describes it approvingly.[10] There is no contradiction in Hegel's affirming this, as we've seen in Chapter 5, and yet maintaining that this form of thought had limitations which had to undergo further development. Intellectualists,

---

[8] The term "Consciousness" refers roughly to the Greeks' unreflective moral consciousness, and the term, "Self-consciousness" to the form of moral reflection that developed out of it. These abstract terms are characterized by a distinctive conception of reality, thought, and self, which I will define in terms of their particular social context.

[9] Hegel, "The Greek World," in *Philosophy of History*, trans. C. Sibree (New York: Colonial, 1900), 253. See Hegel's allusions to Socrates and the Sophists in his *Lectures on Fine Art*, 510.

[10] On this issue of whether the young Hegel's use of the term *Sittlichkeit*, with its positive connotations of unreflective acceptance of social norms and its rejection of reflectivity, later took on a pejorative sense in the *Philosophy of Right*, see Allen Wood, *Hegel's Ethical Thought* (Cambridge: Cambridge University Press, 1990), 217–223; see also Allen Wood, "Hegel's Ethics, " in *Cambridge Companion to Hegel* (Cambridge: Cambridge University Press, 1992), 228–229.

however, rush beyond this point to the end of the story; they assign a positive value to critical reflection and a pejorative sense to unreflectivity and rely on this to explain the Greeks' adoption of the former and their abandonment of the latter. But while the story of Socrates and the Sophists might be a plausible explanation of the process as part of the running commentary "for us," this tale cannot be a compelling explanation to ordinary Consciousness of how the change necessarily arose within its own experience. "We," of course, may point out some flaw in Consciousness, viewing its development from a later, more advantageous standpoint in history, at a cool, reflective distance from how Consciousness comes to find out this flaw about itself. But while our identification of this defect may give Consciousness a legitimate reason to undergo self-criticism, these justifying reasons themselves do not automatically yield an explanation of why Consciousness underwent revision, unless they were the reasons *for which* conceptual innovation took place. The very use of such terms as "pejorative" and "positive" presupposes that there is a single, independent scale of values to which these judgments refer, a standard which would have to be illicitly imported into the dialectic at this node from outside the ongoing process. Only "We," who have culled a rich, extensive biography of Consciousness' thought from reading the *Phenomenology* to the end, can know that there is a tension hidden in its composition. But Consciousness could not have arrived at the same determination by itself, without the benefit of reading the book of its life.

We may cast our critique wider to catch any purely intellectualist understanding of the development, whether or not it is tied to a historical, intellectual movement. One commentator, for instance, identified the fatal defect as "anti-individualism": "[Greek ethical life] denied individuals their full realization by refusing the right to individual conscience, choice, and criticism, and by demanding the unreflective acceptance of given social rules and customs."[11] But no matter how commentators variously identify this defect—as narrow "parochialism," "anti-individualism," or whatever—all intellectualist accounts as such suffer from a common problem.

To conform to the official methodology of the *Phenomenology*, intellectualists must start from the given composition of Ethical Consciousness and derive from it alone a rival system of new concepts for judging and

---

[11] A. Walton, "Hegel: Individual Agency and Social Context," in *Hegel's Philosophy of Action*, ed. Lawrence Stepelevich and David Lamb (Atlantic Highlands, NJ: Humanities Press, 1983), 85–87.

criticizing the beliefs of its old social order. But Hegel thinks this society had not developed enough to formulate a critical theory about its ailments in theoretical, philosophical constructions, and their artistic and religious materials, we saw, had to serve as a substitute. Thus, they could not, in principle, have articulated their culture's problems using the theoretical or speculative concepts "parochialism" and "anti-individualism." Moreover, even if these "happy peoples," as Hegel called them, could have criticized their tranquil, stable ethical life, intellectualist accounts fail to give a reason why they would want to. Hegel writes, "[T]he individual is *content* with the limitations of his existence and has not yet grasped the unrestricted thought of his freer self" (PhG §701). A similar problem arises in trying to explain what purely internal stimulus would prompt the early Greeks, as represented by Plato's prisoners in the cave, to be vexed with the kinds of doubts, conjectures, and epistemological worries that would get reflection started. The complacent prisoners, it is said, were certain of what their sense perceptions reported and were content to sit immobilized in this passive posture "throughout life."[12] Similarly, in Hegel's account, nothing internal to the Greeks' stable, unreflective, and happy state (nothing less than "unrestrained joyfulness") could have prompted them to assume the kind of critical, questioning, testing attitude toward their customs and laws, or their allegiance to them, let alone articulate all this in theoretical concepts, as is required by the intellectualists.[13]

The irony is that intellectualists don't intend their account as a *criticism* of Hegel; yet their presupposition that the emergence of subjective reflection is just an unexplainable primitive datum, apparently something that "just happened," which Hegel supposedly takes as a reasonable premiss,

---

[12] Plato, *Republic*, trans. G. M. Grube (Indianapolis: Hackett, 1974), 515b. Julia Annas points out that there is a real question as to what internal moving force is prompting the prisoners to ask the kinds of questions they would need to ask to get philosophical inquiry (and their movement out of the cave) started. Julia Annas, *An Introduction to Plato's Republic* (Oxford: Oxford University Press, 1981), 259.

[13] Thus, we may understand the intellectualists' urge to invoke an agent, like Socrates, and the destructive power of the elenchus, for all the unexplained knowledge, beliefs, and heightened reflection that stimulated the Greeks to take the next step in Hegel's story or Plato's allegory. But these references to world historical agents are not explanatory because what needs prior explanation are the factors that could give rise to a Socrates in the first place, someone whose mere *questioning* of the conventional norms put him so radically out of sync with his contemporaries that it was perceived as a threat to Athenian law.

saddles his account with a vicious circularity—a sin which blatantly violates the philosophical rigor that he claims for it. For the intellectualists must start from the given composition of the Greeks' thought as a primitive datum and suppose that they can derive from their local conceptual materials alone a rival system of new concepts for judging and criticizing the old social order. But talk of subjective reflection arising in vacuo presupposes an independent, self-conscious awareness that Consciousness could not possess prior to the "act" that Hegel claims was required to bring it into existence. This false account leads to incoherence by Hegel's own lights. Therefore, for exegetical and philosophical reasons, we need an alternative understanding and explanation of the transition to Self-consciousness.

6.2 Structure of the Transition

Something special is happening at the transition. What is puzzling about it is vividly illustrated in the biblical story of the Fall. In this event, the earliest, most innocent form of Consciousness attained a richer self-conception through an original act. Although this example is not Hegel's, he himself was fond of casting the drama of Consciousness' fall, from an original state of ignorance and innocence to a state of knowledge and guilt, in just these biblical terms (PhG §19, §21). Adam and Eve attained a richer self-conception by committing an act that put them in possession of the reflective moral concepts, guilt, and sin. In their blessed ignorance, they knew that they should obey God's law, and the consequences of not doing so, but they could not know the act was wrong prior to committing the very act that would put them in possession of this moral concept.[14] Although they could not have had bad intentions in acting, punishment came swiftly in the form of a punishing self-conception.[15]

---

[14] I'm focusing on the more familiar version of the story, which does not appear in Genesis at all. Elements of it appear in Alcimus Avitus's version in "The Fall of Man," in *De Spiritalis Historiae Gestis* Libri I–III, ed. Daniel Nodes (Toronto: Pontifical Institute for Mediaeval Studies, 1985), 31–46.

[15] Avitus even implies that their fall was predetermined: " . . . interea beata, *venturi nescia casus*/libertas secura bonis . . . " (meanwhile, the blessed one, *ignorant of the fall about to come*, untroubled freedom from what is right . . .) (my translation). "Incipit de Originali Peccato," in *De Spiritalis Historiae Gestis*, Liber II, lines 1–2.

As an unforeseen consequence of their choice, in their awakened self-consciousness, they saw that they were naked and they were ashamed. What is puzzling is that they felt guilty about their act, even though they could not have possessed the concepts of good and evil before committing the very deed that gave them the relevant distinction. Yet, paradoxically, they underwent a form of self-punishment for their act, the full, self-conscious awareness of which was available to them too late and was something that had to be later reinterpreted into their actions *ex post actu.*

This paradox arises even more forcefully in Hegel's own paradigms of the passage to Self-consciousness. He culls his examples from literary texts written around the time that he dates the collapse of Greek ethical life—that is, significantly before the intellectual constructions of Socrates—in the transition from the Homeric epics up to the Aeschylean and Sophoclean tragedies. Oedipus, for instance, exemplifies the difficulty of ascribing to this innocent, unknowing agent the full, conscious awareness of his deeds that could make sense of the moral dimensions of his experience, guilt, and self-punishment. Setting aside the issue of whether others were right to blame him, there was something puzzling about Oedipus blaming himself for his unintentional actions, a case, it would seem, of blaming the victim. For before the full, horrific meaning of his deeds was disclosed to him, there was nothing under their initial description, qua self-defense at the crossroads and getting married, which could warrant his self-lacerating guilt and self-punishment, which were appropriate only to his acts under their subsequent and richer description, qua patricide and incest. What makes the end of the play paradoxical, at least to us moderns, is that we think such a moral judgment is appropriate only if his deeds were the product of this richer, self-conscious reflection. Owing to Kant, modern theories tend to emphasize an agent's intentions over bad results brought about by involuntary factors. And since Oedipus acquired true self-understanding of his actions only as the result of acting, we think he unfairly confronted himself with an evaluation of his deeds that was made independently of his conscious reflection on the matter. Adventitious actions, no matter for good or bad, ought to be immune, it would seem, from moral censure. Yet, in both examples, original sin and *Oedipus Rex,* retrospective judgments attributing guilt to these persons were made without reference to their prior conscious intentions and volitions at the moment of choice, but rather, to a reinterpretation of their actions ex post facto.

One might object that the paradox is generated only for moderns by imposing anachronistic suppositions onto *Oedipus Rex*. If somehow we have contrived a paradox for the ancients, not from their own beliefs but from an anachronistic Kantian standpoint that ties culpability to intentions and not to unlucky consequences, then, like the intellectualists, we are guilty of presupposing the end of the story and we are backsliding all the way back to the false Hegel we criticized at the beginning. So it deserves mention that while the Greeks started out with different moral intuitions from ours, they too would have been perplexed by the end of the play. Consider first: Blinding went well beyond what was required by the oracle and was not part of their scapegoat ritual, which required banishment or murder by murder (*Oedipus Rex*, 100–101). Oedipus himself later questions in the successor play whether blinding was really necessary. Second, pollutants were not to be spoken to or touched (1424–1426), but Oedipus insisted on taking a nontraditional attitude toward his own pollution and showing his dreadful face to the public—blood, gore, gashed eye sockets and all—saying, "approach and deign to *touch* me" (1413). Third, Creon and the community were dilatory and shrank from their collective responsibility to exile the pollutant, and the burden fell on Oedipus himself to insist on exile. Oedipus in his dying days will also question whether exile appropriately fit the crime (more about this later). Thus, we need not impose Kantian associations onto the end of the play to suppose that these three discrepancies would have thrown the Greeks' moral intuitions into confusion. And if we think *Oedipus at Colonus* was intended as a comment on the earlier play, then Oedipus' bewilderment, embitterment, indignation, and resentment in the later play may serve as a paradigm for the Greeks' response to the paradoxical ending. Who better to represent a Greek's opinion about the outcome of that play than someone who was there?

What is relevant for our purposes is that this paradox arises vividly in the paradigms driving Hegel's explanation of the development to moral self-consciousness: unresolvable value conflicts. We may model the kinds of unresolvable conflicts he had in mind on the kind of conflict that would arise if the rules of a much-loved and long-enduring game were shown to be formally inconsistent. For instance, an ardent sports fanatic might follow baseball for decades and might know its rules in the weak sense that he can play by them and adjudicate complex plays with considerable sophistication and baseball erudition. But the rules are extremely complex and the typical athlete or sports fan doesn't know them in the stronger sense of being able to give a proof of their consistency, that is, a proof that will cover all possible and unforeseen cases that might arise in the future. If no hard cases arise to test their knowledge, then the weakness of their performative knowledge need never disrupt the practice. As long as the inconsistency in the system remains dormant, there is no reason why the contradiction in the game need be regarded as defective and intolerable. But suppose a weird, accidental convergence of factors were to cause just such a borderline case to arise and a player were declared "safe" under one rule, but "out" under another.[16] One rule isn't superior and doesn't override the other in practice. So this case is not just hard to call; it's undecidable. More than just spoiling the present game, it calls into question the fairness of rules. For if the rules can't decide whether a move is allowable, then this calls into question the meaningfulness of a win and the whole point of the game. Suddenly, our athlete's ignorance of the rules in the stronger sense has become intolerable because this undecidable case has revealed a tension in his weak sense of knowing them. Still, it would not be right to say the defect is in his blind, unquestioning acceptance of the rules. Rather, all along the game has held a contradiction lurking dormant in its rules, which only became intolerable once the player's understanding of the contradiction had been awakened through action.

To carry this game analogy over to the Greeks' ethical system, Hegel thinks that the Greeks knew their ethical rules with certainty and conviction in the weak sense that they could act according to them, but couldn't give explicit grounds or reasons for thinking they were sound or even consistent. They trustingly deferred to their community's prescriptions and prohibitions, a method of decision that lay beyond the reach of rational deliberation. Yet, nothing need be defective in their harmonious relation to their moral order, the point being not to locate the defect in their weak knowledge, as the intellectualist would. The defect lies squarely in their ethical system because it was governed by inconsistent customs, laws, and rules (PhG §468). As long as the conflicts lay dormant, they were harmless and didn't call out for any remedial action. But once the rules were discovered to be inconsistent or defective in the way that, say, a first-move win makes winning a mechanical and meaningless end, then the game

---

[16] This example is not so far-fetched. See Ted Cohen's "proof" that the rules of baseball are inconsistent in "There Are No Ties on First Base," *Yale Review* 70, no. 2 (1990): 315–322.

was spoiled. Just as a conflict might have arisen in their athletic games and exposed the tension hidden in their rules, compare this situation with discovering that undecidable value conflicts exposed contradictions in their moral game and their weak sense of knowing the rules by which they played. This conflict was exemplified in the *Oresteia*, Aeschylus' version, in which Orestes was torn between two equally valid, but jointly unfeasible duties: duty to carry out blood vengeance forced him to violate an equally valid obligation, duty to honor parents. On the analogy of an inconsistency in the rules of a game, Orestes was declared "safe" under the rule of blood vengeance, but judged to be "out" under the rule of filial piety. Although both principles were required by his community, and Hegel thinks both sides in the conflict were equally right (PhG §740), the dispute was not settled by declaring it a moral "tie."

The game analogy isn't meant to trivialize moral conflicts, only to bring out what is intolerable about solutions based on expedience rather than principle. The political settlement between the Furies and the gods in *The Eumenides* doesn't count as a moral tie because it requires the high-handed intervention of a deus ex machina, Athena, to step outside the limits of the given ethical order and invent a jury to acquit Orestes. This divine protection program is unsatisfactory because it artificially brackets Orestes' case off from the given rules. For suppose we carried this logic over to a game in which the stakes were similarly high and important consequences turned on the outcome. Suppose an inconsistency were revealed in the rules of poker, and by the same logic, we stepped outside the rules of a high-stakes poker game still in progress and invented a new ad hoc rule, one that declares all such unresolvable conflicts null and void, and requires everyone to return all the money, including the person holding the winning hand. This solution, if it may be properly called a "solution," finds a space in the gap left by the fact that knowing what to do lies beyond the reach of rational decision. It doesn't compensate the winner in the game situation, or redress the grievances of the loser who perished in the ethical situation, Clytemnestra. By switching rules in mid-game, the ad hoc solution only changes the game. That is, it replaces the old moral order with a new one.[17]

Another aspect of our game analogy is useful for understanding how incompatible laws could lurk passively in the Greeks' ethical system all

---

[17] The Furies represented an older moral order and the court of Athena, joined by Apollo, represented a new order.

along without the Greeks noticing them for a long time. Hegel must distinguish the relevant historical actions that brought Self-consciousness into existence from ordinary, contingent actions that occur spontaneously all the time. He mustn't convey the impression that Self-consciousness emerged at some historical point at which people began to act. This would be absurd because people act all the time. Not all acts radically transform our attitudes or demand remedial action of us to repair the inconsistency. So he needs to qualify that the kind of value conflicts that produced sober reflection (of the kind that spoil a game or practice) were rarer, more unusual than modern value conflicts that admittedly arise all the time. The disruptive kind of value conflicts had to be rare enough so as not to be likely to arise so often that they constantly threatened to undermine ordinary ethical life. For then one would wonder why the Greeks did not notice or exploit them sooner than they did, and this would undermine Hegel's claim that the development to Self-consciousness occurred when it did, in early Greek culture, not earlier. But he has to avoid the other extreme of referring to actions that are too rare, too improbable. For then we would have to wonder how the Greeks could think they were likely to recur often enough to pose an urgent threat to their practice, much less how they could have found their tragedies depicting these events intelligible. Indeed, he thinks that the rare actions that led to specifically tragic double binds were still possible—a view reinforced by Aristotle, who called such actions "probable" (*pithanos*). Not "probable" in the sense that there's a high statistical probability that such unusual events will occur, have actually occurred, or could happen to us all. One need not regard the tragedies as newspaper reports on actual current events to suppose that they drew on a stock of familiar beliefs, concepts, and conflicts that reflected the Greeks' worldview. Rather what has a high degree of probability is how the characters responded to these events, which plausibly represent how any one of us would respond in a similar situation.[18] And just as it is plausible that an unusual, accidental convergence of freak circumstances would reveal the

---

[18] While the aristocratic heroes represented in tragedy are larger-than-life figures, their actions must still be enough like ours to invite our identification and pity. We, the spectators, are invited to sympathetically identify with sudden reversals of fortune that befall high-placed kings and queens because the way they acted and responded to such situations plausibly represents how any one of us would respond in a similar situation. Cf. Aristotle, *Poetics*, and Hegel's *Spirit of Christianity*, ETW, 233.

inner tension in the rules of a game in time, so an undecidable conflict was inevitably bound to arise in the Greek moral game of a kind serious enough to bring to light a defect in its rules.

6.3 Irresolvable Value Conflicts

Returning to our main paradox: It arises with particular force in cases of unresolvable conflicts, although as we have seen it is not exclusive to them. When Orestes' choice was challenged, his plea was that he played fairly by the rules his community prescribed (with no less than the backing of a god), and in a sense he was right and was not just making excuses. But his defense, a blind trust in the authority of his community, couldn't keep the Furies at bay because it could be adduced to justify the competing and opposite action as well. Since his own community split down the middle about whether he was just, it couldn't provide a standard independent of both conflicting values for ranking one above the other. The paradox in Orestes' case differs slightly from the others because he felt guilty about something he did intentionally and voluntarily. So notice that the paradox doesn't depend on a dubious claim that classical agents did not have intentions, or couldn't reflect in any degree whatsoever on even mundane matters.[19] Although Orestes acted intentionally, his subjective reflection on reasons for acting was not a factor in evaluating his actions because on matters of blood vengeance, and all other fundamental moral matters, Hegel thinks he unquestioningly deferred to his community and to its divine enforcer, a tribunal that was decisive and stood in the place of reasons. Antigone too was an absolutely purposeful agent in her right mind, yet her reflection was not a factor in morally assessing her, for she could only gesture toward the "unwritten" divine laws that simply "are" and always have been, and could adduce nothing more to ground her faith in them (PhG §437).[20] Yet, the paradox still arises in

---

[19] Bernard Williams argues convincingly that, indeed, they had intentions and engaged in practical deliberation: as when a sea-tossed and brine-besmirched Odysseus is beached on a Phaeacian shore, and reflects on his most prudent course of action (Bernard Williams, *Shame and Necessity* [Berkeley: University of California Press, 1993], 34–35).

[20] *Antigone*, in *Sophocles*, vol. 1, trans. Elizabeth Wyckoff (Chicago: University of Chicago Press, 1954), 456–457. Strictly speaking, *Orestes* is better than *Antigone* for Hegel's purpose of focusing on irresolvable value conflicts *within* a person,

these rare cases because these classical agents were required to do two duties, but acting on one precluded the other; thus, either was wrong and caused them to feel deep regrets. Once again, we see an attribution of guilt made without reference to any prior calculations; and once again our agents' postmortem guilt and regret seem to be out of sync with the structure of moral experience.

Notice also that the paradox is not generated by the familiar fact that the Greeks held agents responsible for the unintentional consequences of their actions. Blaming agents for unintentionally bringing about bad results by mistake or negligence was not unique to the ancients.[21] There is nothing "paradoxical" about Telemachus admitting he is to blame for unintentionally leaving the door to the weapons armory ajar.[22] For in the more commonplace cases, ancient and modern, the course of action was not rigidly prescribed in advance of an agent's reflection on the matter (or lack of it), so there is still space to imagine an alternative outcome, if only the agent had been more attentive. But in unresolvable conflicts of the peculiarly disruptive kind that we are considering, this space was closed by the fact that the agent could do his best and still find himself locked into a lose-lose situation. The paradox of holding Orestes responsible for what he did, although he did it intentionally, is felt more strongly than in cases of blaming agents for what they did *unintentionally*. For in Orestes' case, powerful forces at work directed him to take a stronger cue from his community's script than from his own conscience.[23] This eliminated the possibility of imagining, counterfactually, there being space for him

---

rather than between people. Antigone is not forced to choose between a necessity and a necessity, two absolutely symmetric duties, but rather, between a law and something someone externally imposes on her using brute force. Her faith in divine law was confirmed by her community.

[21] Consider Hegel's example which resembles felony murder under New York law: When an agent does something awful, and even worse consequences follow than he intended, he may be punished for all the horrible consequences of his act. So, for example, if an arsonist sets fire to a building and unintentionally kills four people, then he is guilty of killing four people (PR §119Z, §132R).

[22] Williams, *Shame and Necessity*, 50–52.

[23] E.g., the principle of blood vengeance, backed up by Apollo's command, and the threat of being pursued by the Furies, who were roused by Agamemnon's murder (*Agamemnon*, 269–296, 1026ff., 269–305, and *Libation Bearers*, 285–290, in *Aeschylus*, vol. 1, trans. Richmond Lattimore [Chicago: University of Chicago Press, 1953]. Cf. PhG §467; §475).

freely to maneuver. And without this room for him to dodge a disastrous outcome, it seems wrong to cast stones at him.

This paradox points to an essential contrast between ancient and modern value conflicts. Coping with modern conflicts can no longer radically change our attitude toward inconsistencies in our ethical rules, as Hegel thinks they did the ancients. We've already been brought to self-conscious awareness that inconsistencies can arise, and when they do, we no longer unquestioningly defer to our community as the univocal, absolute authority for resolving them. It is no longer shocking or revolutionary to learn that we can self-consciously entertain a bewilderingly rich array of options for deciding our conflicts, including our subjective preferences.[24] But no anguished moment of reflection on such a plurality of options led up to Orestes' and Antigone's choices. The moment of genuine reflection, in which classical agents freely ranked their feasible options, couldn't come before what ought to be done is resolved and acted upon, as some modern decision theorists maintain it should. At this early point in history, this luxury of subjective reflection and inquiry wasn't available to these agents. In classical dilemmas there was a reversal in the chronological order of choosing over reflection. Thus, they differ from modern versions, in which the choice itself usually coincides with the resolution of the conflict. In the classical prototype, reflection wasn't undertaken prospectively; thus, the matter wasn't resolved satisfactorily with the act of choosing. Only after the moral conflict was over, and tragic collision ensued, did the agent retroactively reflect that he did not know what ought to have been done. Rather, the conclusion of his moral struggle marked the beginning of the kind of reflection and inquiry that is regarded as imperative in the modern situation before any course of action has been undertaken.

Pointing out this difference between ancient and modern conflicts is not meant to reduce the Greeks' moral scheme to the patronizing, primitive portrait that Bernard Williams rightly tries to overturn by minimizing the basic conceptual differences between us and the Greeks. Certainly, it is not meant to imply that the Greeks were generally incapable of prospective reflection over their moral and mundane dilemmas in any degree whatsoever. A single example indicates that the matter is more

[24] On modern value conflicts, see Thomas Nagel, "The Fragmentation of Value," in *Mortal Questions* (Cambridge: Cambridge University Press, 1979); and Bernard Williams, "Conflicts of Values," in *Moral Luck* (Cambridge: Cambridge University Press, 1981), 74.

complex than our paradigm initially suggested. When Orestes hesitates to kill his mother in the pivotal passage of the play, Pylades prompts him with the line, "What then becomes thereafter of the oracles declared by Loxias at Pytho? What of sworn oath?" (*The Libation Bearers*, 900–902). This moment of paralyzing doubt represents both an internal conflict in which Orestes is evenly divided against himself and an objective conflict between two duties. Still, basically the same point can be made because on the internal side, Orestes' conflict was not as extensive or deeply felt as a modern hero's, for example, Hamlet's. Orestes' subjective feelings and desires may have come into play to the extent that he might have felt vexed at having an impossible set of demands placed on him, or he might have resented being cast in the bloody role of classical avenger. Hamlet exhibited just such resentment at being unwillingly cast into this stereotypical role. He mocked having to carry out the duties befitting this overly dramatic role by playing his part literally on a stage. But we can gauge the extent of an agent's reflection by how long it interrupts his action in the play.[25] Orestes' internal conflict was not as extensive because it disrupted what he was doing for only a split second, while Hamlet's heightened introspection postponed his action almost interminably. Just to respect this difference need not imply that the Greeks didn't possess the basic moral concepts of responsibility, freedom, agency, guilt, and shame that we moderns enjoy. Hegel's view of history may be progressivist, but he avoids the crude, simplistic picture that Williams associates with vulgar progressivist theories by preserving certain conceptual similarities between us and the Greeks, while respecting the differences, in the complex notion that their moral consciousness underwent an *Aufhebung*, a transformation, meaning both to preserve and to destroy.

Thus, given the paradoxical nature of the transition to critical moral reflection, one which introduces reflective moral concepts like guilt and shame into the dialectic, an account should try to do justice to this important dimension of moral experience and not just dismiss guilt and regret as pathological neurosis or irrational self-laceration. While it may very well turn out that agent regret has to be uncoupled from the structure of moral conflict altogether, we may still demand that a theory of moral agency explain these moral feelings and their related experiences.

---

[25] This phenomenon also occurs in *Oedipus Rex*, when Oedipus marks his moment of reflection by *symbolically* disrupting what he has been doing with his mother by gouging out the eyes that looked upon their sexual relations together with the brooches she used to fasten her nightgown (*Oedipus Rex*, 1266–1271).

In what follows, I argue that Hegel's account succeeds where intellectualist accounts fail, precisely on this point and another crucial point: Hegel makes his claims through this particular shape of Consciousness, instead of, as the intellectualist does, "behind its back." That is, Hegel gives a practical analysis in terms that would have been accessible to the Greeks' moral consciousness because it turns on their awareness of the limitations of their moral system, brought to light by deficiencies in their way of resolving moral dilemmas. While I can't here pursue the larger question of whether genuine cases of unresolved conflicts could ever arise, it is well known that a decisive point of disagreement between Kant and Hegel is that Kant denied that an unresolvable conflict of duties is even conceivable.[26] We also note that some contemporary commentators maintain that such cases are ruled out by a certain classical principle of deontic logic.[27] Let us now turn to the business at hand: to show how Hegel's pragmatic explanation of the emergence of moral reflection responds to the special paradox arising at the transition.

6.4 Ancient Resolution to Conflicts

One prevalent attitude toward contradiction that Hegel questioned is the assumption that the very presence of contradiction indicates an "error" that we simply can't tolerate. Not all contradictions demand some sort of rational resolution. The Greeks' attitude toward contradictions in their mythical and ethical beliefs provides fertile ground to explore the assumption that the mere presence of contradiction when it comes to light always demands that we do something to remove the contradiction. The two areas of belief invite comparison in this regard because Hegel thinks that the same general attitude that allowed the Greeks to regard their community as the authoritative source of ethical canons and customs also supported and sustained their beliefs in myth.[28] He thinks their automatic, unreflective acceptance of mythical truths depended on

---

[26] Kant, *Metaphysics of Morals*, Cambridge Texts in the History of Philosophy, ed. Mary Gregor (New York: Cambridge University Press, 1996), 16.

[27] Bas Van Fraassen, "Values and the Heart's Command," *Journal of Philosophy* 70, no. 1 (1973): 12.

[28] Hegel treats Ethical Consciousness as a perfectly general mode of thought underlying the Greeks' relation to their various ethical, political, and artistic-religious norms.

taking a predecessor's word for it or deriving information about them from an unquestioned authoritative source.[29] Yet, when contradictions and inconsistencies arose in their accounts of the same myth—not just in unimportant details, but over substantive facts, like whether Helen ever went to Troy, or whether Iphigenia or just her wraith was sacrificed at Aulis—the Greeks' attitude toward such inconsistencies was one of good-natured indifference and their response was simply to tolerate the inconsistency.[30]

This is not to suggest that the Greeks didn't really *believe* in their myths, and thus had a high tolerance for errors and genuine inconsistencies as we might have of our modern fiction. Certainly they had the necessary conceptual resources to question the truth of their myths.[31] Nor is it to suggest that hidden contradictions are less disruptive than revealed ones. For even an explicit awareness of contradictions in the rules of some games may not be disruptive enough to keep one from being happy to go on playing. In a friendly game, one might even perversely delight in discovering that such conflicts exist and let them be. It's only to suggest that there's no reason why a contradiction by its very presence in a game must be regarded as fatal.[32]

Both hidden and revealed contradictions are tolerable in the mythico-poetic context because the ground rules for belief commitment are modified. The Greeks' mythical mode of belief didn't require them to commit themselves to inconsistent theoretical beliefs about the way things *really*

[29] On this special status that the young Hegel accorded the Greeks' mythical beliefs, see H. S. Harris, *Hegel's Development: Toward the Sunlight, 1770–1801* (Oxford: Oxford University Press, 1972), xxv.

[30] On this issue, see Paul Veyne, *Did the Greeks Believe in Their Myths?* (Chicago: University of Chicago Press, 1988), 7.

[31] If they attempted to check the veracity of the fantastic and marvelous events in the Homeric epics against their present reality in which no such supernatural occurrences were observed, then a parti-pris style of argument was available to them, which goes: our experiences in the present are more veridical than those occurring in some mythical, atemporal past just because this is *our experience now*, and since what is described in myth clashes with our present experiences, it must, therefore, be false.

[32] To bring out our wrong-headed attitudes toward contradictions arising in mathematics, Wittgenstein similarly distinguishes between the bad and the harmless kind of contradiction. What makes the bad kind intolerable doesn't amount to explicitly knowing about them. See Crispin Wright, *Wittgenstein on the Remarks on the Foundations of Mathematics*, chap. 16, "Consistency," in *Wittgenstein on the Foundations of Mathematics* (London: Duckworth, 1980), 295–317.

are, which for empirical reasons can't be true. Contradictions in their mythical beliefs were local and insulated from other more fundamental beliefs and were of the kind that didn't spread and infect their whole system of beliefs. Since their mythical mode of belief didn't have to bring in any background assumptions, such as what a proper grounding for a belief is, their mythic statements didn't make the kinds of unacceptable contradictory claims about present-day reality (an alarming thing to do) that would commit them to dangerous practical beliefs about reality. Rather, their myths affirmed things about an atemporal mythical past, and pertained to a realm existing prior to and remote from their present, everyday world.[33] It cost the Greeks nothing to believe that Ares and Aphrodite were caught committing adultery. They had nothing to gain from taking a stand on whether they were realists about Minotaurs. When contradictions came to light in their myths, it was not a case of the alarming kind of inconsistency that calls for remedial action to remove the contradiction since nothing in experience was to be gained or lost from doing so. We might add that in a later, quite different approach, Sextus Empiricus gave excellent advice about conflicting myths and endorsed a suspension of judgment.[34]

It's only shocking and disturbing to allow that people are willingly, even cheerfully, endorsing bona fide contradictions if they are of the urgent kind that infect whole practices and hence demand some remedial action. Hegel's explanation of what led to revision in the Greeks' moral concepts turns on this: the Greeks' tolerant attitude toward contradictions in their mythical beliefs doesn't apply as a general method for resolving their ethical beliefs. Tolerating ethical conflict or, alternatively, gliding into a position of suspense about it, will not yield the kind of dynamic oppositions and struggles that Hegel is relying on necessarily to bring about revision in moral concepts. We have seen that agents don't have to *do* anything when faced with conflicting mythical beliefs—truths that will not hurt or help them. But, as far as Hegel is concerned, they have thus gained very little in self-understanding. A quietist attitude toward contradiction is incompatible with his reliance

---

[33] Veyne, *Did the Greeks Believe in Their Myths?* 18.

[34] Sextus Empiricus' 10th mode in "Customs and Persuasions," in *The Modes of Skepticism*, ed. Julia Annas and Jonathan Barnes (Cambridge: Cambridge University Press, 1985), 151–153.

on the mechanism of action and conflict to occasion active inquiry and reflection, not tranquil detachment. Good-natured indifference or the skeptics' advice to suspend judgment may be appropriate when the matter is morally indifferent and no practical action is urgently required, or when inconsistent commitments do not generate life-threatening consequences. But for Hegel, this skeptical solution comes later, historically and conceptually, than the development at issue.

This sharp contrast between the ancients' attitude toward contradictions in their ethical and mythical beliefs brings out a distinctive feature in their method of deciding value conflicts that forced them to an arbitrary resolution. Hegel's historical explanation of the transition brings in some psychological materials at this point. Tragic conflicts provide a crucial context in which to explain revision in their beliefs because of the extraordinary psychological pressure they put on an agent to find a method for coping with them. Ethical conflicts presented agents, not with the indifference of two opposed sides, but with conflicting demands that produced a psychological tension that urgently required some release in action. One would have to resist intolerable psychological pressure to pretend that they do not exist, or just to let the contradiction be. Unlike the mythico-poetic context, the practical context carries with it a demand to act—a practical necessity, which Hegel thinks threw into confusion the skeptics' commitment not to affirm beliefs (PhG §205).

The idea that the Greeks could believe a norm to be binding but couldn't reveal this conviction in their actions, in the sense of asserting it, defending it, staking their life on it—or weren't willing to act on it in any or all of the above senses out of fear for their life, yet they claimed to believe they should do it—is to Hegel an incoherent description of purposive, assertive agents on their way to realizing Spirit's freedom. Accordingly, in a famous passage in the Preface, Hegel proclaims the manifesto of the life of Spirit: "The life of Spirit is not the life that shrinks from death and keeps itself untouched by devastation, but rather the life that endures it and maintains itself in it. It wins its truth only when, in utter dismemberment, it finds itself" (PhG §32). Built into the Greeks' way of knowing their ethical norms, Hegel claims, was a necessity prescribing them to forcefully assert them and resolutely act on them, even if it meant risking an irrevocable and unforeseen outcome. No reference to motivational reasons need be made because motivation was internal to obligation, and it was impossible for virtuous agents to see they had an obligation, yet fail to see they had no motivation, actual or dispositional, for acting on it. Thus, conflicts of the modern duty-desire kind at the heart of Schiller's and Kant's ethics, in which even virtuous people struggle against their desires (PhG §603), didn't arise for virtuous people. Therefore, the Greeks didn't need the kind of exhortation, aesthetico-moral therapy, or psychic-therapeutic education of their desires required by their anguished modern counterparts. Rather, in Schiller's idealization of their "noble naïveté," their actions flowed gracefully from doing a duty that was perfectly aligned with their desires and impulses.

This inseparable connection between believing something and resolutely acting on it is what Hegel thinks led the Greeks to resolve their dilemmas by silently bypassing the reflective process of citing reasons and instead acting intuitively and decisively on whichever principle expressed their strongest value commitment (PhG §466). He thinks Antigone's intransigent resolve to act on her stronger commitment to family than to the state was predetermined by Nature, for example, by her gender (PhG §465), and she could not at will abandon her strongest commitment. Notice that Hegel does not call her absolutist, one-sided perspective "simplified" or "falsified," which would imply she was suffering from cognitive confusion or a delusion which sound counseling about the other available options might have dispelled. She was of sound mind and had to act uncompromisingly on the prescribed rules, selectively attending to certain commitments, while coolly ignoring others. In the passage that offended Goethe so much, Antigone cites a chilling formula as evidence that she is just following the prescribed rules (*Antigone*, 905–912). Hegel later converted what in her speech might seem to us a vice into an exemplar of Greek universalism (PhG §457).

But the problem with this distinctively classical solution is that it resolves through instinct and nature what can't be resolved by decisive moral argument and a rational calculation of values. In the ancient solution, deleting one of the conflicting principles in favor of the other couldn't be justified without riding roughshod over the demands of the other principle. This resulted in regret and remorse over the consequences. Since the outcomes were irrevocable, there was room for nothing more than the kinds of gnawing regrets and futile longings that modern philosophers try assiduously to avoid. Something is obviously wrong with the classical resolution because such outcomes were irrevocable; they provided no benefit for retrospective judgment and regret; they left no room for reparative or compensatory actions. Thus, the ancient resolution that we have arrived at has a quite primitive look. But this should not be surprising, considering the still very short history of the problem.

Hegel's explanation of the transition to moral reflection turns on what is problematic about their flawed method of decision making. He seeks to explain how moral reflection emerged, solely in psychological terms internal to the Greeks' mode of thought, from their awareness of the limits of their moral reasoning, brought to light, in particular, by their flawed methods for solving dilemmas. Recall the unhappy paradox that I alluded to earlier: namely, that in situations of tragic conflict, guilt was generated by an action that violated a moral obligation, without regard to the agent's intentions and volitions in acting. Intentions and volitions are uncoupled from moral experience at this early stage of history, and Hegel thinks there is no inconsistency in this being so. He follows the ancients, who blamed agents for their unintentional actions by maintaining that their reactions of guilt and self-punishment were not irrational, ones which ideal, reflective moral agents in perfect command of themselves would not indulge in. Rather, he thinks their negative reactive attitudes toward conflicts, feelings of guilt and shame, were *appropriate* (PhG §§468–469, §740).[35] But appropriate in a far more interesting sense than that some recompense was owed the victims. Hegel is relying on shame and guilt to serve as noncognitive signs that these agents have done something very bad for which they can't evade responsibility. But a pronouncement of guilt captures only one aspect of the whole action and leaves out the equally essential aspect in which these agents were blameless. On Hegel's holism, these agents are both innocent and guilty. We will return to this contradictory and problematic result in the next chapter. Here, I wish to explore the significant role that Hegel assigns to our negative reactive attitudes toward conflict in order to see our way clear through these paradoxical cases.

---

[35] He writes: "Guilt is not an indifferent, ambiguous affair, . . . as if with the doing of it [the deed] there could be linked something external and accidental that did not belong to it, from which aspect, therefore, the act would be innocent" (PhG §468). Also, see his remarks that " . . . consciousness cannot deny its guilt, because it committed the act" (PhG §740). On this issue see Wood, *Hegel's Ethical Thought*, 138–139.

6.5 Negative Reactive Attitudes toward Contradiction

Hegel's rejection of the authority of the first person standpoint makes his view of moral agency especially well suited to handling these paradoxical cases that saddle agents with guilt and responsibility without reference to intentions. Agents fail to arrive at a true self-understanding of their actions and purposes, he thinks, prior to their goal's being fully articulated and qualitatively transformed in being played out in their actions. He writes, "[T]he absolute right of Ethical Consciousness is that once an action is finished, the form of its actuality should be nothing more than what that Consciousness *knows*" (PhG §467). Oedipus doesn't arrive at the right description of what he has done just by inspecting his intentions and volitions at the crossroad, but only when he is confronted with a retrospective interpretation of his acts. By taking the stance of a historian toward the facts of his own personal history, Oedipus gradually reads back into his acts their truer significance. He derived this second, richer description of his deeds from their revealed interconnections within the wider network of past events in which they were embedded. His retrospective self-interpretation transformed his beliefs about what he actually did, irreversibly altering what he earlier thought he did. This demanding way of relating to himself was supported by his redescription. More than neurotic misdescription, his later redescription justified taking a self-critical stance, changing his acts from courageous to base, from deeds that were innocent, to ones for which he was rightly blamed (PhG §474). In response to altering his beliefs about what he actually did, not what he intended, his emotional response to his action accordingly underwent an appropriate reversal, from feeling praiseworthy to feeling guilt and shame.

The effect of individual guilt and shame in revising beliefs was similar to the shame, perplexity, confusion, and numbness that Socrates' dialectical method aroused in his interlocutors and bystanders at the theoretical level, which led to the aporia required to rupture their prejudicial views and purge them of false beliefs. Just as the specific emotion, shame, is evoked by Socratic dialectic to dismantle an interlocutor's unwarranted assumptions (and set an example to deter bystanders),[36] guilt

---

[36] Cf. Spirit of Christianity, ETW, 230–231. When an agent chooses to adopt a strict moral posture such as Oedipus', he may be set up as a morally praiseworthy example to inspire others. Similarly, when an agent *fails* to adopt the appropriate

and regret served an index to the unsatisfactoriness of the distinctively ancient resolution to unresolvable conflicts. This emotional response served as a warning to all those who would accord absolute status to their norms.

As we've seen in previous chapters, Hegel relies on psychological, not formal, considerations in response to contradictions. Here, he assigns a significant practical role to the whole range of negative reactive attitudes—shame, guilt, regret, remorse—in response to moral conflicts. Rather than seeing them as signs of error, or an irrational mistake that ought not to have happened, Hegel invokes the torments of guilt and regret in the bloody aftermath of tragic conflicts to falsify the agents' unwarranted trust in their community as final ethical arbiter. The cumulative residual sorrow produced by these serial killings compelled the community to abandon its flawed methods of coping with and containing these conflicts. It was in their attitudes, Hegel thinks, that their fate really began. And he quotes Sophocles lovingly to the effect that this therapeutic belief revision can't be attained without someone suffering: "Because we suffer we acknowledge that we have erred" (PhG §470). When Creon, for example, surveyed the landscape of his life in the guilty aftermath of enforcing his edict and saw it littered with the corpses of his wife, his son, and his son's bride, it's unlikely that this mortifying sight only reinforced his belief that he was right all along. In Hegel's words, "[T]he right which lay in wait is not present in its own proper shape to the consciousness of the doer, but is present only implicitly in the inner guilt of the resolve and the action" (PhG §470). This transitional, aporetic moment, in which agents find they can no longer identify with their own acts, or with the community that prescribed them, transformed their way of thinking through and through. As he moralizes, "The accomplished deed completely alters [the agents'] point of view" (PhG §470). Their reactive attitudes toward what was already sealed by fate involved an exercise of their agency, not over external circumstances, but in their active response to what was done to them.

To add to the significance that Hegel assigns these negative reactive attitudes, we may distinguish further within this class of emotions between an unhealthy, paralyzing kind and a healthier, forward-looking variety.

---

moral posture, his bad example may be held up as a warning for others to learn from, e.g., as Agamemnon's fate served as a warning throughout the *Odyssey* to Odysseus and Telemachus.

A passive, backward-looking grief dwells futilely on the irremediable defects of an unchangeable past. A passive regret accepts fatalistically that one could not have acted otherwise. In its passive variety, remorse consists of futile longings for what might have been if only life hadn't been disrupted by a disfiguring fate. By contrast, reactive emotions in their healthier, active variety have a transformative effect by pointing to a warrant for revision of the settled assumptions that led to the outcome.[37] Regret initiates inquiry into, and reflection on, those happier alternatives that might have been actual if only the agent had acted differently. In its active aspect, remorse produces reflection on some precious quality of a life that was had, but lost, and a poignant sense of just what it was that we lost. It provokes active reflection on why those qualities were important to one, and why one lacked the fortitude of character to hold onto one's happy life. "In suffering we acknowledge that we have erred."

Hegel further links up this model of individual agent-blame, with its distinctively psychological response to contradiction, to community-wide belief revision. But to analyze global changes in the Greeks' moral consciousness through changes in their local responses to dilemmas, he needs to claim more than that the Greeks' moral system possessed intransigent conflicts and contradictions. For intractable contradictions are present in every community and system—whether a game, a myth, or a language—which don't bring about globally disruptive changes causing them to fall apart. In a language game, our linguistic rules may not uniquely determine their application, as Wittgenstein said, but while they may present us with incommensurable, yet equally valid, interpretations, we manage to obey our linguistic rules, and it would be wrong to describe our language practice as on the verge of collapse. Such conflicts may be fatal to theories; they may entangle our understanding in some kind of intellectual mistake. But no one ever died from acting one-sidedly on a linguistic rule. Whereas, where ethical conflicts are concerned, Hegel wants to show that they resulted in actual practices collapsing. Something more is needed to show that the Greeks' ethical conflicts had more globally disruptive consequences than conflicts that might arise inconsequentially in their myths, which we saw could remain local and not infect their more fundamental beliefs.

---

[37] On the active aspects of guilt and regret, cf. Hegel's discussion in *Spirit of Christianity*, ETW, 230, 231, 233.

What makes these intransigent contradictions more insidious than those arising inconsequentially in any system is that the social consequences of ascribing blame extended well beyond an individual coping privately with his guilt. Tragic conflicts that arise at the individual level were particularly disruptive to the whole community because they persisted well beyond the initial problem they presented. The consequences stretched across a social network of identificatory ties. An individual acting one-sidedly on a rule activated a larger network of strong identificatory ties with others, which generated a cycle of murders that disrupted the order and solidarity of whole communities. In *Philosophy of Right*, Hegel criticizes the primitive revenge theory of punishment implied in the ancients' way of coping with these crimes, not as isolated, unrepeatable events, but as a self-sustaining series of events with systematic connections (PR 102, R; see *Spirit of Christianity*, ETW 229). An individual's choice to kill a relative did not remain a quiet, private family affair. It was a wrong that required a repetition of an offense to right it, which then set off an equally necessary chain of responses in others, spreading to future generations. In the Oresteia, Thyestes' initial curse on Atreus is passed down to Agamemnon, whose assertion of a right had to entail a second wrong; and for Clytemnestra to right that second wrong entailed a further wrong; and strict compliance with the rules required Orestes to right that third wrong with a fourth wrong; and so on. The stain spread through successive generations of the house of Atreus in a potentially endless cycle of revenge. To terminate the series of acts of revenge at any one generation for a "time-out" was arbitrary. Still another chain of necessary reactions may be traced along the Oedipal line: Jocasta and Laius' efforts to avoid fate proved to be just the thing needed to bequeath to Oedipus his sorrowful legacy, a curse which he in turn passed down to Polyneices and Eteocles, who then handed it down to their surviving sisters, and so on. The cumulative residual sorrow these serial killings produced, Hegel thinks, compelled the community to begin to reflect rationally on its flawed methods of coping with and containing these conflicts.

Hegel's strategy is to analyze global changes in the Greeks' shape of consciousness through changes in their local responses to dilemmas. He adopts this strategy because he thinks revising their local responses brought with it a change that was absolutely fundamental to the Greeks' moral consciousness. An alteration in the whole shape of this moral consciousness occurred simultaneously with a change in their response to

value conflicts. The Greeks' local value conflicts led them to a first awareness that their conventional morality could confront them with equally
valid, but opposed, principles, an awareness that led them simultaneously
to question and search for reasons for these principles. The search for
grounds, Hegel thinks, inevitably led to an awareness of the limitations
of their principles. For once the Greeks began testing and questioning
the grounds of their laws, he thinks this signaled a decline in their immediate, trusting acceptance of them, a decline which started the slide
toward immorality and eventually to the collapse of their laws. For of two
conflicting laws, Hegel writes, "I could make whichever of them I liked
the law, and just as well neither of them, and as soon as I start to test
them I have already begun to tread an unethical path" (PhG §437).

Hegel's practical account of the transition from moral consciousness
to moral self-consciousness, then, far from being sketchy, vague, and incomplete, provides the basis for a richly interconnected theory of action,
moral action, expression, knowledge, and self-knowledge. Against purely
intellectualist interpretations, I have argued that there was nothing intrinsically more desirable about reflective inquiry over unreflecting acceptance for the young Hegel. He tries to show that, without negative
moments of crisis in the practical sphere to get reflection started, conceptual revision in the theoretical sphere would never have taken place.
Unlike Socratic dialectic, however, these negative moments in Hegel's
dialectic do not end in aporia. On the positive side, these negative moments provide the impetus to adopt an alternative mode of thought, one
involving the kind of subjective reflection and inquiry that is available
to modern agents in similar situations. As we'll see in the final chapter,
Hegel's own account of moral agency and responsibility is not meant
to provide us with a solution to all ethical dilemmas that improves on
the ancients' solution. Rather, critical reflection emerges as superior at a
particular historical stage on pragmatic grounds because it promises to
yield more success in effecting mutually acceptable resolutions to tragic
conflicts.

The transition to Self-consciousness on Hegel's account occurred
gradually over a long historical period, but inevitably, the two moral conceptions had to meet somewhere. In the next chapter, I analyze the moral
worldview that emerges at this juncture of the dialectic, where ancient
and modern conceptions meet. Already we've seen some elements of
ancient and modern conceptions beginning to merge within the Greeks'
literature. More than just a passive media for mirroring their culture's

conceptual scheme, concepts, ailments, and values, the Greeks' artistic media were essential both to grappling with tensions in their morals that they could not yet articulate in theoretical propositions and to bringing about further conceptual innovations. We've already seen evidence that the Greeks' moral consciousness was moving closer to a Kantian moral conception in the successor play, *Oedipus at Colonus,* in which a wrecked and dying Oedipus says he was not to blame and regards himself as something of a victim. Turnabout is fair play, and now he stresses a distinctively modern-sounding link between culpability and intention. Since he did not intend the act, he reasons, his self-punishment did not fit the crime. The two plays may be seen as trying out two incompatible moral intuitions, and the move from *Oedipus Rex* to *Oedipus at Colonus* reflects a movement toward abandoning one set of moral intuitions and adopting another that came nearer to our own.

Finally, I will end this chapter by pointing to an ambiguity in interpreting the necessity of this particular transition. Hegel's account of necessity at this transition combines two senses of necessity, weak and strong. If his historical explanation were strictly a posteriori and derived from historical fact, then we should be able to confirm or disconfirm it by checking it against the empirical facts. If all that Hegel is giving us were just an empirical description of what happened in history, then his views on historical necessity would commit him only to saying that this development was bound to happen. Then the crises setting it into motion could be regarded as contingent and need not have occurred when he said they did, in early Greece, but could have happened sooner, later, or not at all (PhG §451, §475). The weak necessity he is committed to at this straightforward level of empirical description consists in the unavoidable conflicts that were presented once the events were arbitrarily set into motion.

But Hegel wants to claim more than that history as a matter of empirical fact happened to follow this rational and intelligible course. His claim is not just a causal one; rather, it is rationally supported in the sense that he thinks the psychological facts created a compelling reason for moral reflection to appear in this particular ethical community when it did. It could not have appeared sooner because he thinks there was no reason for the community to be "ripe" to receive it (PhG §71). But at the level of human history, he can't make this stronger claim that the development to Self-consciousness was a necessary one and had to take the course it did, when it did. To make the stronger claim that the development had to follow necessarily, he has to give an explanation which brings in his speculative logic. Historical transitions, he thinks, are, at bottom, logical transitions that get manifested in a temporal dimension; historical actions also express thoughts of historical agents and thus may be explained by reference to agents' thoughts. Since thought exhibits a rational development captured by his logical categories, historical events at bottom just are logical processes, and, accordingly, the shapes of consciousness just are the categories in the *Logic*. For Hegel to make his stronger claim that the transition had to occur when it did, not sooner, later, or not at all, one has to descend with him to the deeper, logical categories of his System. While one can understand his empirical explanation without knowing this aspect of his System, without undergoing further initiation into it, the novice is barred from gaining insight into the strong necessity of this development. For the stronger necessity governing the logical categories occurs "behind the back of Consciousness." And without this deeper knowledge, these events can only appear contingent to the uninitiated unbeliever.

7

Two Aspects of Holistic Agency

7.1 Problem of Moral Indeterminacy

Certain cases of moral ambiguity are too strange and unclassifiable to be judged evil or innocent, yet too disturbing and disruptive to let go as undecidable. Thus, consider the primal scene of moral ambiguity: Oedipus' act at the crossroads. On an ancient reading, which omitted reference to intentions, his external bodily movements were described under their unintentional aspect as "patricide." By contrast, in the sequel at Colonus, Oedipus described his intention as "self-defense," and he identified, instead, with a proto-Kantian assessment of pity and pardon.[1] Merely by shifting to the Kantian stance, which makes morality immune to bad luck, Oedipus made his act pardonable by tying his culpability to subjective intentions rather than external consequences. This dramatically reversed the value of his act, turning it into something innocent. Better to be born later into a modern Kantian world, which switches the moral value of an act from guilt to innocence by describing the same act under an internal aspect that recognizes the permissibility of one's intentions.

---

[1] More than two decades later at Colonus, an aging, dying Oedipus raises a single, isolated voice to protest his innocence above the chorus of condemnations (*Oedipus at Colonus*, lines 258–264). He tries to evoke mercy, forgiveness, and sanctuary by crafting a positive redescription of what his intentions and motives were at the crossroads: "retaliation" or self-defense in response to being wronged (270–273). Hegel also describes Oedipus' act as "courageous self-defense," in *Spirit of Christianity*, 233–244. See also PR 117Z).

Hegel calls this abrupt switch in the value of a moral act the "inverted world" (*verkehrte Welt*) effect, by which he means, roughly, that the moral shiftiness within an individual psychology can make an act forbidden or permissible, depending on whether moral assessment is directed at intentions or consequences. Hegel formulates the problem of shifting values in the *Phenomenology of Spirit* in connection with attempts to neutralize the effects of moral luck on responsibility.[2] The problem has more than just a local significance in the *Phenomenology*. He links certain shifts in value to elaborate historical paradigms, to the collective consciousness of a historical people, to the general character of a whole nation and its citizens (*realen Geister*, PhG §441/*Werke 3*:326; *Bewußtseins realisiert*, §447/*Werke* 3:329). The ideas being tested here are perfectly general, and Nietzsche describes the inverted world effect in remarkably similar terms, as a conflict between classical and Kantian-Christian interpretations resulting in a transvaluation of values.[3] The general issues at stake here, whether consequences or intentions are morally relevant, also enter as a strand in contemporary analytic debates about the doctrine of double effect.[4] Moreover, the contemporary relevance and importance of this phenomenon lies in its power to critically engage two prominent moral theories, consequentialism and Kantianism.

[2] PhG §§157–160. Hegel describes the inverted world thus: "The punishment which under the law of the *first* world disgraces and destroys a man, is transformed in its *inverted* world into the pardon which preserves his essential being and brings him to honour" (PhG §158). The first world Hegel identifies with early Greek morality, the second, with Kantian morality. His later account of the inverted world effect in *Philosophy of Right* remains remarkably consistent with his account in the *Phenomenology*, as he himself explicitly notes (PR §135R). In a parallel passage, he writes, "This [innocent] content is only one of the many elements of an action as a concrete whole, and the others may perhaps entail its description as 'criminal' and 'bad'. . . . Thus there arises a contradiction between descriptions: according to one the action is good, according to the other it is criminal" (PR §140R, T. M. Knox translation).

[3] Nietzsche, *Beyond Good and Evil* §22, §23; *Genealogy of Morals*, essay I, §10.

[4] See Warren Quinn, "Actions, Intentions, and Consequences: The Doctrine of Double Effect," *Philosophy and Public Affairs* (Fall 1989); Warren Quinn, "Actions, Intentions, and Consequences: The Doctrine of Doing and Allowing," in *Killing and Letting Die*, ed. Bonnie Steinbock and Alastair Norcross (New York: Fordham University Press, 1994); Francis Kamm, "Non-consequentialism, the Person as an End-in-Itself, and the Significance of Status," *Philosophy and Public Affairs* 21 (Fall 1992); and Philippa Foot, "The Problem of Abortion and the Doctrine of the Double Effect," in *Virtues and Vices* (Berkeley: University of California Press, 1978).

The problem at issue is not that such morally indeterminate acts have a vague moral content, falling into a gray moral area that blurs the lines between good and evil. The inverted-world effect is more like the "seeing as" phenomenon in the ambiguous duck-rabbit figure. We see the reversible duck-rabbit figure sharply now as a duck, and then in a sudden gestalt-switch, just as resolutely as a rabbit. Similarly, the morally ambiguous figure resolves on one moral view sharply under its consequential aspect, but on another under its intentional aspect (PhG §617). Just as we can't see the reversible figure as both duck and rabbit at the same time, similarly, the reversible moral figure involves an abrupt and unstable shift between two mutually incompatible self-descriptions: "I, Oedipus, whom all men call the great" (*Oedipus Rex*, line 8) doesn't build gradually and continuously on Oedipus' later self-description as "a sinner and a son of sinners" (1398), but is abruptly displaced by it.

We may thus demand of our practice of moral judgment that it generate univocal, determinate verdicts that conform to a rule of moral bivalence, according to which a moral act is either evil or innocent, but not both at the same time. But morally ambiguous cases, conflict cases, and cases of bad moral luck would seem to fall afoul of this minimally rational rule. For in such cases it would seem we can make an act forbidden or permissible, depending on which aspect of action we direct our attention to. Nothing, in principle, prevents Oedipus from shifting between contrasting verdicts in a potentially endless series of sequels. The ancient verdict was overly demanding; but resting content with the forbearing modern verdict may raise suspicions that this aging, embittered, confused, and possibly self-deluded man is conveniently picking the description under which his act comes out looking best. Without a rational basis for seeing his act under one aspect rather than the other, as in the gestalt-figure, both aspects are to be weighed equally. This makes it arbitrary to terminate the potentially infinite series of evaluations at either verdict.[5] Thus, to fix a stable interpretation, one minimally in conformity with the rule of moral bivalence,

---

[5] Commentators on *Oedipus Rex* tend to be sharply divided between these two opposed verdicts. At one extreme, for example, Paul Fry gives a flattering, promotional portrait of the kind we might find in a personal ad: Good leader with extraordinary powers for rational inquiry; hates secrets and mystification; loves openness; insists on thrashing things out in public; successful, but possesses one slight physical defect (Paul H. Fry, "Oedipus the King," in *Homer to Brecht*, ed. Michael Seidel and Edward Mendelson [New Haven: Yale University Press, 1977], 180, 175–176). At the other extreme, Theodore

Hegel asks of such morally ambiguous actions, "Which of these sides of the action [inner or outer] is really the essential one?" (PR §140R).

Hegel's holistic approach to morality rejects this tendency to focus on intentions or consequences as it gets reflected historically in early Greek ethics and Kantian moral thought (PhG §633). His holistic critique of these two prominent moral views brings to light the failure of one-sided approaches to capture all that he takes to be relevant to moral assessment. From the early Frankfurt manuscripts onward, he exhibits a humanistic streak in defending the rights of morally ambiguous figures, such as Oedipus, Orestes, Antigone, and Mary Magdalene, against society's impersonal moral and legal institutions (*Spirit of Christianity*, ETW 242–244; GW 185–186). His discussion of Conscience in the *Phenomenology*, as I understand it, proposes just such a holistic, intuitive standpoint from which it might be possible to reconcile individuals to the impersonal demands of moral life. In this chapter, I show how Hegel dialectically derives the need for this third holistic, intuitive standpoint out of the contradictions arising in the two positions around their one-sided responses to morally ambiguous cases. This will require me to take a somewhat extended detour through some of the ancient scenarios that Hegel has in mind; in particular, Sophocles' Oedipus cycle, and repetitions of these ancient paradigms in modern analogues. My aim is not primarily historical, and there will be a great deal of idealization in my reconstruction of the historical problematic that Hegel thinks led up to Conscience.

7.2 Ancient Causal Account

Beginning with the ancient view, Hegel singles out a causal account of attribution, which he identifies with the early Greeks or the "ancients," as I'll call them rather vaguely.[6] The ancients, on his account, derived their assignments of responsibility from a prior conception of mind taken

---

Buttrey gives a criminal profile of Oedipus of the kind we might find in a police report: Homicidal maniac, who struck four grown men with enough force to kill them; much less would have been needed to render them harmless in self-defense (Theodore V. Buttrey, "Understanding *The Oedipus Rex*: Why Do They Pay Us a Salary?" Ida Beam Lecture, University of Iowa, spring 1997).

[6] PhG §§444–483, and supplementary material from "Force and the Understanding" (PhG §§132–165), and parallel passages in "Purpose and Responsibility" in PR §§115–118, and EG §§503–517.

over from an early monistic tradition beginning with Homer, which conceived of the psyche as inseparable from the body, not as a distinct locus of mental activity.[7] On this monistic outlook, intentions and motives were not conceived of as separable mental occurrences distinct from bodily actions. Accordingly, as others have done before him, Hegel remarks on the "emptiness" or silence of the Greeks' inner thoughts (PhG §146).

One implication of this unified theory of mind and body for morals is that it offers some defense of the Greeks' neglect of intentions in moral assessment: "What . . . does not appear, is for Consciousness nothing at all." Rather, on this ancient model, agents' actions were standardly assessed in causal terms, independent of their internal attitudes and self-understanding.[8] While the Greeks were able to deliberate rationally and reflectively about various choices before acting, Hegel thinks the role that conscious deliberation and reflection played in arriving at moral assessment was different from that of the moderns in important ways (PhG §163).[9] All the internal meanings available to Oedipus introspectively, before acting at the crossroads, were useless for helping him recognize the significance of what he had done. Consequences of actions on this

---

[7] In this ancient monistic theory, Michael Forster writes, "all those psychological faculties, which do perform mental functions, such as thumos, the kardia, and the phren, are analogous with physical organs and parts of the body—the chest, heart, diaphragm, respectively." Michael N. Forster, *Hegel's Idea of a Phenomenology of Spirit* (Chicago: University of Chicago Press, 1998).

[8] The ancient causal account is not to be confused with modern causal theories of action, which explain action in terms of *internal* mental causes, e.g., intentions, motives, desires, or beliefs as causes. Charles Taylor contrasts Hegel's theory of mind and action with this type of causal theory in Davidson. See Charles Taylor, "Hegel's Philosophy of Mind," in *Human Agency and Language, Philosophical Papers*, vol. 1 (Cambridge: Cambridge University Press, 1985), and Donald Davidson, "Actions, Reasons, and Causes," *Journal of Philosophy* 60, no. 23 (1973). Reprinted in *Actions and Events* (Oxford: Oxford University Press, 1980).

[9] Hegel remarks that, "What has simply *happened* becomes rather a *work deliberately done*" (PhG §462), which suggests that before acting, one might act with only an intuitive grasp of what was right, and afterward, it might just happen that one's act has the unconscious result of being universal. Hegel writes of this phenomenon in connection with Antigone, whose act "has as its object and content this *particular* individual who belongs to the family, but *is taken as* a universal being freed from his sensuous, i.e., individual, reality" (PhG §451). Recognizing the universal aspect of actions on this ancient model, Hegel thinks, is something that "just happens," not something consciously and deliberately done (PhG §461, §465).

model were traced back to their external bodily causes, whether or not agents intentionally caused them, with an eye to praising, blaming, and passing other forms of judgment (PhG §132).[10] By identifying ascriptions of causal responsibility with assignments of moral agency, this model evoked the double senses of the Greek word for cause, *aitía*, meaning both cause and guilt.[11]

Another, still general, feature of early Greek ethics was derived from prior Homeric notions of the heroic virtues. It was the success or failure of acts for which agents deserved credit or blame (PhG §322), not prohibitions against intending them. For instance, the archaic heroic ideal that Phoenix held up to inspire Achilles in the *Iliad* was to be "a doer of deeds" (*Iliad* 9.443). Similarly, a warning was held up to bystanders after Oedipus was disclosed to be a "doer of dreadful deeds" (*Oedipus Rex* 1327). Acting out of good motives and virtuous dispositions wasn't

[10] This neglect of psychological materials in ascriptions of agency and responsibility need not imply that these agents didn't have virtuous motives, dispositions, or any inner life whatsoever; or that their criteria of right action didn't require, minimally, that they act out of virtuous motives and dispositions. It implies only that psychological motivations didn't serve as the decisive authority in their understanding and assessment of their actions. On whether the ancients had intentions or perceived themselves as having any, Bernard Williams argues convincingly that they did. The concept of intention, he argues, is already clearly present as early as Homer, although there is no noun or verb equivalent to intention in Homer. Bernard Williams, *Shame and Necessity* (Berkeley: University of California Press, 1993), 33, 56–64. For other accounts of the Greeks' causal conceptions of agency, see Werner Jaeger, *Paideia* (Oxford: Oxford University Press, 1934), 1:161; Georg Henrik von Wright, *Explanation and Understanding* (Ithaca: Cornell University Press, 1971), 64–65; and J. Walter Jones, "The Mental Element in Wrongdoing," chap. 14 of *The Law and Legal Theory of the Greeks* (Oxford: Clarendon Press, 1956), 261–262, 267, 268–269. See Davidson for a roughly comparable modern view, which ascribes blame even in cases of unintended mishap. If a person's bodily action may be described under an aspect that makes it intentional, then, Davidson maintains, that person is the agent of that action. Donald Davidson, "Agency," in *Actions and Events* (Oxford: Oxford University Press, 1980), 46.

[11] Hegel evokes this double sense of *aitía* in such remarks as: "Consciousness cannot deny its guilt, because it committed [caused] the act" (PhG §740); and "By the deed [cause], therefore, it becomes *guilt*. For the deed is its own doing, and 'doing' is its inmost nature. And the guilt also acquires the meaning of crime" (PhG §468); and "the *doer* [causer] cannot deny the crime or his *guilt*" (PhG §469, cf. §322, §372, §738). Von Wright notes that the Finnish word for cause, *syy*, has exactly the same double meaning as aitía. Von Wright, *Explanation and Understanding*, 65.

sufficient for right action unless *areté* was manifested in actual deeds that were appropriate to one's particular social role and station in life. This emphasis on the impersonal facts reduced an act to its public significance within an aretaic system. Courage, for instance, an exemplary virtue in the catalogue of heroic virtues, was evaluated, not on the basis of having a desire, willingness, or freedom to cultivate the virtue, but by its manifestation in courageous deeds.[12] We see this inseparable connection between virtue and realized actions even in involuntary outcomes due in part to lucky chance, constitutive luck, and other goods of fortune (PhG §475, PR §124).[13] Although lucky chance, not just admirable character traits, enabled Oedipus to solve the riddle of the Sphinx, he and others happily identified with the result.[14]

What Hegel found intuitively appealing about the ancient paradigm was the following simple idea: If an outcome was caused by someone's direct intervention, and if that harm would not have occurred without their contribution, then that person was responsible for the outcome. In Oedipus' case, one unlike any other the Greeks had seen before, assignment of responsibility was based on the following gross, literal, causal facts: Someone's striking movements at the crossroad initiated a long

[12] Hector, for instance, could be publicly recognized for his courageous achievements, befitting a warrior of his class and stature, yet, still confess in private that he had no particular desire to risk his life in the forefront of the fighting. In a rare, domestic scene in the *Iliad*, Hector confesses to Andromache that being brave does not come naturally, but is something he had to learn (*Iliad* 6.440–446). Similarly, Hegel's view of courage in modern ethical life is that individual character traits and inner motives don't determine a person's courage because "the culmination of courage is not intrinsically of a spiritual character" (PR §327, §325, §328).

[13] Paris no doubt counted himself courageous and fortunate to have achieved a measure of celebrity for having killed Achilles with Apollo's help (*Iliad* 22.358). Also, in Paris' dual with Menelaus, it requires the intervention of a goddess to save Paris. There is no indignity in this because Aphrodite also intervenes on Aeneas' behalf, no mean warrior (*Iliad*, bk. 5). Achilles, for his part, intensely identified with his gifts of superhuman strength, although it was said he possessed them by dint of the gods (*Iliad* 1.178).

[14] Oedipus declared himself "a child of fortune, beneficent fortune." His physical deformity requires him, presumably, to lean on stage with a cane; thus, we may imagine that he is feeling old and enfeebled by his deformity, and his two limbs and cane represent the part of the Sphinx's riddle that goes, "But when the number of its limbs is largest, then it is weakest." Hence, his physical deformity, which was due to luck, makes him part of the answer, and this stroke of luck perhaps suggests to Oedipus the answer. Fry, "Oedipus the King," 186.

series of causally connected events, each entailing the next, ultimately culminating in killing the stranger, among others. Due to bad luck of the most alien and external kind, the stranger turned out to be identical with Laius. The initiating act must belong to someone, and the most pertinent causal fact in this case was observed to be that Oedipus did it, not another. Undeniably, Oedipus was causally instrumental in killing his father, and his father would not have died without Oedipus' direct intervention. It wasn't this patsy or just anyone who caused this murder. We need not cast about for someone better to blame, or for someone to share jointly in the shame. Blame in Oedipus' case thus resists being reduced to vicarious responsibility, or to scapegoating, as is often wrongly supposed.[15]

This emphasis on the impersonal causal facts gives the ancient view a prima facie appeal. On it, an act is reduced to its public significance, not to prohibitions against intending it. The rule assessing acts as permissible or forbidden was guided by the brute, empirical facts alone. On this view, Hegel writes, we can say in clear, determinate moral concepts what the significance of an act is, no matter the fluctuations in the agent's

---

[15] In the primitive scapegoating practice, there was a looseness in the tie between agency and causal efficacy that can't be tolerated on the causal model, which links blame inescapably to causal connections. In the scapegoating rite, under the rules, a faultless bystander or messenger could take over blame for an outcome, independent of an intentional or causal connection between the person held responsible and the harm done. In scapegoats of myth and ritual, the scapegoat assumed responsibility for something he not only did not intend, but was not, in some cases, even causally responsible for, where the liability mechanically transferred over from someone or something causally responsible, to this innocent proxy. This is not to say, of course, that the Greeks themselves always kept these distinctions sharply in mind in practice. Robert Parker writes, "The fundamental idea [of scapegoat rituals] is obviously that of 'one head' [or rather two, in most cases] 'for many,' but there is ambiguity as to who the one should be" (Robert Parker, *Miasma: Pollution and Purification in Early Greek Religion* (Oxford: Clarendon Press, 1983), 258; see also all of chap. 9, 257–280.

What's more, Oedipus' case also resists being reduced to certain modern analogues of vicarious responsibility. For instance, under French and German law, parents or guardians can be held responsible for damages caused by their children. Under English law, a master (employer) is responsible for damage caused by his servants (staff) acting within the scope of their duties (H. L. Hart, *Causation in the Law* [Oxford: Oxford University Press, 1959], 60, 61). In Hegel's treatment, the reason Oedipus' act can't be reduced to vicarious responsibility in this sense is that a fully mature, sane adult was not acting under the auspices of any higher authority, and there was no such prior or even tacit assumption of liability transferred over to him from another party. See *Spirit of Christianity*, ETW 226.

subjective understanding: "The deed is something simply determined, universal, to be grasped in abstraction; it is murder, theft, or a good action, a brave deed, and so on, and what it is can be said of it" (PhG §322, cf. §134; PR §119R). A patricide is not seen as a patricide in this context for one person and yet as something different for another. A patricide is universally the same act for everyone in every context uniformly, without exception (PhG §§467–468). Oedipus' initial judgment of what he did relied on expert eyewitness testimony about the brute empirical facts.[16] He and his community were in fundamental agreement that what he had done was a patricide (PhG §461, §462, §633).[17] No matter the fluctuations in Oedipus' self-understanding, there was little room for pardon, forgiveness, or evasion in the Greeks' moral and legal concepts of transgression and retribution. Thus, the punishment befitting this parricide's crime was clear (*Oedipus Rex* 100–102, 1367–1368) and should have followed inexorably from their laws and prevailing customs (why it didn't, is an interesting but entirely different matter).[18]

[16] The honest old shepherd, who rescued Oedipus on the hillside, and Laius' sole surviving servant are expert witnesses summoned to testify for the purpose of arriving at an objective and publicly ascertainable proof of guilt, or absence of it. These third-party witnesses testified to the empirical facts (of the plainest sort) that gave evidence of Oedipus' causal involvement. The reliance on empirical evidence and inferences to bring about recognition is taken over from a prior tradition in Homer. For example, in the recognition scenes between Eurakleia and Odysseus in the *Odyssey*, a Homeric digression of more than seventy lines relates the origins of the scar on Odysseus' thigh significantly to their shared past (*Odyssey* 19.393ff.). Similarly, Odysseus and Penelope rely on their shared empirical knowledge of the bedpost, around which their bed was built, to effect a recognition (*Odyssey*, bk. 23). Following Homer's use of external signs and shared memory, Euripides' recognition scene between Electra and Orestes rejects Aeschylus' simple reliance on a lock of hair, footprint, and bit of cloth as absurd (*Electra* 513–544) and depends, similarly, on empirical evidence combined with shared memory and testimony.

[17] According to Hegel's idealization of early Greek moral thought, individuals trustingly and unreflectively deferred to communal authorities on the matter of patricide, and all other fundamental moral and legal matters (PhG §448, §476). The attitude that a virtuous classical agent brought to his community's ethical and legal judgments was one of intuitive, unwavering identification. In this attitude, Hegel writes, "there is no caprice and equally no struggle, no indecision since the making and testing of law has been given up; on the contrary, the essence of ethical life is for this consciousness immediate, unwavering, without contradiction" (PhG §465).

[18] Why, for instance, in certain versions, are Oedipus' crimes of incest and parricide left unpunished? Why is Oedipus allowed to continue ruling in *Seven*

I've reconstructed this historical paradigm in more detail than Hegel himself does, in order to bring out some of the virtues that he takes to be imperative to moral assessment. While his own ethics will represent a development that takes him beyond this model's historical peculiarities, what he'll preserve from it is the special role that identification and recognition play in retrospective judgment. The stance of moral judgment is essentially retrospective, directing moral scrutiny backward toward the past, to comprehensively include all of an action's consequences. To formulate this requirement at the level of generality that he intended, Hegel demands as a general requirement of any moral view that individuals recognize in their own deeds, realized concretely in the world, something proceeding from their own essence that elicits intense identification. This demand is reflected in his definition of freedom in action—in one formulation of it anyway—which involves comprehending your own acts in a way that makes them cease to appear as something alien to your deepest interests and aspirations. This desire for identification and recognition, he thinks, is a commonsense, pretheoretical goal of all humans who strive for happiness.[19]

With these background principles in place, we can now explain why Hegel, in pioneering new moral concepts and principles, finds anticipations of these concepts in nontheoretical sources in Homer and the Greek tragedians, who offered no technical theories or generalizable

---

against Thebes? Why is Oedipus allowed to marry again? These puzzling questions notwithstanding, I'll limit my discussion of causation to the Greeks' moral realm, not to the counterpart of causation in their legal realm. Hegel doesn't think that questions concerning how to relate Oedipus' case to the prevailing laws and customs concerning patricide would have arisen. He thinks interpreting or questioning the laws didn't arise in Greek moral, social, and legal life: "These laws . . . of the ethical substance are immediately acknowledged. We cannot ask for their origin and justification, nor can we look for any other warrant" (PhG §421; cf. §437). Elsewhere, he says, "This realm of laws is indeed the truth for the Understanding, and that truth has its *content* in the law" (PhG §150).

[19] Hegel doesn't give a technical, deductive proof that his formula for practical freedom is the sought-after and realizable standard. The commonsense origins of his concept of practical freedom are salient even in one of his most technical formulations of it: "To be free, is to be at home with oneself [*bei sich*] in what is the other," where "*bei sich*" can commonly mean "at one's own home." This relation of self-identity, achieved through something other than oneself, is expressed in the technical formula "Bei-sich-selbst-sein-in-einem-Anderen," and is often translated "being *at home* in an other."

formulas about morals and law. He selects this strand of Greek thought, from among more or less developed strands of thought coexisting inconsistently within the same culture, without implying that its neglect of intentions in morals was true of all Greek thought.[20] This particular strand of Greek thought interests him because its pretheoretical intuitions represent a brute immediacy in morals, which he thinks accords better with everyday common sense than the theoretical optimism in, say, the Platonic-Socratic tradition or the technical/legal viewpoint in Antiphon's *Tetralogies.* Hegel uses ordinary German words to describe the value that the ancients placed on doing deeds (*tun, Tat, Handlung, handeln, Handelnde,* and so on), in order to stress the agreement between its concept of causing harm and an ordinary, commonsense notion of doing harm.[21] While he does not uncritically identify himself with commonsense

---

[20] Certainly this omission of intentions is not true, as Forster pointed out in discussion, of the dualistic, Platonic-Socratic strand of thought, which conceived of the soul as distinct from the body. In Socrates' court case in the *Apology,* Socrates argues that no one would intentionally corrupt the youth (*Apology* 25e–26b), which suggests that considerations of his intentions alone ought to absolve him. Socrates maintains, optimistically, that "a virtuous man is always safe," and the doctrine of Socratic intellectualism further reinforces this general optimism that legal/moral blame is appropriate only if one intentionally or knowingly does wrong. Socrates' moral intuitions do not necessarily reflect a newer, innovative tradition. We need not suppose that the Socratic-Platonic tradition, and after it Aristotle, discovered a novel concept, "intention," and thus reflected a newer, transitional tradition in the minority, as against older traditions and beliefs of an overwhelming majority. Antiphon's imaginary court cases in the *Tetralogies,* concerning homicide and other crimes, don't date much later than the period of Sophocles' Oedipus cycle, and yet they contain similar evidence that the Greeks did, indeed, care about intentions in morals and law. On these exceptional cases, see Jones, who points out that already in Sophocles' *Oedipus at Colonus* we see the emergence of intentions as a basis for evaluation. Jones, *The Law and Legal Theory of the Greeks,* 259–261, 263–264.

[21] For example, "Es wird also durch die Tat zur Schuld. Denn sie ist sein Tun, und das Tun sein eigenstes Wesen; und die Schuld erhält auch die Bedeutung des Verbrechens" (PhG §468/*Werke* 3:342). Hegel avoids using causal language that would be less familiar to common German usage (such as *Ursache, ursächliche, Gründe vorbringen, verursachen,* and *veranlassen*), which would explain why commentators, as far as I know, have missed Hegel's causal analysis of the Greeks' conception of agency in PhG. The textual evidence for this causal account is partly in "Force and the Understanding," where Hegel refers to the Greeks' pretheoretical grasp of laws and forces (e.g., motion, gravity, electricity, magnetism, velocity, and causal efficacy), as they appear in their natural science

morality, his prior commitment to a unity between theory and common sense leads him to seek to preserve certain commonsense causal concepts in his account of moral agency, while insisting that they must undergo important modifications in order to accommodate some of the relevant philosophical distinctions available from a higher standpoint of reflection. By doing so, he means to emphasize the unity between moral thought and ordinary experience, and to raise the virtues that he sees exemplified in this historical paradigm to a general requirement of any moral view.

7.3 Alienation and Impersonality

The trouble with the ancient verdict is that it gets this and other indeterminate cases intuitively wrong. Hegel brings to light the flawed metaphysics of responsibility that follows from the ancients' flatly causal conception around cases of honest agents who fare badly. He relativizes his criticisms of it in proper dialectical fashion to the beliefs of the historical agents he's discussing. He construes the ancients' lack of control on this picture from the perspective of their own archaic beliefs by linking their conception of agency to fate.[22] If Oedipus' acts were preordained by some inscrutable, but purposeful agency—be it fate, the gods, divine necessity, or supernatural causes—then not only did Oedipus lack global control over all the distant antecedents and remote consequences of his acts, but we can't even narrow down the area of his genuine agency to

---

and philosophy. The counterpart to causation in the practical sphere is their pretheoretical grasp of laws and causal concepts as they are involved in causal explanations of moral agency (PhG §§158–159). If metaphysicians talk of causation as one of the fundamental axioms of science, and yet the word "cause" doesn't occur at the highest levels of natural science and theoretical physics, then it should come as no surprise that the causal concepts that Hegel thinks were so fundamental to Greek moral experience don't appear at all in his *phenomenal* rendering of the most ordinary levels of their practical experience.

[22] Hegel's references to fate (in PhG §316; cf. §464, §653; PR §356) have a textual basis in *Oedipus Rex* only if the passage at line 103 is translated, "Who is this man whose fate the God pronounces?" Paul Woodruff stressed in discussion, however, that there are no clear references to fate in this work. Instead, Woodruff translates the line: "Who is this man whose fate has been revealed?" (*Oedipus Tyrannus* 102; trans. with notes by Peter Meineck and Paul Woodruff [Indianapolis: Hackett, 2000]).

a local fragment of it, which he intended under some description—that is, to some control he had over his bodily acting self when he purposely fled his first set of parents, only to acquire a second set, who were just the thing needed to fulfill the oracle's decree.[23] Nor can voluntary control be linked to the clearheaded knowledge he had of what he did at the crossroads under some limited intentional description. For at that intersection between human agency and fate, Oedipus' intention to avoid fate was itself subject to the influence of fate. Paradoxically, actively intending to avoid the predicted outcome passively brought about the very outcome he intended to avoid.[24]

This makes impersonally assigning responsibility within a fatalistic framework even more demanding than assigning it within a deterministic one. Even if determinism were true, there would still be at least a fraction of our acts under our control, on a compatibilist reading anyway, and we would still be responsible for the effect of our intentions and desires on our behavior, though not for anything more than that.[25] But on a fatalistic account, not even this fragment of Oedipus' behavior was subject to any change or adjustment by his conscious, voluntary activity. Even with respect to that narrow fraction of his act which seemed under his active control at the crossroads, he was later shown to be passive at the deepest level. No amount of prospective deliberation on his part

[23] The first Delphic oracle arms Oedipus early on with a contrastive conception of his life and deeds: namely, what he might do, and could expect to happen, if he doesn't take active steps to avoid it. This contrastive conception of his actions essentially defined what in the course of leaving his foster parents was of value to him. This, combined with his resolute and purposeful character, determined which course of action he would take, rather than reflective choice or rational deliberation. Thus, Hegel may be drawing on Aristotle's remark that Oedipus' act was not entirely contrary to expectation, given his character when he writes, "[The doer] takes his purpose from his character" (PhG §737).

[24] Nietzsche describes this paradox aptly: "The old man [at Colonus] . . . suggests to us that the hero attains his highest activity, extending far beyond his life, through his purely *passive* posture, while his conscious deeds and desires, earlier in his life, merely led him into passivity" (Friedrich Nietzsche, *The Birth of Tragedy*, trans. Walter Kaufmann [New York: Random House, 1967], 68).

[25] Susan Wolf, "Sanity and the Metaphysics of Responsibility," in *Responsibility, Character, and the Emotions,* ed. Ferdinand Shoeman (Cambridge: Cambridge University Press, 1987), 51; Thomas Nagel, *Mortal Questions* (Cambridge: Cambridge University Press, 1979), 28; Richard Brandt, "Determinism and the Justifiability of Moral Blame," in *Determinism and Freedom* (New York: Collier Books, 1961).

could have altered the result even at the local level, if his tragic destiny was decreed in advance by fate at the deepest level.

This assignment of responsibility is far worse than on a deterministic picture. Oedipus is not only held responsible for that stripped-down act of his will, not under his control at the time, but also for the bad, far-reaching, global effects of his act, laid out in advance by a brutally indifferent fate. He is blamed for many of the posterior phases of his act, proliferating forward indefinitely, because of the causal tie linking several related phases to the same act. His agency stretches out like an "accordion," to use Feinberg's term, over the total compass of his deed, as it develops unpredictably in time.[26] Causal efficacy dredges up distant traces of his crime buried deep in his past, which propagate forward along an extended chain of causal connections, linking remote past antecedents (preordained before his birth) to the pollution that is presently killing his citizens. What makes this totalizing conception of agency and responsibility disturbing for morality is that Oedipus can be blamed for a proliferation of effects on it, without even the presumption of voluntariness on his part, or even the possibility that he could have done otherwise (PhG §365). Thus, an implausible metaphysics of responsibility flows from this picture. This is just one of two general defects that Hegel thinks make a flatly causal picture of agency untenable.

Hegel's second objection concerns the way these metaphysical tensions manifest themselves to classical agents from the inside. We may sharpen this psychological effect around a contrast between personal and impersonal standpoints. When Oedipus adopts a self-evaluation based on something expressing the self of another, he thinks about, and comments on, his actions in the coldly formal speech of a detached spectator (see PhG §633). The deep incoherence in assuming this dual position is that it leads him to behave as a person divided within himself. This incoherence is brought to light earlier in *Oedipus Rex*, but only "for us," when he unknowingly brings personal and impersonal standpoints into

---

[26] Joel Feinberg, "Action and Responsibility," in *Philosophy in America*, ed. Max Black (Ithaca: Cornell University Press, 1965), 146. This complex combination of antecedents and consequences takes on a life of its own: "This reality is a plurality of circumstances which breaks up and spreads out endlessly in all directions, backwards into their conditions, sideways into their connections, forwards in their consequences" (PhG §642).

uneasy proximity. The incoherence in assuming a third-person posture toward his own actions is expressed in his testimonies and avowals after his act, as part of his attempt to come to terms with what he has done. It is symptomatic of his estrangement from his own bodily movements that he speaks of himself literally as of a stranger. He disguises his own agency from himself right up to the end of the play, by the use of language that implies he is a stranger to his own deeds, not fully acquainted with himself, speaking about them from the remote distance of a spectator gazing upon another's deeds: "If with my knowledge he lives at my hearth/I pray that I myself may feel my curse" (*Oedipus Rex* 250–251). In imperial language more appropriate for use with a stranger, he formally issues an order to himself in an impersonal voice lacking a self: "May I be gone out of men's sight" (832–833).

What makes his spectator's knowledge psychologically untenable is that he can't identify with anything in his own actions that would point to himself as the determining source. He can't sustain a meaningful relation to his own actions when construed impersonally as the product of a higher power—a terrible necessity, an incomprehensible fate—standing outside and above him. His spectator consciousness, as Hegel puts it, is "conscious only of a paralysing terror of this movement, of equally helpless pity, and at the end of it all, the empty repose of submission to Necessity" (PhG §734). Yet, on the ancient account, as a spectator of his own deeds, he can't repudiate his own bodily movements or their consequences. They belong to him because he caused them (PR §115R, §118). These contradictions of an internal nature, Hegel thinks, drive the dialectical process of restructuring moral consciousness forward to an alternative intentional conception.

Already, we see signs that intentions are emerging as a basis for evaluation in the later play, *Oedipus at Colonus*. At Colonus, Oedipus copes with his inability to sustain a meaningful internal identification with his own acts by dissociating himself from his own bodily actions, as if they were something external to him, mere vessels of an incomprehensible fate, to be classed with other inessentials that merely "happened" to him. He withdraws his claim of agency from what in the causal model was thought to be essential (bodily actions) and in a dramatic dialectical reversal draws his self-assessment from what was thought to be inessential (inner intentions). In retrospect, in a public disclaimer at Colonus, he now judges that he did the deed in ignorance and self-defense and states in language more expressive of his inner self his personal conviction that he did not intend to do the things for which he suffered, but, rather, he complains, "I suffered those deeds more than I acted them" (*Oedipus at Colonus* 266–267).[27] His later declamation of innocence, made from an internal standpoint, is not merely in juxtaposition to his earlier self-condemnation, made from an external standpoint. The two judgments are irresolvably in contradiction.

This moral gestalt switch, as it manifests itself through agents consciously reflecting on what they have done, brings into play from a place still within ordinary experience a subjective faculty that points to a much more complex interior structure of moral consciousness than seen earlier. Now, as Hegel puts it, "In the *deed*, they exist as beings with a self, but with a diverse self; and this contradicts the unity of the self" (PhG §472). With the realization that a causal construal of action is too coarse to capture this more complex psychological structure of consciousness, the transition to an intentional conception has already taken place.

---

[27] Hegel calls all such disclaimers a "language of complaint and regret" (cf. PhG §317, §653). Examples of such disclaimers—sincere, self-deluded, and fraudulent alike—abound in the classical literature. Orestes, for instance, declares his conviction that he acted impersonally and innocently on a law backed by a higher authority. He dissociates himself from any wrongdoing of his bodily actions by declaring, "I give you in chief the seer of Pytho, Loxias [Apollo]. /He declares that I could do this and not be charged with wrong" (1026ff.). In two famous disclaimers from the *Iliad*, Agamemnon and Achilles dissociate themselves remorselessly from their actions as the personification of alien forces (*Iliad* 19.85–90). In response to bad publicity about them both, they are no longer able to see their preferred conception of themselves in their acts, which, if construed impersonally, caused the slaughter of their own compatriots, including Achilles' best friend, Patroclus (19.56ff., 19.61–62). Agamemnon claims he was passive with respect to his own passion ("*atê*") that caused him to take Briseis from Achilles, and blames a god for influencing his inner volitions (318–322). Achilles, for his part, blames the slaughter of the Achaeans on impersonal forces, the enemy, although he had earlier intentionally entreated Thetis to call down destruction on his own men (1.407–412). The examples multiply. In response to growing bad press about her from Greeks and Trojans alike, Helen finds she can no longer identify with her liaison with Paris, which, if construed in terms of remote causal antecedents and distant terminal effects, caused the disaster of the ten-year Trojan war and the death of her own brother. While she admits she did not follow Paris unwillingly (3.174), she nevertheless dissociates herself from the original desire that led her to elope, by naming Aphrodite as the determining agency (3.259ff.).

7.4 Modern Intentional View

Kantian ethics appears as the next most prominent development that can accommodate the internal background that was missing in the causal account. Hegel gives a sustained critique of the rational testing process that he thinks gets essentially expressed in Kant's moral individualism in *Religion within the Bounds of Reason Alone,* in "Morality" (PhG §§601–625), in "Reason as Lawgiver" (PhG §§419–428), and "Reason as Testing Laws" (PhG §§429–437), and correspondingly in "Intention and Welfare" (PR §§118–128, especially PR §118, §117Z). I won't attempt to reconstruct the historical Kant here in as much detail as I devoted to the classical model since Hegel thinks the Kantian model is already implicated in its inverted world classical counterpart. The inversion consists in shifting the ancients' priority away from external deeds to internal motives, while still conceiving of inner motives under a universal aspect. In the inverted Kantian model, the split between the two aspects of action now gets expressed in even more sharply dualistic terms: in terms of a conflict between desires and rationality and the impartial authority of one's rational self detached from one's own desires (PhG §603, §622). Kant tries to capture the positive connotations of universality and impartiality, by abstracting away all features specific to the personal standpoint, except those universal features discernible from an impersonal standpoint.[28]

Consider how the Kantian approach would respond to a morally indeterminate case from Goethe's *Sorrows of Young Werther,* still in terms that reference the classical approach. In a crisis moment, Charlotte hands

---

[28] I'm using the key term "impersonality" to cover a broader range of meanings, including the positive Kantian meanings of impartiality, objectivity, and universality, as well as alienation, dissociation, and estrangement. Kant tries to avoid the negative connotations of alienation and dissociation arising on the causal account by internalizing the impersonal stance, in the form of a principle of universalizability, representing the universal will of all. My use of "impersonality" is meant to evoke Hegel's concept of alienation (*Entfremdung*)—which has purely negative connotations of passive resignation, or subdued, dampened response— yet also to be flexible enough to capture a broader, more nuanced scale of meanings, both positive and pejorative. Michael Hardimon is good on this issue of cashing out *Entfremdung* and *Versöhnung* into philosophically precise, yet broader, meanings, and themes. See Michael Hardimon, *Hegel's Social Philosophy: The Project of Reconciliation* (Cambridge: Cambridge University Press, 1994), 86–87.

over a brace of pistols to a suicidally deranged Werther, who asks for them for protection on an upcoming trip. Charlotte summons every means in her power, we'll presume, to bring about her good intentions. Yet, Werther uses the guns shortly thereafter to shoot himself in the head. By Kant's lights, if Charlotte was acting permissibly in lending Werther the pistols, then the bad consequences can't be imputed to her. Charlotte may even feel "content" with herself in advance of the tragic outcome, since her meritorious aim was to help Werther, not to harm him. But in the analogous ancient case, Socrates condemns such a person who would hand over the weapons for doing wrong. In the inverted ancient world, Socrates thinks he talks good common sense when he says, "Everyone would surely agree, that if a friend had deposited weapons with you when he was sane, and asks for them when he is out of his mind, you should not return them. The person who returns them is not doing right."[29] Werther himself, who lives in an inverted world of a kind, similarly implicates Charlotte in guilt. His suicide note stresses the literal, causal facts of the kind that were emphasized by the ancients: "You, Lotte, hand me the weapon; you, from whom I wished to receive death and now receive it."

When such rare cases arise, Kant's theory may not be able to solve them, but Hegel is not so much criticizing Kant's theory for failing to do a kind of work it was never designed to do. Instead, Hegel generates a tension in the intentional view between theory and practice, by drawing on a wider network of beliefs to uncover a commonsense belief about agency, which he thinks Kant himself must be committed to if his theory is to conform to commonsense morality, as he claims it does.[30] If Charlotte had acted merely permissibly, and in accord with duty, in lending Werther the brace of pistols, then on Kantian theory no good or bad consequences (intentional or not) can be imputed to her. However, if Charlotte acted meritoriously, doing more in the way of duty than was required of her, then Kant would allow that the good results of her action,

[29] The Platonic Socrates presents this case in the *Republic* as a counterexample to Cephalus' popular ethic that there are moral absolutes derivable from common experience (*Republic* 1.331c).

[30] Kant, *Groundwork of the Metaphysics of Morals*, ed. Mary Gregor, intro. Christine M. Korsgaard (Cambridge: Cambridge University Press, 1998), preface; and "On the Common Saying: 'This may be true in theory, but it does not apply in practice,'" in *Kant's Political Writings*, trans. H. B. Nisbet (Cambridge: Cambridge University Press, 1970).

but not the bad, can be imputed to her.[31] Thus, if Charlotte had achieved her meritorious aim of providing Werther with the pistols in order to protect him on his trip from a band of murderous marauders, then Kant would say, with common sense, that she could rightfully derive "satisfaction" from the good results (PR §124R).

Where Kantian moral theory goes wrong, Hegel thinks, is in trying to hold apart in theory two standpoints that are shown to be irresolvably in tension in practice. A tension arises between theory and practice since we don't forgo our satisfaction in the fortunate cases. Our spontaneous satisfaction reveals our commonsense belief that in such cases "the lack of fit between purpose and reality [consequences] is not taken seriously at all. On the other hand, the action itself does seem to be taken seriously" (PhG §619).[32] Thus, when our aims go wrong in the unfortunate cases, it strains common sense to insist that the bad consequences can't be imputed to us. Hegel's prior commitments to a holistic unity between theory and practice make it imperative to weigh Charlotte's residual guilt about the outcome equally against her good intentions. In the tragic aftermath, she no doubt agonizes over her guilt and holds herself responsible for much more than what she's answerable to on the forbearing Kantian verdict. Yet, Kantian theory severs this vital, commonsense connection to realized actions, which Charlotte shows she is still committed to in her affective response.[33] To insist that she *should* be internally constituted so as to be able to displace her identification with what she values onto abstractly considered universalizable motives doesn't mean

---

[31] Wood draws this interpretation from textual support in Kant's *Metaphysik der Sitten*, Akademie Edition 6 (Berlin: Walter de Gruyter, 1902–83), 227–228; *Lectures on Ethics*, in *The Cambridge Edition of the Works of Immanuel Kant* (New York: Cambridge University Press, 1992), 80ff./Ak. 6:228; and "On an Alleged Right to Lie," Ak. 8:425–430.

[32] PhG §399, §§601–602, §618. Hegel writes, "[I]n the accomplished deed, consciousness knows itself to be actualized as this particular consciousness . . . and enjoyment consists in this" (PhG §618). He adds further that, "therefore, it is to take higher moral ground to find satisfaction in the action" (PR §121Z).

[33] On the alienation resulting from the Kantian dualisms between sense and reason, desire and duty, happiness and virtue, Hegel writes, "For the consciousness which does what is right, action and its own actual doing remains pitiable, its enjoyment remains pain" (PhG §§228–230). Elsewhere, Hegel writes, "[F]or the particular—impulses, inclinations, pathological love, sensuous experience or the universal is necessarily and always something alien and objective" (*Spirit of Christianity*, ETW 211).

much in the tragic aftermath. For what is the force of "should" at the end of the novella when it is said, "They feared for her life"?

In this chapter, I've set up a framework around a contrast between ancient and modern theories brought to light around their deficiencies for solving ethically indeterminate cases. My purpose has been to provide Hegel with a motivation for bringing about a synthesis in the final moral position most resembling his own view: he appeals to an intuitive form of moral consciousness that he calls "Conscience," which tries to overcome the dualistic conception of purpose and result arising on ancient and modern approaches. In the next, final chapter, I show how Hegel extends his principle of organic wholes to ethical actions in Conscience, in order to provide a genuine organic synthesis of the two preceding views: one which involves a holistic way of seeing cause and effect, purpose and result, and means and ends as parts of an inseparable whole.

8

Hegel's Final Synthesis

The culminating viewpoint that ends the Spirit chapter in Hegel's *Phenomenology* is such a rich and tangled synthesis of strands from past positions that the demarcation between where other people's thought leaves off and Hegel's own begins is not always cleanly and sharply drawn (PhG §§632–671; cf. PR §§129–141). We may thus understand the tendency among commentators to dismiss the passage on Conscience as presenting an untenable Romantic intuitionism that Hegel earlier discredited in Sense Certainty (see also GW 149–150). W. H. Walsh, for one, finds it hard to reconcile the appeal to intuition in Conscience as an infallible criterion for arriving at moral knowledge with the rationalism in Hegel's ethics. He backs away from ascribing to Hegel a belief in ethical intuitions because it runs contrary to his rational, ethical objectivism.[1] Michael Forster allows that Conscience is an immanent critique of Fichte's view in the *Wissenshaftslehre* (1794), but not a view that Hegel himself endorses.[2] Charles Taylor stresses the intuitionist elements in the position that Hegel is assimilating to his own view, as well as elements in the position that he's criticizing, and thus allows that the positive elements make Conscience "a vision which is close to Hegel's." But Taylor ultimately backs away from his own insight because he thinks the intuitionist elements veer too close to the Romanticism that Hegel had distanced himself from by the time of the *Phenomenology*: "Hegel could not accept the Romantic notion of

[1] W. H. Walsh, *Hegelian Ethics* (London: Macmillan, 1969), 26.
[2] Michael N. Forster, *Hegel's Idea of Phenomenology* (Chicago: University of Chicago Press, 1998).

an immediate unity with the universal, or the belief in intuition which aspires to a kind of ineffable encounter with God."[3]

However, Allen Wood allows that there are intuitionist elements preserved in Hegel's own rationalist ethics, but in a way that makes it clearly distinguishable from its untenable Romantic precursor. Wood argues that Hegel gives a partial, though ambiguous, anticipation of his own ethics through an immanent critique of Fichte's ethics of conscience: "In the *Phenomenology of Spirit*, Hegel follows Fichte in regarding 'conscience' as the final criterion of duty from the moral standpoint (PhG §632–71)."[4] Wood reinforces this elsewhere: "Hegel also regards conscience as a necessary element in morality, which not even the structures of ethical life can displace. This positive side of Hegel's theory of conscience also deserves emphasis."[5]

In this chapter, following Wood, I wish to emphasize the positive side of Hegel's theory of Conscience. Conscience, as I understand it, is an elaborate expansion of Hegel's earlier remarks sketched briefly at the end of the Reason chapter (PhG §§435–437). Earlier, in "Reason as Lawgiver" and "Reason as Testing Laws," Hegel has dialectically criticized the limitations and drawbacks associated with rational reflection and the inevitable state of demoralization that he associates with a growing reliance on reason following the collapse of Greek ethical life (*Sittlichkeit*). The two concluding paragraphs of the Reason chapter, then, urge a return to what he calls a "Sense Certainty of moral knowing" (PhG §635)—a return that was predicted all along by the theory (PhG §423)—to an immediate, intuitively certain mode of knowledge associated with ancient Greek ethical life in which certain moral truths are known spontaneously through intuition rather than a process of reflection on reasons. Understood as an expansion of these earlier paragraphs, Conscience has preserved in it intuitive elements reminiscent of the early Greeks' intuitive knowledge of their ethical norms.

My interpretation will differ from Wood's, however, in one important respect. I will arrive at my conclusions by taking a circuitous route through Hegel's logic of organic wholes. By taking this route off the beaten path, I think I can give a positive account of certain ambiguities

[3] Charles Taylor, *Hegel* (Cambridge: Cambridge University Press, 1975), 193.

[4] Allen W. Wood, "Hegel's Ethics," in *The Cambridge Companion to Hegel* (Cambridge: Cambridge University Press, 1992), 223–224.

[5] Allen W. Wood, *Hegel's Ethical Thought* (Cambridge: Cambridge University Press, 1990), 174–175.

in the position. Given Hegel's methodological commitments to a principle of organic unity, I'll argue that the ambiguities in the view are not a drawback, as on Wood's account, but predictable and even *necessary* consequences of the contradictory operation that such an organic synthesis implies. Quite the opposite of provoking ambivalence, I'll argue that the ambiguities in the position are precisely a reason for thinking it merits Hegel's wholehearted endorsement.

8.1 Organic-Holistic Actions

The morally indeterminate cases we've been examining have exhibited the following contradictory structure (brought to light through a clash of standpoints, inverted worlds, competing conceptual schemes, what have you): When two parts of an action, inner volition and outer consequences, are driven by moral reflection into conflict, one aspect of the act has the value of crime, another aspect the value of innocence. On the two dualistic approaches described in the preceding chapter, one aspect of action taken in isolation from the whole indicates the value of the action. Conscience (*Gewissen*) represents Hegel's final synthesis of elements from the preceding dualistic moral worldviews in a way that brings intentions and consequences under the same organic whole and restores to us this holistic vision of our actions as integrated, self-unified, and whole. He overcomes the one-sidedness of these dualistic approaches by extending his principle of organic wholes to ethical actions in a holistic way of seeing cause and effect, purpose and result, means and ends as parts of an inseparable whole: "The action, then, as a completed work has the double and opposite meaning of being either the inner individuality and *not* its expression (consequences), or, *qua* external, a reality *free from* the inner, a reality which is something quite different from the inner" (PhG §312).[6]

From this holistic viewpoint, the Kantian standpoint from which an agent's intentions stand in an accidental relation to the outcome vanishes.

---

[6] Hegel writes that "Actuality therefore holds concealed within it the other aspect which is alien to this knowledge, and does not reveal the whole truth about itself to consciousness" (PhG §469). To deny this would put a strain on our commonsense idea that, as John McDowell puts it, "natural powers that are actualized in the movements of our bodies are powers that belong to us agents." (John McDowell, *Mind and World* (Cambridge: Harvard University Press, 1994), 91.

No single aspect of action (part) can capture the essence of the whole. Good intentions that come to nothing can't be understood without being "organically related" to the action taken as a completed whole. Hegel emphasizes the continuities between organic processes and human activities in order to extend his principle of organic unity to human actions and activities (VA 147; cf. 149). In nature, everything within an organism—its parts and the interconnections among the parts—exists for the sake of the whole. If the parts of an action have no significance apart from the whole, then both intentions and consequences must be conceived as organic moments of the whole.

Hegel extends his holism even further: to see the "rationality realized" in a single isolated action emerges only if we look at it in the light of the whole cycle of an individual's complete life: "In his immediate reality [the spiritual individual] appears only fragmented in life, action, inaction, wishing and urging, and yet his character can be known only from the whole series of his actions and sufferings" (VA 147). A person's deeds appear only as a mass of individual details, particular occupations, and activities, which are sundered and split into infinitely many parts, so that the point of unity of an individual's life's projects and aims is not visible (VA 149). Their aims appear trifling in comparison with the greatness of the whole. When conceived of as a whole completed series, a vision of the unity of the whole opens up.

But we don't have access to the significance of the action over a completed lifetime since the finite mind can't take in the action as a complete totality. To grasp the action as a completed series, we would have to run through all the phases and appearances of the act in conscientious moral reflection: from forming an intention, externalizing the intention in bodily movement, which gives rise to consequences that spread out like an "accordion" in all of their causal connections over a completed lifetime. But if the point of unity of the action is not comprehensible as a concentrated center (sum), how do we assign a determinate value to an action that all of its parts have when taken together? How does an organic approach arrive at determinate values in hard cases where a dualistic approach has failed?

8.2 "Conscience: The 'Beautiful Soul,' Evil and its Forgiveness."

In the morally ambiguous cases we've been examining, where the conflict occurs within the same action, Hegel extends his use of the logical term "contradiction" to describe the relation between the values of the parts.[7] But two contradictory parts that are implicated in one and the same action are inconceivable as a unity, except as aspects of the whole action to which they belong. This results in holding two contradictory judgments about the same action in an unstable equilibrium: "Hence, supreme guilt is compatible with supreme innocence," Hegel writes (*Spirit of Christianity,* ETW 236; PhG §603, §622, §161, §356). Oedipus' act, taken merely as a sum of its parts, no more counts as guilty patricide than innocent self-defense. For what is the sum of the values of two parts with contradictory values? If the concept of virtue is shown to have its opposite, vice, organically implied within it, then they are one unity in the sense that in each, the other is expressed at the same time. Since the two parts of the whole have opposed values, vice and virtue, the contradiction between them is not one which a *rational* consciousness can use to confer value intelligibly upon the whole act. The unified value of the act (or state of affairs) can't be reduced analytically to a sum of the value of its parts. How then can the determinate value of the whole act, conceived of as an organic unity, be *rationally* comprehensible?

These cases are "pathological," in the sense that they are inherently resistant to resolution by rational means. These intractable cases point to the existence of a moral significance that falls through the cracks, as it were, one that eludes a classically bivalent logic: "[T]he deed is not evil, but not innocent, and equally as much evil as not evil." Taken as an organic totality, such acts are not graspable by ordinary identity logic. For trying to hold two contradictory determinations within moral thought violates our most minimal rational constraints on determinate meaning: namely, that the antecedent conditions under which something can be thought of as a unified action with a determinate moral content is that it cannot exceed logical possibility. And if we accede to the dependency of practical action on the ordinary laws of logic, then such actions taken as a totality have no unity. What, then, becomes of our commitments to morally determinate verdicts and to a principle of moral bivalence on Hegel's organic-holistic model?

---

[7] The same goes for cases where the contradiction exists between two opposed parties, as between Antigone and Creon. Both opposed parties are equally right, Hegel concludes, and equally wrong (PhG §740). Both sides suffer the same destruction, and neither power has any advantage over the other (PhG §472). That's what makes it a contradiction (*Spirit of Christianity,* ETW 234).

To arrive at determinate moral verdicts on an organic view of agency, we will need an alternative way of expressing moral significance (VA 152). On this view, the truth of vice and virtue consists only in their relation to one another; each in its very concept contains the other. In thinking of one, we can't give up this implied relation to the other, nor can we give up our knowledge of the distinction. When vice and virtue form parts of a connected whole, they have to have a determinate value different from that which they would have if they were not related in this way. That is, the organic whole must confer on the action a value which none of its parts could have when taken in isolation, or as a sum. What organicism has introduced further is a mediating relation that gives us some alternative means of judging the value of the action as a unified whole. We do in fact grasp actions as a unified whole, Hegel thinks, with common sense. But this moment, at which we hold firmly in moral reflection two contradictory aspects of action, both good and evil, in a relation of unity is only something accessible to "the inwardness of intellectual reflection"—what he calls "Conscience."

8.3 Hypocrisy and Moral Evasion

This peculiar ambiguity in the position gives immediate cause for concern: If we can't seem to distinguish between good and wicked actions on it, this would seem to open the floodgates for moral shiftiness, moral evasion, and hypocrisy (PhG §432, §437, §617). This would make Hegel's appeal to intuition nothing more than a throwback to Romantic intuitionism. If private convictions were to remain confined to the subjective level of feelings, inclinations of the heart, love, and faith, as Fichte, Jacobi, Schelling, and the German Romantics thought they must, then there would be nothing to provide rational constraints on moral experience to distinguish conscientious actions from wicked actions. Terrible crimes have been committed in the name of fanatical moral and religious convictions. When convictions lead us astray, self-deluded appeals based on personal convictions are worth no more than those based on impersonal authority. Whether appeals to conscience are honest or insincere will depend on the force of an individual's circumspection. Without some corroborating evidence to provide independent confirmation of a person's sincerity, a Romantic appeal to intuition is no more than a capitulation to human badness.

Hypocrisy and moral evasion seem to pose a threat to Conscience particularly in the morally indeterminate cases we've been discussing. For morally ambiguous cases have built into their structure something that allows one to shift to whichever standpoint one's act comes out looking best under. The flexibility and discretion built into these cases may trigger the natural susceptibility of bad and self-deluded people to try to realize their self-interested ambitions under the guise of being moral, through the same action a moral person would undertake to do as a duty (PhG §432, §660, §644). With Kant, Hegel thinks that it's a characteristic human failing to be particularly susceptible to the self-deceptive illusions of the "dear self."[8] What troubles Hegel even more about modern life, in contrast to the simplicity and homogeneity of Greek ethical life, is this potential for conflicts to give rise to moral evasion as modern life becomes increasingly complex, pluralistic, and varied.[9]

---

[8] Kant concedes that self-delusion is a prevalent human failing in his remark about the ultimate inscrutability of our inner motives: "[F]rom this it cannot be inferred with certainty that no covert impulse of self-love, under the mere pretense of that idea, was not actually the real determining cause of the will; for we like to flatter ourselves by falsely attributing to ourselves a nobler motive, whereas in fact we can never, even by the most strenuous self-examination, get entirely behind our covert incentives" (*Groundwork of the Metaphysics of Morals*, 19/Ak. 4:407).

[9] Conflicts are more likely to arise in modern times, Hegel thinks (PhG §642), though moral evasion is by no means limited to modern cases. In the *Agamemnon*, for instance, Clytemnestra hypocritically maneuvers in the space left open by the fact that her action was morally ambiguous between being an opportunistic crime and, in her words, "a rite of purification," "a sacrament," a duty (*Agamemnon* 1574–1577, 1638, 1673–1675; cf. PhG §475). From an impersonal standpoint, Clytemnestra's act could be construed to be in conformity with duty. She tried to exploit this disparity between her impartial duty and her inner conscience by crafting language to make her appear a bereaved mother exacting revenge for her child's murder. She could bring this off for a time because the kind of hidden, internal evidence, which would reveal her lofty talk as a pretext for seizing Agamemnon's enormous wealth and power, was inaccessible from a neutral observer's standpoint, so successfully did she bury her duplicitous motives under layers of equivocal language (*Agamemnon* 1522–1529, 1396, 1431). We get a glimpse into her true motives when she alludes to Agamemnon's affair with Cassandra while conveniently suppressing mention of her own affair with Aegisthus. Certainly, she has suffered the loss of a child and a husband for years, and has even tried to kill herself, so she claims (*Agamemnon* 866–876). But this imperious woman, emerging embittered and hard-hearted from her war experiences, reveals her true colors in a remorseless description of what she has done. She reveals that her true motives were an unnatural ambition and self-seeking lust for money and power. In her final, chilling line, she gloats to her accomplice, "You and I have the power" (*Agamemnon* 1673–1675).

Thus, consider a case with a timeless structure, which gets repeated over and over again in modern life. A philanderer gets a girl pregnant, due to bad luck of the most unforeseeable kind, but did not intend to do so. Supposing he strenuously took every precaution to avoid the outcome, nothing is in place at this stage to prevent the philanderer from shifting to whichever standpoint happens to conform to his preferred moral image of himself (PhG §644). If the philanderer had succeeded in his aims, Kant would allow that he could have derived "satisfaction" from the result. It puts no strain on common sense to say the philanderer would have whole-heartedly identified with, and derived "satisfaction" from, the bodily result. But since his intentions were thwarted, the Kantian luck-neutralizing solution allows the philanderer discretionary room to shift, from locating what he valued in his bodily act, to the conformity of his motives to the impersonal stance. He hypocritically displaces what is really of value to him onto something incorporeal and abstract, a good will, and is allowed to feel quite content with himself for having done so. Hegel writes, "Consciousness comes to see that the placing apart of these moments [effects] is a 'displacing' of them, a dissemblance, and that it would be hypocrisy if, nevertheless, it were to keep them separate" (PhG §631).

While the philanderer's forbearing stance toward his motives may be consistent with every man's opinion about such matters, this does not necessarily indicate a commitment to impartiality. We can see through the girl's eyes the intuitive appeal of taking a hard-line causal stance. On a strict causal conception, there is no discretionary room for the philanderer to shift to the intentional stance, if by chance his act were thwarted. Imagine him trying to trivialize the causal tie between his act and the girl's condition with the remark, "There was just a causal connection. It could have been me; it could have been anyone!" Certainly this man conceives of his responsibility in impersonal terms, but coldly, with none of the positive connotations of objectivity, impartiality, and universality that we have alluded to so far. To keep up the ancient tension in this modern case, the girl can keep this transvaluer from crafting language in order to get off on a modern technicality. She can cut through his caviling rhetoric, and reduce what has happened to the simplest possible causal language. She can say to the offending male, be he ancient or modern, "But that's just the point. It wasn't just anyone who caused this to happen. You did it. So you are responsible—no one else!"[10]

---

[10] This still doesn't make it a clear-cut case. Consider some cultural variations: In modern Zaire, a man can take a second wife and not be held responsible for

Thus, the moral ambiguity built into Conscience, which seems to make it vulnerable to such cases, is cited by commentators as a reason for thinking the position could not be one Hegel is wholeheartedly endorsing. Even Wood, who emphasizes the positive side of Hegel's theory of conscience, concedes that the contradictory elements in it make it a position that could not merit Hegel's unequivocal endorsement: "Conscience selects an act because it is good in some respects, but in other respects the act may appear to be bad even wrong. . . . Hegel's treatment of conscience is correspondingly ambivalent." Wood adds the further qualification that "conscience cannot altogether avoid an attitude of self-worship. Taken together with the possibilities of deception and hypocrisy that accompany it, this puts conscience very close to moral evil."[11] Hyppolite writes in a similar vein about the instability of this position: "Hegel does not begin by criticizing this individual morality, although he soon shows the ambiguity of such formulas and reveals within good conscience (*Gewissen*) a bad conscience that is not yet aware of itself."[12] Hegel himself acknowledges that Conscience is a morally ambiguous position: "Others, therefore, do not know whether this conscience is morally good or evil. Or rather, they cannot know but they must also take it to be evil" (PhG §649). In fact, he generalizes this to all actions, not just morally indeterminate and conflict cases. He insists that "all acting implicates one in evil"—all actions have an admixture of good and evil. Hence, the title of the subsection: "Conscience: The 'beautiful soul,' *evil* and its forgiveness."

Such an ambiguity would certainly be a flaw in a moral position if Hegel's ethics were a purely rationalist one. But Hegel's ethics is not purely rationalist, as I've been arguing, but rather, organic-holistic. This doesn't make Conscience *nonrational*, for it possesses a kind of immanent rationality tied naturalistically to his organic model. The proper location of "rationality," in his organic sense of the word, lies in the inner

---

supporting his first wife and her children, unborn or living. They are simply "her problem." Consider a variation closer to our own culture: The girl deceives the man into thinking she can't get pregnant, for whatever reason, in order to force him to make a commitment to her. Or perhaps she is intent on acquiring a child by any means necessary. Then who the father is certainly is a matter of indifference: It could have been him, it could have been anyone.

[11] Wood, *Hegel's Ethical Thought*, 174; cf. "Hegel's Ethics," 1992, 224; and PhG §660; PR §139.

[12] Hyppolite, *Genesis and Structure of Hegel's Phenomenology of Spirit* (Evanston: Northwestern University Press, 1974), 500.

logic of the Will's activity. He locates the ground of this unity in a transcendental source: the unity of the self. To see one's inner intentions related to one's external actions as parts of an organic unity, one must see it as issuing from the organically unified powers of the Will. The organic unity of the Will implies that it is a single, unified Will which provides the volition and carries out the action. The inner unity that overcomes conflicting aspects of action springs from the organically unified powers of the will. And if the ground of our consciousness of this unity falls outside the purview of pure rational thought, being guided and constrained by logical, discursive laws, then this suggests that we know the unity by some other means than purely rational thought alone proceeding in accordance with logical, discursive laws.

8.3 Internal Causality and Constitutive Interpretation

"Conscience" is Hegel's term for an intuitive faculty of the Will that gives us this intuitive, noncognitive access to the unifying ground of our moral experience. Becoming a living, conscientious agent involves retreating from the external world of causes into oneself to find there a kind of internal causality needed to grasp one's own act as a unity. Without this recognition of the unity in one's own action, one's action has little value or, at the very least, a neutral, indifferent value. Hegel writes, "Life points to something other than itself, viz. to *consciousness,* for which Life exists as this unity, or as genus" (PhG §172). Conscience supplies this unity in the form of simple, unanalyzable, immediate intuitions, convictions, affects, feelings of approval, pricks of conscience, assent and dissent (PhG §635)—all of which arise spontaneously from an intuitive, nonrepresentable unified core of the self, and which can't be prompted or commanded, or produced by argument, reasoning, testing, or a rational calculation of values. The convictions that Conscience produces are said to be absolutely particular to the situation, infallible, and require no further proof of their correctness than that they possess this unfaltering relation to the self.

Although Oedipus was passively mutilated by forces beyond his control, it is in his active attitudes, responses, and convictions that he brings to his fate, that his fate really begins. At Colonus, his "voice" of conscience delivers the conviction that he acted under the description, "self-defense." Retrospectively at Colonus, Oedipus brings the potentially infinitely shifting series of valuations of what he has done to an end, by resolving, with unwavering conviction, on a morally determinate content. He locates what is morally essential in his deed taken as a whole by linking his morally significant inner attitudes to the outer aspects of his act. He relates himself decisively, with unwavering conviction, to his deed, through this act of identification ("acknowledgment," "recognition"). He can intensely identify with aspects of his actions, even those that go wrong,[13] as an authentic expression of his will because what his actions are, essentially, are construed as the products of his inner willing and its expressions (PhG §650).[14] By actively revising and altering the meaning of his earlier deed, his self-knowledge is in some important sense constitutive of his action. He recognizes himself in what he has done because a *constitutive*, not a flatly causal, relation to actions, engenders more meaningful identification with his act. If Oedipus should later, in yet another sequel, forsake or dissociate himself from the significance of his act, his act would lose its significance. For a conscientious agent knows he still doesn't possess complete knowledge, and could never have complete knowledge over a lifetime. But his incomplete knowledge is held to be sufficient just because it is *his own* knowledge (PhG §642).

Since Hegel himself acknowledges that Conscience is morally ambiguous, the point is not whether the conscientious agent can justify himself to others or to all others. The point is whether Oedipus can live with himself and what he's done. For, Hegel writes, "Others, therefore, do not know whether this conscience is morally good or evil. Or rather, they cannot know but they must also take it to be evil" (PhG §649). In cases involving guilt without crime, Oedipus' grief and regret over what was done indicate the contradiction between recognizing his right to self-defense and lacking the forces to actually hold on to this right (*Spirit of Christianity*, ETW 233). On Hegel's retributive theory punishment, if Oedipus' punishment is to be rationalized, then in some sense he has to

[13] Hegel's notion of identification is meant to be flexible enough to cover situations that warrant joyful affirmation, as well as painful situations that nonetheless elicit passionate identification. Saint Francis, for instance, is said to have identified so wholeheartedly with Christ's stigmata to the point where he felt the pain himself.

[14] Here, I have benefited from Harry Frankfurt's theory of identification in "Identification and Wholeheartedness" and "Identification and Externality," in *The Importance of What We Care About* (Cambridge: Cambridge University Press, 1988).

will his own punishment. Through self-punishment, in the form of pangs of conscience, actively produced by himself, Oedipus has to sense that he's injured in himself the same life that he has injured (*Spirit of Christianity*, ETW 232).

Notice there are no "hard facts" on Hegel's organic-holistic account of agency. That is, actions are not to be regarded as having dated, irreversible properties, but are to be regarded as temporally extended, living expressions of life-forms that are continuously undergoing change and revision. The morally relevant facts come into existence in retrospective judgment after the dated, causal, chronological facts for they are construed in such a way that their unity depends on the self's willing and its practical activity. As he writes, "What is to be valid and to be recognized as a duty, is so, only through the knowledge of oneself in the deed." An agent's act is the way it is only in the way that he knows it to be. Objective moral facts are constructed out of subjective, fact-creating volitions (PhG §640, §635).[15] In constitutive self-interpretation, you get an identity between the knower and the thing known. In this sense, the knower's inner act of identification is primitive and the moral content of his act is derivative. That means that even events in the past can lose their essential nature if they lose this constitutive relation to the self. As Hegel writes, "If the deed ceases to have this self within it, it ceases to be that which alone is its essence" (PhG §650). This fluid, constitutive relation of the self to action leaves value judgments open to later revision in the light of new evidence.[16] Their significance is open to further revision since what gives an act its content is a relation of fixity and commitment of a conscientious agent to a unified conception of that content.

This dependence of moral facts on the knower converts what one knows one's act to be, as something initially produced by alien external causes, into knowing it as something caused by one's own convictions. This means that a different kind of causality is at work than the external causality we encountered in the ancient conception. Hegel replaces the

---

[15] For a contemporary account of intersubjectivism concerning values, see Christine Korsgaard, "The Reasons That We Share," chap. 10 of *Creating the Kingdom of Ends* (Cambridge: Cambridge University Press, 1996), 278.

[16] The moral truths revealed to you through moral intuition produce judgments that apply only to particular situations, and can't be generalized to like social situations or to hypothetical or imagined cases, because there is no discursively statable rule or implicit, internalized standard, which you tacitly consult, which is underlying your intuitive capacity to judge new cases.

notion of an external or relative cause with a natural conception of an internal animating principle of purposive movement. A sign of life in organisms is that they are self-causing (self-generating), such that the cause of a thing that makes it what it is originates from within itself. For what causes the action to be essentially what it is can't be located in an uncomprehended, uninterpreted action, but only in the self-knowledge of a reflective living subject in whom you get an identity of the knower and the thing known.

In order to distinguish the intuitionist elements of Conscience from its untenable, Romantic version, notice that Hegel departs significantly from the Romantic Intuitionists over the issue of whether convictions can stay private and unarticulated. The specific defect of Fichte's ethical intuitionism, one which Hegel thinks he shares with the Romantic Intuitionists Jacobi and Schelling, gets expressed in Fichte's claim that this self-constituting act of intuition is *ineffable* (GW 167, 151). To overcome this defect of indiscursivity, Hegel insists that intuitive convictions can't stay at the inarticulate level but must be expressed in corroborating public behavior, including verbal behavior. Publicly articulating my conviction isn't just a way of translating it or restating in a different way that I had a conviction all along. I may have had some dim, inchoate awareness, a nascent conviction already there to be further cultivated and reinforced.[17] But inner convictions don't get translated into an outer language, as if language were a passive medium directed at some pregiven, preexisting conviction. For Hegel, there is no preexisting conviction with a fully pre-constituted identity existing independently of my declarations and disclaimers. My inchoate, inner awareness of my conviction has to be shored up because my convictions aren't at some distance from the conceptualizing effect of my declarations. My public expressions are my only means of knowing what my convictions are because my inner convictions are inseparable from the form in which they get expressed.

Hegel's demand of public discursivity raises Conscience to a higher level of communally sharable meanings, and moves intuitive moral experience into a realm of communicatively shared meanings. "Consciousness declares its *conviction*; it is in this conviction alone that the action is a duty; also it is valid as duty solely through the conviction being *declared*"

---

[17] Although the convictions Conscience produces are said to be infallible, requiring no further proof of their correctness, Hegel follows Fichte's ethics of conscience in allowing that convictions can sometimes be "darkened," "clouded over, " or mistaken.

(PhG §653). Moving from the purely affective dimension of my moral experience given in intuitive feelings to describing my experience in moral concepts raises my private conviction to something intersubjectively comparable and capable of being recognized and acknowledged by like-minded others (PhG §654). My subjective experience must have some aspect of the universal in it for it to be reachable by general moral concepts. By using public concepts, I affirm and reinforce my affective response to the universal features of particular concrete situations (PhG §647) and make explicit to you in sharable concepts my sense of the importance of the situation as I experienced it. My conviction is "mine," but you can recognize in my declarations and assurances an element of the universal. My judgments are ratified by intersubjective agreement and recognition among other members of my moral community, with whom I share certain basic moral convictions.[18] The more my convictions are in conformity with the shared convictions of my moral community, the more my behavior and judgments conform to the duty as acknowledged and recognized by others, the more my convictions take on an aspect of universality.[19]

Still, contradictions and ambiguities will arise anew at even higher levels of Conscience in the form of conscientious objectors diverging from their community's moral convictions. Rare cases will still arise in which one's convictions fail to conform to one's community, and when they do, Hegel thinks there is no moral fact of the matter for resolving moral

---

[18] Allen Wood emphasized in comments that these richer elements of discursivity and community are also already anticipated in Fichte and are not at all inconsistent with Fichte's notion of conscience as providing infallible intuitions.

[19] A parallel between moral intuitions and linguistic intuitions might be useful here. Hegel thinks that people brought up in the same moral and linguistic community have a shared ability to appreciate and judge certain cases alike. Just as linguistic intuitions are shared by members of the same linguistic community, moral intuitions are shared by individuals living in the relevant moral community (PhG §652, §654). The right substantive moral terms and concepts to describe your moral experience are supplied at the intuitive level in the form of linguistic intuitions. The substantive ethical terms you use to pick out a universal property of your action are drawn from intuitive experience and known through intuition. Your formulations, through which you express your moral convictions, aren't insulated from intuitiveness but are inseparable, reciprocally related elements. Cf. John McDowell, *Mind and World* (Cambridge: Harvard University Press, 1994), lectures 1, 2; and Bernard Williams, *Ethics and the Limits of Philosophy* (Cambridge: Harvard University Press, 1985), 95–99.

disagreements—if by "fact of the matter," you mean an objective, mind-independent fact, existing independently of how the self interprets it. For such talk cuts against his Idealist thesis that agents' self-interpretations and expressions constitute a norm for arriving at determinate moral meanings. On his view, contradiction in the form of dissent and disagreement over communal norms has to arise continually because it is required essentially by dialectical theory. Too much happy consensus and compromise paralyzes debate and promotes static stability. Hegel relies on freely dissenting opinions and disagreements to serve as the catalyst for bringing about radical concept revision.

At the highest levels, Hegel envisions a holistic form of conscientiously guided thought and expression, guided normatively by shared convictions and communal recognition, which preserve and embrace the contradictions within a holistically unifying attitude. When viewed against a background of shared convictions, a restorative unity is achieved within agents by virtue of their knowing that their convictions are shared by like-minded individuals. Admittedly, Conscience is not a position which Hegel unqualifiedly endorses, or presents as a terminal solution, if by "solution" you mean a criterion that eliminates the appearance of contradiction altogether in every rare, borderline case. In an imperfect world, good intentions come uncoupled from consequences, and when they do, they inevitably entangle us in messy contradictions, ruptures, and errors. But Conscience gives us a holistic way of understanding moral actions, as they appear unified through contradictory appearances in a way that doesn't eliminate, suppress, or deny the contradictions even at the highest levels. By accommodating the contradictory aspects of action in an organic unity, the ontic conflict in the act doesn't vanish. Conscientious identification and recognition remove the epistemic conflict within the agent (PhG §596). Moral conflict is just the local appearance of contradiction to be understood against the background of this deeper, organic self-unity.

8.4 Concluding Remarks

This book began with wonder: What does Hegel mean when he says we must regard concepts as "living"? I set off on this odyssey from Hegel's treatment of life in the *Naturphilosophie*. My search for the conditions that make it possible to cognize living concepts set out from eighteenth-century pre-formation theory. Goethe's notion of an inner intuitive vision of the unity of nature led us through the Romantic *Naturphilosophen*'s idea that a special kind of intuition is needed to recognize the contradictory unity of organic wholes. This ended with a call to restructure the human cognitive faculty to make its structures more receptive to the contradictory structures in nature.

I sought to clarify the status of contradiction in Hegel's dialectical thought on the more technical side of things by arguing that a paradox arises in our ordinary understanding of the law of contradiction. These reflections were motivated by the intuition that Hegel's doctrine of contradiction was powerful and compelling, yet it had been willfully misunderstood by hyper-rationalistic commentators or overly sanitized by well-intentioned sympathizers. I located the motivation for his doctrine of contradiction in the peculiar logic governing his model of organic wholes and argued that this logic entailed, not a rejection of the law of contradiction wholesale, but a synthetic reconstruction of our ordinary understanding of the law in its analytic form.

My initial theoretical reflections were meant to set up a general organic framework for understanding life in connection with value. I began practically applying the organic model to value by looking to Hegel's aesthetic Idea of life in natural beauty for what it could tell us about becoming living subjects. Hegel arrived at an Idea of life that was aesthetic in nature, I argued, through the influence of Kant's *Critique of Judgment*. Through an analysis of Hegel's appreciation, and appropriation, of the most radically subjective aspects of Kant's aesthetics, I tried indirectly to bring out the epistemological significance of Kant's third *Critique*. I argued that the holistic conditions Hegel places on knowledge led him to incorporate elements of Kant's subjective, emotivist analysis as a springboard for characterizing a form of intuitive comprehension that overcomes the problem of part/whole in organisms. In particular, Hegel revives Kant's insight into the intellectus Archetypus for giving us a holistic, unifying vision of nature: a kind of intuitive comprehension that doesn't move from the parts to the whole, but which allows us to glimpse aesthetic unities noncognitively through partial totalities.

I wondered further what kind of nonstandard, logical world such artistic imaginative experience must take place in. Although there is no difference for Hegel in truth-value between the pictorial version of a truth and the same truth taken philosophically in his System, it seemed that a nonstandard logic must govern aesthetic experience. For he allows that some performative kinds of artistic knowledge enjoy the status of partial knowledge or "half" knowledge, falling in a gray, shaded middle ground between truth and falsity. Nonpropositional, pictorial expressions embody "half" truths, which don't count as determinately true or determinately false, but occupy a third middle ground that the law of excluded middle said could not exist.

In the third part of the book, I explored the relevance of Hegel's organic-holistic logic for moral agency and responsibility. I reconstructed his conception of moral agency in relation to a historical debate between classical and Kantian moralities. I brought out the defect of focusing one-sidedly on intentions or consequences, as it got reflected historically in early Greek ethics and Kant's ethics, to illuminate their responses to indeterminate and conflict cases. Cases of moral luck and value conflicts served as a diagnostic for revealing problems in applying Hegel's organic logic to actions and arriving at determinate moral verdicts. The problem with applying the logical relation between part and whole, in which the value of the whole is different from the sum of the value of the parts, to the relation between means and effects was that it required us to tolerate the simultaneous assertion of two contradictories. I argued that Hegel proposes an alternative synthesis that tries to succeed where one-sided accounts fail, by finding a unique standpoint from which it is possible to meet both individual and impersonal demands of moral life.

Finally, I tied up loose ends by showing how Hegel's final synthesis of dualistic positions integrates inner agency with outer behavior by relating inner attitudes stably to resulting actions in a relation of expressive identification. It seemed fitting to end this book with the image of an aged, dying Oedipus, glancing regretfully backward at the ruins of his wrecked life, retrospectively from the standpoint of a whole completed lifetime. Yet, somehow still finding within himself, in one last defiant act of expressive identification and constitutive self-understanding, a way of living with himself and what he's done as a way of embracing life itself. His distinctive attitude and posture represents a genuine synthesis that retains the ancients' notion that responsibility rests undeniably with causal agency, but adds the internal element missing on that model with a Fichtean notion of conscience.

I feel privileged to have been born into a time that is witnessing an explosion of interest in Hegel. The wave of interest on the Anglo-American continents and in Germany, spreading as far as the shores of Korea, Japan, and China, amounts to an exciting Hegel Renaissance in our own time. My hope is that this book—inevitably a product of my time—will speak to the timely need for a radical new way of thinking about conflict, contradiction, and conceptual incommensurability, which will explode many of our assumptions about what should count as knowledge. If we have understood the soul of Hegel's meaning, as conveyed in this book, then we must us discard our rigid, pigeon-holing concepts and culturally specific categories and let our living concepts range freely over a wider, more nuanced field of meanings. We must stop patrolling the fixed, conceptual borders to rule what's in, what's out. We must give up our arrogant assumption that everything is, in principle, comprehensible and translatable into *our* foreign concepts. And if we can't give up our absurd sense of entitlement, then let the limits of our culturally relativized concepts be the limits of our culturally impoverished world. We deserve it.

Bibliography

Primary Sources by Hegel

Books and Lecture Cycles

Werke: Theorie Werkausgabe. 20 vols. Edited by Eva Moldenhauer and Karl Marcus Michel. Frankfurt am Main: Suhrkamp Verlag, 1970–71.
Phenomenology of Spirit. 1807. Translated by A. V. Miller. Oxford: Oxford University Press, 1977.
Science of Logic. 1812. Translated by A. V. Miller. London: George Allen and Unwin, 1969.
Philosophy of Right. Edited by Allen Wood and translated by H. B. Nisbet. Cambridge: Cambridge University Press, 1991. Consulted with translation by T. M. Knox. Oxford: Oxford University Press, 1952.
Encyclopedia. Part I: *Logic.* 1817. Translated by A. V. Miller. Oxford: Oxford University Press, 1970.
Encyclopedia. Part II: *Philosophy of Nature.* Translated by A. V. Miller. Oxford: Oxford University Press, 1970.
Encyclopedia. Part III: *Philosophy of Spirit.* Translated by William Wallace and A. V. Miller. Oxford: Oxford University Press, 1971.
Lectures on Fine Art. Vols. I–II. Translated by T. M. Knox. Oxford: Oxford University Press, 1975.
Lectures on the Philosophy of World History: Introduction. Translated by H. B. Nisbet. Cambridge: Cambridge University Press, 1975.

Essays and Letters by Hegel

Early Logic 1802: Excerpt in Introduction to *Faith and Knowledge,* edited by Walter Cerf and H. S. Harris. Albany: State University of New York Press, 1977.

The Jena System, 1804–5: Logic and Metaphysics. Edited and translated by John Burbridge and George di Giovanni. Kingston: McGill-Queen's University Press, 1986.

Early Theological Writings. Translated by T. M. Knox. Chicago: University of Chicago Press, 1975.

System of Ethical Life (1802/3) and *First Philosophy of Spirit* (1803/4). Edited and translated by H. S. Harris and T. M. Knox. Albany: State University of New York Press, 1979.

The Difference between Fichte's and Schelling's System of Philosophy. Translated by H. S. Harris and Walter Cerf. Albany: State University of New York Press, 1977.

Faith and Knowledge. Edited by Walter Cerf and H. S. Harris. Albany: State University of New York Press, 1977.

Natural Law. Translated by T. M. Knox. Philadelphia: University of Pennsylvania Press, 1975.

"On the Actuality of the Rational and the Rationality of the Actual." *Review of Metaphysics* 23 (June 1970).

"On the Essence of Philosophical Criticism Generally and its Relationship to the Present State of Philosophy" in *Between Kant and Hegel.* Edited by George di Giovanni and H. S. Harris. New York: State University of New York, 1985.

Hegel: The Letters. Edited by Clark Butler and Christiane Seiler. Bloomington: Indiana University Press, 1984.

Secondary Sources

Acquila, Richard. "Predication and Hegel's Metaphysics." *Kant-Studien* 64 (1973): 231–245.

Adkins, Arthur. *Merit and Responsibility: A Study in Greek Values.* Oxford: Clarendon Press, 1960.

Aeschylus. *Agamemnon. Aeschylus I.* Translated by Richmond Lattimore. Chicago: University of Chicago Press, 1953.

Allison, Henry. *Kant's Theory of Taste: A Reading of the Critique of Aesthetic Judgment.* Cambridge: Cambridge University Press, 2001.

Ameriks, Karl. "Recent Work on Hegel: The Rehabilitation of an Epistemologist?" *Philosophy and Phenomenological Research* 52, no. 1 (1992).

Annas, Julia. *An Introduction to Plato's Republic.* Oxford: Oxford University Press, 1981.

Aristotle. *Metaphysics.* Translated by Richard Hope. Ann Arbor: University of Michigan Press, 1960.

———. *Physics.* Translated by Richard Hope. Nebraska: University of Nebraska Press, 1961.

———. *On Poetry and Style*. Translated by G. M. Grube. New York: Macmillan 1986.

Avitus, Alcimus. *The Fall of Man, De Spiritalis Historiae Gestis Libri I–III*. Edited by Daniel Nodes. Toronto: Pontifical Institute for Medieval Studies, 1985.

Barnes, Jonathan. "The Law of Contradiction." *Philosophical Quarterly* 19, no. 77 (1969): 302–309.

Barry, Brian. "Tragic Choices." *Ethics* 94 (January 1984): 303–318.

Beiser, Frederick. *German Idealism: The Struggle against Subjectivism, 1781–1801*. Cambridge: Harvard University Press, 2002.

———. *The Romantic Imperative*. Cambridge: Harvard University Press, 2003.

Belting, Hans. *The End of the History of Art?* Translated by Christopher S. Wood. Chicago: University of Chicago Press, 1987.

Berstein, M. "From Self-Consciousness to Community: Act and Recognition in the Master-Slave Relationship." In *The State and Civil Society: Studies in Hegel's Political Philosophy*, edited by Z. A. Pelczynski. Cambridge: Cambridge University Press, 1984.

Bett, Richard. "Rationality and Happiness in the Greek Skeptical Traditions." In *Rationality and Happiness: From the Ancient to the Early Medievals*, edited by Jiyuan Yu and Jorge Gracia. Rochester: University of Rochester Press, 2004.

Bloom, Harold. *The Anxiety of Influence*. Oxford: Oxford University Press, 1973.

———. *A Map of Misreading*. Oxford: Oxford University Press, 1975.

Bole, Thomas J., III. "Contradiction in Hegel's *Science of Logic*." *Review of Metaphysics* 40 (March 1987): 515–534.

Bradley, A. C. "Hegel's Theory of Tragedy." In *Oxford Lectures on Poetry*. London: Macmillan, 1959.

Brandom, Robert. "Holism and Idealism in Hegel's *Phenomenology*." *Hegel-Studien* Band 36 (Summer 2002): 57–92. Felix Meiner Verlag, 2001. Reprinted in *Tales of the Mighty Dead: Historical Essays in the Metaphysics of Intentionality*. Cambridge: Harvard University Press, 2002.

———. "A Sketch of a Program for a Critical Reading of Hegel." *Internationales Jahrbuch des Deutsches Idealismus*, Band 3, (2005): 131–161. Special issue on German Idealism and Contemporary Analytic Philosophy, edited by Karl Ameriks and Jürgen Stolzenberg. Berlin: Walter de Gruyter.

———. "Some Pragmatist Themes in Hegel's Idealism: Negotiation and Administration in Hegel's Account of the Structure and Content of Conceptual Norms." *European Journal of Philosophy* 7, no. 2 (1999): 164–189. Reprinted in *Tales of the Mighty Dead*.

Brandom, Robert, with Nicholas Rescher. *Logic of Inconsistency*. Oxford: Basic Blackwell, 1980.

Brandt, Richard. "Determinism and the Justifiability of Moral Blame." In *Determinism and Freedom*. New York: Collier Books, 1961.

Bubner, Rüdiger. "Gibt es ästhetische Erfahrung bei Hegel?" In *Hegel und die "Kritik der Urteilskraft*," edited by Hans-Friedrich Fulda and Rolf-Peter Horstmann. Stuttgart: Klett-Cotta, 1990. Reprinted in English translation as "Is There a Hegelian Theory of Aesthetic Experience?" in *The Innovations of Idealism*, translated by Nicholas Walker. Cambridge: Cambridge University Press, 2003.

Bungay, Stephen. *Beauty and Truth: A Study of Hegel's Aesthetics.* Oxford: Oxford University Press, 1987.

Burbidge, John. "Language and Recognition." In *Method and Speculation in Hegel's Phenomenology,* edited by Merold Westphal. Atlantic Highlands, NJ: Humanities Press, 1982.

Butler, Clark. "Hegel's Dialectic of the Organic Whole as a Particular Application of Formal Logic." In *Art and Logic in Hegel's Philosophy,* edited by Warren Steinkraus and Kenneth Schmitz. Atlantic Highlands, NJ: Humanities Press, 1980.

Buttrey, Theodore V. "Understanding *The Oedipus Rex*: Why Do They Pay Us a Salary?" Ida Beam Lecture, University of Iowa, spring 1997

Čapek, Milič. "Hegel and the Organic View of Nature." In *Hegel and the Sciences,* edited by R. S. Cohen and M. W. Wartofsky. Dordrecht: D. Reidel, 1984.

Casey, John. "Beauty, Truth, and Necessity," *TLS,* no. 3851, 2 (January 1976): 14–16.

Clark, Malcolm. *Logic and System: A Study of the Transition from "Vorstellung" to Thought in the Philosophy of Hegel.* The Hague: Nijhoff, 1971.

——. "Meaning and Language in Hegel's Philosophy." *Revue Philosophique de Louvain* 58 (1960): 557–578.

Cohen, Ted, and Paul Guyer, eds. *Essays in Kant's Aesthetics.* Chicago: University of Chicago Press, 1982.

Colletti, Lucio. *Marxism and Hegel.* London: Lowe & Brydon, 1979.

——. "Marxism and the Dialectic." *New Left Review* 93 (1975): 3–29.

Cook, Daniel J. "Language in the Philosophy of Hegel." *Janua Linguarum,* no. 135. The Hague: Mouton, 1973.

Corngold, Stanley. "Hölderlin and the Interpretation of the Self." *Comparative Criticism* 5 (1983): 187–200.

Crawford, Donald. *Kant's Aesthetic Theory.* Madison: University of Wisconsin Press, 1974.

Dahlstrom, Daniel. "The Aesthetic Holism of Hamann, Herder, and Schiller." In *The Cambridge Companion to German Idealism,* edited by Karl Ameriks. Cambridge: Cambridge University Press, 2000.

——. "Hegel's Appropriation of Kant's Account of Teleology of Nature," In *Hegel and the Philosophy of Nature,* ed. Stephen Houlgate. Albany: State University of New York Press, 1988.

Dancy, R. M. *Sense and Contradiction: A Study in Aristotle.* Dordrecht: D. Reidel, 1975.

Davidson, Donald. "Actions, Reasons, and Causes." *Journal of Philosophy* 60, no. 23 (1973). Reprinted in *Actions and Events.* Oxford: Oxford University Press, 1980.

——. "Agency." In *Actions and Events.* Oxford: Oxford University Press, 1980.

——. "What Metaphors Mean." In *Inquiries into Truth and Interpretation.* Oxford: Oxford University Press, 1984.

Debrock, Guy. "The Silence of Language in Hegel's Dialectic." *Cultural Hermeneutics* 1 (1973): 285–304.

De Man, Paul. "Sign and Symbol in Hegel's Aesthetics." *Critical Inquiry* 8 (Summer 1982): 761–775. Reprinted in *Aesthetic Ideology*, edited by Andrzej Warminski. Minneapolis: University of Minnesota Press, 1997.

Des Chene, Dennis. *Life's Form: Late Aristotelian Conceptions of the Soul.* Ithaca: Cornell University Press, 2000.

Dodds, E. R. *The Greeks and the Irrational.* California: California University Press, 1951.

Drees, Martin. "The Logic of Hegel's *Philosophy of Nature*." In *Hegel and Newtonianism*, edited by Michael J. Petry. Dordrecht: Kluwer, 1993.

Düsing, Klaus. "Die Idee des Leben in Hegels Logik." In *Hegels Philosophie der Natur*, edited by Rolf-Peter Horstmann and Michael Petry. Stuttgart: Klett-Cotta, 1986.

Empiricus, Sextus. *The Modes of Skepticism.* Edited by Julia Annas and Jonathan Barnes. Cambridge: Cambridge University Press, 1985.

Feinberg, Joel. "Action and Responsibility." In *Philosophy in America*, edited by Max Black. Ithaca: Cornell University Press, 1965.

Findlay, John. *Hegel: A Re-Examination.* London: George Allen & Unwin, 1958.

——. "The Contemporary Relevance of Hegel." In *Language, Mind, and Value.* London: George Allen & Unwin, 1963.

——. "The Hegelian Treatment of Biology and Life." In *Hegel and the Sciences*, edited by Robert Cohen and Marx Wartofsky. Dordrecht: D. Reidel, 1984.

Förster, Eckart. "The Importance of §§76, 77 of the *Critique of Judgment* for the Development of Post-Kantian Philosophy." *Zeitschrift für philosophischen Forschung* 56, no. 2 (2002): 169–190.

Forster, Michael N. *Hegel and Skepticism.* Cambridge: Harvard University Press, 1989.

——. "Hegel's Dialectical Method." In *The Cambridge Companion to Hegel*, edited by Frederick Beiser. Cambridge: Cambridge University Press, 1993.

——. *Hegel's Idea of a Phenomenology of Spirit.* Chicago: University of Chicago Press, 1998.

Frankfurt, Harry. *The Importance of What We Care About.* Cambridge: Cambridge University Press, 1988.

Fraasen, Bas van. "Values and the Heart's Command." *Journal of Philosophy* 7, no. 1 (1973).

Fricker, Miranda. "Intuition and Reason." *Philosophical Quarterly* 45, no. 179 (April 1995): 181–189.

Friedman, R. Z. "Hypocrisy and the Highest Good: Hegel on Kant's Transition from Morality to Religion." *Journal of the History of Philosophy* 24, no. 4 (1986): 503–522.

Fry, Paul H. "Oedipus the King." In *Homer to Brecht*, edited by Michael Seidel and Edward Mendelson. New Haven: Yale University Press, 1977.

Gadamer, Hans-Georg. "The Idea of Hegel's Logic" and "Hegel's Inverted World." In *Hegel's Dialectic: Five Hermeneutical Studies.* New Haven: Yale University Press, 1976. Originally published as *Hegels Dialektic.* Tübingen, ©1971.

Gammon, Martin. "Dynamic Resemblance: Hegel's Early Theory of Ethical Equality." *Review of Metaphysics* 50 (December 1996): 315–349.

Gardiner, Patrick. "Kant and Hegel on Aesthetics." In *Hegel's Critique of Kant*, edited by Stephen Priest. Oxford: Oxford University Press, 1987.

Geuss, Raymond. "A Reply to Paul de Man." *Critical Inquiry* 10, no. 2 (1983): 375–390.

Ginsborg, Hannah. "Kant on Aesthetic and Biological Purposiveness." In *Reclaiming the History of Ethics: Essays for John Rawls*, edited by Andrew Reath, Barbara Herman, and Christine Korsgaard. Cambridge: Cambridge University Press, 1997.

——. "Kant on Understanding Organisms as Natural Purposes." In *Kant and the Sciences*, edited by Eric Watson. Oxford: Oxford University Press, 2001.

Giovanni, George di. "The Category of Contingency in the Hegelian Logic." In *Art and Logic in Hegel's Philosophy*, edited by Warren Steinkraus and Kenneth Schmitz. Atlantic Highlands, NJ: Humanities Press, 1980.

——. "More Comments on the Place of the Organic in Hegel's Philosophy of Nature." In *Hegel and the Sciences*. Dordrecht: D. Reidel, 1984.

——. "Reflection and Contradiction. A Commentary on Some Passages of Hegel's *Science of Logic*." *Hegel-Studien*, Band 8 (1973): 131–161.

Goethe: Scientific Studies. Edited and translated by Douglas Miller. New York: Suhrkamp, 1988.

Goethe's Botanical Writings. Translated by Bertha Mueller. Woodbridge, CT: Ox Bow Press, 1952.

Goethe's Way of Science: A Phenomenology of Nature. Edited by David Seamon and Arthur Zajonc. New York: State University of New York Press, 1998.

Gray, J. Glenn. *Hegel's Hellenic Ideal*. New York: Columbia University Press, 1941.

Green, Murray. "Hegel's Concept of Logical Life." In *Art and Logic in Hegel's Philosophy*, edited by Warren Steinkraus and Kenneth Schmitz. Atlantic Highlands, NJ: Humanities Press, 1980.

Greenspan, P. S. "Guilt and Virtue." *Journal of Philosophy* 91, no. 2 (1994): 57–70.

Gregor, Mary. "Aesthetic Form and Sensory Content in the *Critique of Judgment*: Can Kant's 'Critique of Aesthetic Judgment' Provide a Philosophical Basis for Modern Formalism?" In *The Philosophy of Immanuel Kant*, edited by Richard Kennington. Washington, DC: Catholic University of America Press, 1985.

Guyer, Paul. "Absolute Idealism and the Rejection of Kantian Dualism." In *Cambridge Companion to German Idealism*, edited by Karl Ameriks. Cambridge: Cambridge University Press, 2000.

——. *Essays in Kant's Aesthetics*. Edited by Ted Cohen and Paul Guyer. Chicago: University of Chicago Press, 1982.

——. "Hegel on Kant's Aesthetics: Necessity and Contingency in Beauty and Art." In *Hegel und die "Kritik der Urteilskraft*," edited by Hans-Friedrich Fulda and Rolf-Peter Horstmann. Stuttgart: Klett-Cotta, 1990.

——. *Kant and the Claims of Taste*. Cambridge: Harvard University Press, 1979.

Habermas, Jürgen. *Knowledge and Human Interests*. Boston: Beacon Press, 1971.

Hankins, Thomas L. *Science and the Enlightenment*. Cambridge: Cambridge University Press, 1985.

Hanna, Robert. "From an Ontological Point of View: Hegel's Critique of the Common Logic." *Review of Metaphysics* 40 (December 1986): 305–338.

Hardimon, Michael. *Hegel's Social Philosophy: The Project of Reconciliation.* Cambridge: Cambridge University Press, 1994.

Harris, H. S. "The Concept of Recognition in Hegel's Jena Manuscripts." *Hegel-Studien*, Beiheft, Band 20 (1980).

———. *Hegel's Development: Night Thoughts* (Jena 1801–1806). Oxford: Clarendon Press, 1983.

———. *Hegel's Development: Toward the Sunlight, 1770–1801.* Oxford: Oxford University Press, 1972.

Hart, H. L. "The Ascription of Responsibility and Rights." *Proceedings of the Aristotelian Society,* 1948–1949.

———. *Causation in the Law.* Oxford: Oxford University Press, 1959.

Hartmann, Eduard von. "Hegel: A Non-metaphysical View." In *Hegel: A Collection of Critical Essays,* edited by Alasdair MacIntyre. Notre Dame: University of Notre Dame Press, 1972.

Heidegger, Martin. *Hegel's Phenomenology of Spirit.* Bloomington: Indiana University Press, 1980.

———. *Poetry, Language, Thought.* New York: Harper & Row, 1971.

Henrich, Dieter. "Art and Philosophy of Art Today: Reflections with Reference to Hegel." In *New Perspectives in German Literary Criticism,* edited by Victor Lange and Richard Amacher. Princeton: Princeton University Press, 1979.

———. "Beauty and Freedom: Schiller's Struggle with Kant's Aesthetics." In *Essays in Kant's Aesthetics,* edited by Paul Guyer and Ted Cohen. Chicago: University of Chicago Press, 1982.

———. "The Contemporary Relevance of Hegel's Aesthetics." In *Hegel,* edited by Michael Inwood. Oxford: Oxford University Press, 1985.

———. "Hegel and Hölderlin." *Idealistic Studies* 2 (1972): 151–173.

Heraclitus. *Fragments: The Collected Wisdom of Heraclitus.* Translated by Brooks Haxton. New York: Viking, 2001.

Hirsch, E. D. *Validity in Interpretation.* New Haven: Yale University Press, 1967.

Hölderlin, Friedrich. *Hymns and Fragments.* Translated by Richard Sieburth. Princeton: Princeton University Press, 1984.

———. Letter to Bölendorf, on December 4, 1801. #236 in *Essays and Letters on Theory,* edited and translated by Thomas Pfau. Albany: State University of New York Press, 1988.

Homer. *Iliad.* Translated by Richmond Lattimore. Chicago: University of Chicago Press, 1951.

———. *Odyssey.* Translated by Richmond Lattimore. New York: Harper and Row, 1965.

Honneth, Axel. "Integrity and Disrespect." *Political Theory* 20, no. 2 (1992): 187–201.

———. *The Struggle for Recognition: The Moral Grammar of Social Conflicts.* Translated by Joel Anderson. Cambridge: Polity Press, 1995. First published by Suhrkamp Verlag, 1992.

Horstmann, Rolf-Peter. "Kantian Elements in Hegel's Method?" (in draft).

———. "What Is Hegel's Legacy and What Should We Do with It?" *European Journal of Philosophy* 7, no. 2 (1999): 275–287.

Hunt, Ian. *Analytical and Dialectical Marxism.* Aldershot, Eng.: Avebury, 1993.

Hyppolite, Jean. "The Concept of Life and Consciousness of Life in Hegel's Jena Philosophy." In *Studies on Marx and Hegel.* New York: Basic Books, 1969.

———. *Genesis and Structure of Hegel's Phenomenology of Spirit.* Chicago: Northwestern University Press, 1974.

———. "The Ineffable." In *Logic and Existence.* Translated by Leonard Lawlor and Amit Sen. Albany: State University of New York Press, 1997.

Inwood, Michael J. *Hegel.* London: Routledge & Kegan Paul, 1983.

———. "Hegel on Action." In *Idealism Past and Present,* edited by George Vesey. London: Cambridge University Press, 1982.

———. "Hegel, Plato, and Greek 'Sittlichkeit.'" In *The State and Civil Society, Studies in Hegel's Political Philosophy,* edited by Z. A. Pelczynski. Cambridge: Cambridge University Press, 1984.

———. *Introduction to Hegel's Lectures on Fine Art.* London: Penguin, 1993.

Isenberg, Arnold. "Critical Communication," and "Perception, Meaning, and the Subject Matter of Art." In *Aesthetics and the Theory of Criticism.* Chicago: University of Chicago Press, 1973.

Jaeger, Werner. *Paideia.* Vol. 1. Oxford: Oxford University Press, 1934.

Jaeschke, Walter. "Early German Idealist Reinterpretation of the Quarrel of the Ancients and Moderns." *CLIO* 12, no. 4 (1983): 313–331.

Jamme, Christopher. "Hegel and Hölderlin." *CLIO* 15, no. 4 (1986): 359–377.

Jones, J. Walter. *The Law and Legal Theory of the Greeks.* Oxford: Clarendon Press, 1956.

Kaminsky, Jack. *Hegel on Art: An Interpretation of Hegel's Aesthetics.* 1962. Albany: State University of New York Press, 1970.

Kainz, Howard P. *Hegel's Philosophy of Right, with Marx's Commentary: A Handbook for Students.* Hague: Martinus Nijhoff, 1974.

Kant, Immanuel. *Critique of the Power of Judgment.* Edited and translated by Paul Guyer. Cambridge: Cambridge University Press, 2000. Consulted translation by James Creed Meredith. Oxford: Oxford University Press, 1952.

———. *Critique of Pure Reason.* Edited by Paul Guyer and Allen Wood. Cambridge: Cambridge University Press, 1997.

———. *Groundwork of the Metaphysics of Morals.* Edited by Mary Gregor with an Introduction by Christine Korsgaard. Cambridge: Cambridge University Press, 1998.

———. *Lectures on Metaphysics.* Translated and edited by Karl Ameriks and Steve Naragon. Cambridge: Cambridge University Press, 1997.

———. *Logic.* Translated by R. S. Hartman and W. Schwarz. Indianapolis: Bobbs-Merrill, 1947.

———. *Metaphysical Foundations of Natural Science.* Translated and edited by Michael Friedman. Cambridge: Cambridge University Press, 2004.

———. *Metaphysics of Morals.* Cambridge Texts in the History of Philosophy, edited by Mary Gregor. New York: Cambridge University Press, 1996.

———. *Prolegomena.* Translated by Paul Carus. Illinois: Open Court, 1988.

Keefe, Rosanna, and Peter Smith, eds. *Vagueness, Truth, and Logic: A Reader.* Cambridge: MIT Press, 1997.

Kelly, George Armstrong. *Idealism, Politics, and History: Sources of Hegelian Thought.* London: Cambridge University Press, 1969.

———. "Notes on Hegel's 'Lordship and Bondage.'" *Review of Metaphysics* 19, no. 4 (1966).

Knox, T. M. "Hegel's Attitude to Kant's Ethics." *Kant-Studien*, vol. 49.

Kojève, Alexandre. *Introduction to the Reading of Hegel.* Translated by James H. Nichols, Jr. Ithaca: Cornell University Press, 1969.

Korsgaard, Christine. *Creating the Kingdom of Ends.* Cambridge: Cambridge University Press, 1996.

Longuenesse, Béatrice. *Kant and the Capacity to Judge.* Translated by Charles Wolfe. Princeton: Princeton University Press, 1998. Originally published Paris: Presses Universitaires de France, 1993.

———. "Point of View of Man or Knowledge of God: Kant and Hegel on Concept, Judgment, and Reason," in *The Reception of Kant's Critical Philosophy,* ed. Sally Sedgwick. Cambridge: Cambridge University Press, 2000.

Lukács, Georg. *Goethe and His Age.* Translated by Robert Anchor. New York: Grosset & Dunlap, 1968.

———. "Hegel's False and His Genuine Ontology." Translated by David Fernbach. Chapter 3 of Part I of *Toward the Ontology of Social Being.* London: Merlin Press, 1978.

———. *The Young Hegel: Studies in the Relations between Dialectics and Economics.* Translated by Rodney Livingstone. Cambridge: MIT Press, 1966.

Lukasiewicz, Jan. "On the Principle of Contradiction in Aristotle." *Review of Metaphysics* 24 (1970–71): 485–509.

MacIntyre, Alasdair, ed. *Hegel: A Collection of Critical Essays.* Notre Dame: University of Notre Dame Press, 1972.

Makkreel, Rudolf. "The Feeling of Life: Some Kantian Sources of Life-Philosophy." In *Dilthey-Jahrbuch für Philosophie und Geschichte der Geisteswissenschaften,* Herausgegeben von Frithjof Rodi, Band 3/1985: 83–104.

———. *Imagination and Interpretation in Kant.* Chicago: University of Chicago Press, 1990.

Manser, Anthony. "Hegel's Teleology." In *Hegels Philosophie der Natur,* edited by Rolf-Peter Horstmann and Michael Petry. Stuttgart: Ernst Klott Verlag, 1986.

———. "On Becoming" in *Hegel and Modern Philosophy.* Edited by David Lamb. Australia: Croom Helm, 1987.

Marcuse, Herbert. *Reason and Revolution: Hegel and the Rise of Social Theory.* Boston: Beacon Press, 1941.

Mates, Benson. *Elementary Logic.* 2nd ed. New York: Oxford University Press, 1972.

McCumber, John. "Hegel's Philosophical Languages." *Hegel-Studien,* Band 14 (1979): 183–196.

McDowell, John. *Mind and World.* Cambridge: Harvard University Press, 1994.

McFarland, J. D. *Kant's Concept of Teleology.* Edinburgh: University of Edinburgh Press, 1970.

McTaggart, John. *A Commentary on Hegel's Logic.* Cambridge: Cambridge University Press, 1910.

——. "Hegel's Theory of Punishment." *International Journal of Ethics* 6 (1896): 482–499.

Morris, Herbert. "Nonmoral Guilt." In *Responsibility, Character, and the Emotions*, edited by Ferdinand Schoeman. Cambridge: Cambridge University Press, 1987.

Mure, G. R. G. *A Study of Hegel's Logic.* Oxford: Oxford University Press, 1959.

Nagel, Thomas. "Ethics." In *The View from Nowhere.* Oxford: Oxford University Press, 1986.

——. *Mortal Questions.* Cambridge: Cambridge University Press, 1979. See especially "The Fragmentation of Value," "Subjective and Objective," and "Moral Luck."

——. "Thoughts from the Outside." In *The Last Word.* Oxford: Oxford University Press, 1997.

——. "Two Standpoints." In *Equality and Partiality.* Oxford: Oxford University Press, 1991.

Neuhouser, Frederick. *Foundations of Hegel's Social Theory: Actualizing Freedom.* Cambridge: Harvard University Press, 2000.

Nietzsche, Friedrich. *Beyond Good and Evil.* Translated by Walter Kaufmann. New York: Random House, 1966.

——. *Birth of Tragedy.* Translated by Walter Kaufmann. New York: Random House, 1967.

——. "On the Truth and Lies in a Nonmoral Sense." In *Philosophy and Truth.* Edited and translated by Daniel Breazeale. New York: Humanity Books, 1999.

Norman, Richard J. *Hegel's Phenomenology: A Philosophical Introduction.* Atlantic Highlands, NJ: Humanities Press, 1976.

——. *The Moral Philosophers: An Introduction to Ethics.* Oxford: Clarendon Press, 1983.

Norman, Richard J., and Sean Sayers. *Hegel, Marx, and Dialectic: A Debate.* First published in Brighton, Sussex: Harvester Press, and by Atlantic Highlands, New Jersey: Humanities Press, 1980.

O'Brien, William Arctander. "Getting Blasted: Hölderlin's "Wie wenn am Feiertage. . . . " *MLN* 94, nos. 1–3 (1979): 569–586.

O'Hagan, Tom. "On Hegel's Critique of Kant's Moral and Political Philosophy." In *Hegel's Critique of Kant*, edited by Stephen Priest. Oxford: Oxford University Press, 1987.

Parker, Robert. *Miasma: Pollution and Purification in Early Greek Religion.* Oxford: Clarendon Press, 1983.

Pinkard, Terry. *German Philosophy, 1760–1860: The Legacy of Idealism.* Cambridge: Cambridge University Press, 2002.

——. *Hegel's Phenomenology: The Sociality of Reason.* Cambridge: Cambridge University Press, 1996

——. "Historicism, Social Practice, and Sustainability: Some Themes in Hegelian Ethical Theory." *Neue Hefte für Philosophie* 35 (1995): 56–94.

——. "The Logic of Hegel's Logic." *Journal of the History of Philosophy* 17 (October 1977): 417–435.

——. "Virtues, Morality, and Sittlichkeit: From Maxims to Practices." *European Journal of Philosophy* 7, no. 2 (1999): 217–238.

Pippin, Robert. *Hegel's Idealism: The Satisfaction of Self-Consciousness.* Cambridge: Cambridge University Press, 1989.

——. "Hegel's Metaphysics and the Problem of Contradiction." *Journal of the History of Philosophy* 26, no. 3 (July 1978): 301–312.

——. "You Can't Get There from Here." In *The Cambridge Companion to Hegel.* Cambridge: Cambridge University Press, 1992.

Plato. *Parmenides.* Translated by Mary Louise Gill and Paul Ryan. Indianapolis: Hackett, 1996.

——. *Republic.* Translated by G. M. Grube. Indianapolis: Hackett, 1974.

Popper, Karl. *The Open Society and Its Enemies*, vol. 2. New York: Harper and Row, 1962.

——. "What Is Dialectic?" In *Conjectures and Refutations.* London: Routledge, Kegan, Paul, 1963.

Priest, Graham. "Contradiction, Belief and Rationality." *Proceedings of the Aristotelian Society*, v.86 (1985–1986): 99–116.

——. "Inconsistencies in Motion." *American Philosophical Quarterly* 22, no. 4 (1985): 339–346.

Putnam, Hilary. "The Analytic and the Synthetic." *Minnesota Studies in the Philosophy of Science*, 3:358–397. Minneapolis: University of Minnesota Press, 1962.

——. "Is Logic Empirical?" *Boston Studies in the Philosophy of Science*, 5:216–241. Dordrecht: D. Reidel, 1969.

——. "Three-Valued Logic." *Philosophical Studies* 8 (1957): 23–80.

Quine, W. V. O. *The Ways of Paradox.* Cambridge: Harvard University Press, 1966.

Richardson, Robert. *The Romantic Conception of Life: Science and Philosophy in the Age of Goethe.* Chicago: University of Chicago Press, 2002.

Riedel, Manfred. "Nature and Freedom in Hegel's Philosophy of Right. In *Hegel's Political Philosophy: Problems and Perspectives*, edited by Z. A. Pelczynski. Cambridge: Cambridge University Press, 1971.

Roe, Shirley. *Matter, Life, and Generation: Eighteenth-Century Embryology and the Haller-Wolff Debate.* Cambridge: Cambridge University Press, 1981.

Rosebury, Brian. "Moral Responsibility and 'Moral Luck.'" *Philosophical Review* 104, no. 4 (1995): 499–524.

Russell, Bertrand. "Logic as the Essence of Philosophy." in *Readings on Logic*, edited by I. M. Copi and J. A. Gould. New York: Macmillan, 1972.

——. "On Denoting." In *Essays in Analysis.* New York: George Braziller, 1973.

Sayers, Sean. "The Actual and the Rational." In *Hegel and Modern Philosophy.* Edited by David Lamb. New York: Croom Helm, 1987.

——. "Contradiction and Dialectic in the Development of Science." *Science and Society* 45, no. 4 (1981–1982): 409–436.

Schaff, Adam. "Marxist Dialectics and the Principle of Contradiction." *Journal of Philosophy* 57, no. 7 (1960): 241–250.

Scheffler, Samuel. *Consequentialism and Its Critics.* Oxford: Oxford University Press, 1988.

Schiller, Friedrich. *Letters on the Aesthetic Education of Mankind.* Translated by E. M. Wilkinson and L. A. Willoughby. Oxford: Clarendon Press, 1967.

———. *Naïve and Sentimental Poetry.* Translated by Julius A. Elias. New York: Frederick Ungar, 1966.

Sedgwick, Sally. "Hegel's Treatment of Transcendental Apperception in Kant." *Owl of Minerva* 23, no. 2 (1992).

———, ed. *The Reception of Kant's Critical Philosophy.* Cambridge: Cambridge University Press, 2000.

Sextus Empiricus. *The Modes of Skepticism.* Edited by Julia Annas and Jonathan Barnes. Cambridge: Cambridge University Press, 1985.

Siemens, Reynold. "Hegel and the Law of Identity." *Review of Metaphysics* 42 (September 1988): 103–127.

Smith, Anthony. "Hegelianism and Marx: A Reply to Lucio Colletti." *Science and Society* 50, no. 2 (1986): 148–176.

Sophocles. *Sophocles,* vol. 1: *Oedipus the King, Oedipus at Colonus, and Antigone.* Translated by David Grene, Robert Fitzgerald, and Elizabeth Wyckoff. Chicago: University of Chicago Press, 1954.

Sophocles: Oedipus Tyrannus. Translated, with introduction and notes by Peter Meineck and Paul Woodruff. Indianapolis: Hackett, 2000.

Stirner, Max. "Art and Religion." In *The Young Hegelians,* edited by Lawrence S. Stepelevich. Cambridge: Cambridge University Press, 1983.

Suchting, W. A. *Marx and Philosophy: Three Studies.* New York: New York University Press, 1986.

Surber, Jere Paul. "Hegel's Speculative Sentence." *Hegel-Studien* Band 10 (1975): 211–230.

Szondi, Peter. "Hölderlin's Overcoming of Classicism." *Comparative Criticism* 5 (1983): 251–270.

———. "The Notion of the Tragic in Schelling, Hölderlin, and Hegel." In *On Textual Understanding and Other Essays,* translated by Harvey Mendelsohn. Theory and History of Literature, vol. 15. Minneapolis: University of Minnesota Press, 1986.

Taylor, Charles. *Hegel.* Cambridge: Cambridge University Press, 1975.

———. "Hegel and the Philosophy of Action." In *Hegel's Philosophy of Action,* edited by Lawrence Stepelevich and David Lamb. Atlantic Highlands, NJ: Humanities Press, 1983.

———. "Hegel's Philosophy of Mind." In *Human Agency and Language, Philosophical Papers,* vol. 1. Cambridge: Cambridge University Press, 1985.

———. "Hegel's Sittlichkeit and the Crisis of Representative Institutions." In *Philosophy of History and Action,* edited by Yirmiahu Yovel. Dordrecht: D. Reidel, 1978.

———. "The Opening Arguments of the *Phenomenology.*" In *Hegel,* edited by Alasdair MacIntyre. Notre Dame: University of Notre Dame Press, 1976.

———. "Responsibility for Self." In *The Identities of Persons,* edited by Amélie Oksenberg Rorty. Berkeley: University of California Press, 1969.

———. "Self-Interpreting Animals." In *Human Agency and Language,* Philosophical Papers, vol. 1. Cambridge: Cambridge University Press, 1985.

———. "Social Theory as Practice." In *Philosophy and the Human Sciences,* vol. 2. Cambridge: Cambridge University Press, 1985.

Thompson, Michael. "The Representation of Life." In *Virtues and Reasons: Philippa Foot and Moral Theory,* edited by Rosalind Hursthouse, Gavin Lawrence, and Warren Quinn. New York: Clarendon Press, 1995.

Unger, Richard. *Hölderlin's Major Poetry: The Dialectics of Unity.* Bloomington: Indiana University Press, 1975.

Van Fraassen, Bas. "Values and the Hearts Command." *Journal of Philosophy* 70, no. 1 (1973).

Veyne, Paul. *Did the Greeks Believe in Their Myths?* Chicago: University of Chicago Press, 1988.

Von Wright, Georg Henrik. *Explanation and Understanding.* Ithaca: Cornell University Press, 1971.

Walsh, W. H. *Hegelian Ethics.* London: Macmillan, 1969.

Walton, A. "Hegel: Individual Agency and Social Context." In *Hegel's Philosophy of Action,* edited by Lawrence Stepelevich and David Lamb. Atlantic Highlands, NJ: Humanities Press, 1983.

Wicks, Robert. "Hegel's Aesthetics: An Overview." In *The Cambridge Companion to Hegel.* Cambridge: Cambridge University Press, 1983.

Wilde, Lawrence. "Logic: Dialectic and Contradiction." In *The Cambridge Companion to Marx,* edited by Terrell Carver. Cambridge: Cambridge University Press, 1991.

Wilkinson, E. M., and L. A. Willoughby. *Goethe: Poet and Thinker.* London: Edward Arnold, 1962.

Williams, Bernard. "Conflicts of Values." In *Moral Luck.* Cambridge: Cambridge University Press, 1981.

———. "Ethical Consistency," *Problems of the Self.* Cambridge: Cambridge University Press, 1973.

———. *Ethics and the Limits of Philosophy.* Cambridge: Harvard University Press, 1985.

———. *Shame and Necessity.* Berkeley: University of California Press, 1993.

Winckelmann, Johann Joachim. *Reflections on the Imitation of Greek Works in Painting and Sculpture.* La Salle, IL: Open Court Classics, 1987.

Wood, Allen. *Hegel's Ethical Thought.* Cambridge: Cambridge University Press, 1990.

———. "Hegel's Ethics." In *The Cambridge Companion to Hegel.* Cambridge: Cambridge University Press, 1992.

———. *Kant's Ethical Thought.* Cambridge: Cambridge University Press, 1999.

Wolf, Susan. *Freedom within Reason.* New York: Oxford University Press, 1991.

———. "Sanity and the Metaphysics of Responsibility." In *Responsibility, Character, and the Emotions,* edited by Ferdinand Schoeman. Cambridge: Cambridge University Press, 1987.

Wolff, Michael. *Der Begriff des Widerspruchs: Eine Studie zur Dialektik Kants und Hegels.* Königstein/Ts.: Anton Hain Verlag, 1981.

———. "Hegel's Organicist Theory of the State: On the Concept and Method of Hegel's 'Science of the State'" in *Hegel on Ethics and Politics.* Edited by Robert Pippin and Otfried Höffe. Cambridge: Cambridge University Press, 2004.

Wright, G. H. von, *Explanation and Understanding.* Ithaca: Cornell University Press, 1971.

Index

Absolute Knowledge, 120
Achilles, 166, 176n
action, 151, 165–66, 170, 183–84, 189–95.
  See also agency
aesthetics: and aesthetic ideas, 82–83, 88–92,
  94, 96; and beautiful form, 108; and intuitive knowledge, 2–3, 81; for Kant, 3; and
  life, 91–92, 95, 98–99; and nature, 82–83,
  196; and the rational mind, 88–89; and
  self-determining motion, 86; and truth-
  value, 196–97. *See also* art
Agamemnon (Aeschylus), 176n, 187n
agency: and causality, 174; and common
  sense, 172, 178–79; and fate, 172–73;
  inner and outer aspects of, 131, 154, 175;
  and intentions, 151–52, 197; and law of
  contradiction, 56; as living expression
  of life-forms, 192; and logic, 3; and the
  organic model, 131–33; and psychology,
  166n; and regret, 165; and responsibility, 166, 172, 179; and self-unity, 4; and
  subjective feelings, 147, 172–73
aitía, 166–67
ambiguity, moral. *See* indeterminacy, moral
analyticity, 28, 64, 73–76
animals, 85–87
ancient skepticism, 61–62
anteriority, threat of, 123–24
anthropomorphism, 34, 115–16
Antigone, 144–46, 152, 164, 165n, 185
anti-individualism, 136–37

Antiphone, *Tetralogies*, 171
appearance, 62, 70
Archetype, 46–47
Aristotle, 63–64, 68, 73, 75, 84–85; on law
  of contradiction, 38, 56, 73; in *Physics*,
  27n, 68; on tragedy, 143, 143n, 173n
art (general): art-religion, 105; contradiction in, 121; and the divine, 106; as
  highest human expression, 88–89; and
  indiscursivity, 114–19; and knowledge,
  89, 121–22; and linguistic expression,
  113–14; and the living subject, 113;
  mimetic, 95n; and nature, 89; perfection
  of, 105; and Sense Certainty, 109–10;
  and Spirit, 107; and truth, 102–3; and
  unified consciousness, 2–3. *See also*
  aesthetics; art, Greek
art, Greek: harmony of, 106; and idealization, 123–27; indiscursivity of, 110; and
  knowledge, 106, 122; mode of understanding in, 104; and moral consciousness, 158–59; and philosophy, 126–28;
  and pictorial thought, 101–3; and spirituality, 105; and truth, 121; unreflectiveness of, 107. *See also* Greeks
Atreus, house of, 157
Aufhebung, 55, 101–3, 101n
Avitus, Alcimus, 138n

baseball rules, 140–41. *See also* game analogy
beauty. *See* aesthetics

213